Glossary of
COGNITIVE
SCIENCE

Jo Glorie
Series General Editor
c/o Paragon House Publishers
90 Fifth Avenue
New York, NY 10011

A PARAGON HOUSE GLOSSARY
FOR RESEARCH, READING, AND WRITING

Glossary of COGNITIVE SCIENCE

CHARLES E. M. DUNLOP
JAMES H. FETZER

PARAGON HOUSE

New York

First edition, 1993

Published in the United States by

Paragon House
90 Fifth Avenue
New York, N.Y. 10011

Copyright © 1993 by Paragon House

Library of Congress Cataloging-in-Publication Data

Dunlop, Charles E. M.
    Glossary of cognitive science / Charles E.M. Dunlop, James H.
Fetzer.—1st ed.
        p.   cm.—(A Paragon House glossary for research, reading,
and writing)
    Includes bibliographical references.
    ISBN 1-55778-566-X   —ISBN 1-55778-567-8 (pbk.)
    1. Cognitive science—Dictionaries.   I. Fetzer, James H.
II. Title.   III. Series.
BF311.D84   1993
153.4'03—dc20   92-27750
                                                            CIP

Manufactured in the United States of America

To David Hemmendinger

Contents

Preface

This glossary has been composed with the aim of providing assistance to students, teachers, and others who seek to understand the key concepts in cognitive science—a highly interdisciplinary subject encompassing work in computer science, psychology, linguistics, and philosophy.[1] Cognitive science is one of the most exciting and fastest growing areas of contemporary intellectual inquiry; our purpose is to make this remarkable and fascinating field easier to study.

A few remarks about the contributing disciplines may be helpful. Cognitive science studies the nature of cognition in human beings, other animals, and machines (if such a thing is possible), typically treating cognition as a set of processes that can at least in theory be carried out by a computer. Cognitive science draws inspiration from

---

[1] Some would argue for the inclusion of the neurosciences on this list. In our view, the neurosciences provide an important set of constraints on theorizing about cognition, since biological brains must be capable of implementing a correct theory of mentality. At the same time, mentality may not ultimately be limited to biological systems, and the architecture of cognition can be described usefully at a level higher than that of brain function. Accordingly, our glossary does not address this area.

theoretical *computer science*, which is concerned with the nature, varieties, and limits of computation, and from the branch of computer science known as *artificial intelligence* (AI), which investigates the extent to which the mental powers of human beings can be captured by means of machines. Two distinct approaches to AI are now apparent. The first, symbolic AI, treats the mind as a processor of information-bearing symbols. More recently, an approach known as connectionism has been gaining a strong following; it attempts to model brainlike interconnections of neurons. The choice between these two approaches essentially involves a commitment as to the correct level of explanation in cognitive science. To a first approximation, symbolic AI regards the mind as akin to a computer program, whereas connectionism looks at the underlying systems on which programs are implemented.

Cognitive psychology, like symbolic AI, views the mind as a processor of information and proposes internal cognitive categories, structures, and mechanisms to capture that idea. Some cognitive psychologists have modeled their theories by building computer programs, whereas others have devised theories of cognitive processing stemming from ingenious experiments on human and animal subjects.

Linguistics, as it pertains to cognitive science, involves the analysis of language structures whose study provides a window into the organization and workings of the mind. Although these structures may be studied in the abstract, they too may be modeled on computers. A practical spin-off of such modeling is the possibility of developing computer systems for natural language communication.

Philosophy's interest in contemporary cognitive science is a natural extension of philosophical theories about the nature of mind, some of which were first proposed more than two thousand years ago by the ancient Greeks. Today's philosopher/cognitive scientist takes a keen interest in empirical results from artificial intelligence, psychology, and linguistics, with the aim of fashioning theories of mind that accommodate, critically evaluate, and synthesize research from those areas.

Some glossaries attempt to be very scholarly, while others are intended to be more down-to-earth. This one definitely falls into the second category. We have tried to produce an introductory compendium of concepts that would be most beneficial for those who are making an initial effort to understand the field. Rather than attempt to trace the origins or etymologies of these notions, we have sought to present them as they are understood by scholars who are working within contemporary cognitive science. We have also tried to be selective rather than exhaustive by focusing attention on the most important ideas—the key concepts. Moreover, while we have described a number of well-known artificial intelligence programs in order to provide an overview of their range and accomplishments, the choice of what to include or exclude in such cases was often rather arbitrary. Fuller accounts may be found in Raymond Kurzweil, *The Age of Intelligent Machines*; Edward Feigenbaum et al., *The Handbook of Artificial Intelligence*; and Stuart Shapiro, *Encyclopedia of Artificial Intelligence* (all listed in the Bibliography).

Terms in **boldface** type within a given entry are themselves defined elsewhere; this provides a convenient way of noting connections among related ideas. (Exceptions are *artificial intelligence* and *cognitive science*, which occur repeatedly throughout the book.) Some entries contain references to specific works, for which complete information is contained in the References section, and for those readers who want to pursue cognitive science in greater detail, we have included a Bibliography for further study.

Finally, in addition to the conventional definition entries, we have included brief biographical sketches of a number of important figures in the field.

We welcome comments from readers. Please feel free to write to us at our respective institutions or to contact us by electronic mail. Our Internet addresses are:

chuck.dunlop@um.cc.umich.edu

and

jfetzer@ub.d.umn.edu.

Special thanks are due to our editor Jo Glorie at Paragon House, who cheerfully revised deadlines several times and who provided ongoing encouragement and excellent critical feedback. Two anonymous reviewers for Paragon House offered many useful comments on the penultimate manuscript, resulting in a much-improved final version. Shelly Hoffman-Grant furnished expert assistance with proofreading, and ingeniously tracked down a variety of recalcitrant biographical data. Ray Ranier was also very helpful in the latter regard.

C. E. M. D. and J. H. F.

A

A priori/a posteriori distinction. A distinction drawn between two kinds of knowledge. A priori knowledge can be acquired *independently* of experience (for example, that $2 + 2 = 4$ or that the president of a republic is an elected official), whereas a posteriori knowledge can be secured only *on the basis of* experience (for example, that some apples are rotten, or that John F. Kennedy was President of the United States). Defense of this distinction requires a supporting theory, traditionally one based on the **analytic/synthetic distinction**.

Abduction/abductive inference. See **Inference to the best explanation**.

Absent qualia problem. A difficulty that some philosophers have taken to refute **functionalism**. According to functionalism, psychological states can be adequately characterized in terms of their interrelationships and the input-output relations of the system to which they belong. But this account ignores the alleged qualitative character of some psychological states (for example, the taste of lemon or the throb of a pain). If such **qualia** are omitted (or are absent) from psychological descriptions, it would seem possible for a robot to have a (functional) psychology identical to yours while lacking many of the experiences that you have. Given that this result is unacceptable, functionalism must be rejected. This argument has generated an extensive literature. See also **Inverted spectrum problem**.

ACT (Adaptive Control of Thought) system. A theory of mind developed by John R. Anderson which holds that a common set of principles—specifically, **production systems**—underlie all higher cognitive capacities, such as memory, reasoning, and language. This approach has been modeled in a series of computer programs. A recent version known as ACT* is described in detail in Anderson (1983). See also **Cognitive architecture**.

Actions. Behaviors brought about by some combination of motives, beliefs, ethics, abilities, and capabilities. When behavior is understood to be bodily motion and other gestures (including the sounds we make), actions are restricted to behaviors that are intentional (deliberate) and exclude behaviors that are involuntary (autonomic), although allowance must be made for unintended consequences of intentional acts.

Activation. (a) The degree of availability of a **memory** at a given moment. A telephone number you have just obtained from the operator and are now repeating to yourself may remain in a state of high activation just long enough for you to complete dialing, after which it will probably be forgotten. This example illustrates activation in **short-term memory**. But items from **long-term memory** may also be activated during periods when they are being consciously thought about. For example, your access to your own memorized Social Security number is apt to be a bit faster if you have just stated it than if someone asks you for it without warning. (b) The level of activity exhibited by a given **processing unit in a connectionist system**.

Activation rule. A rule applied to a **processing unit in a connectionist system** relating the inputs to a given unit

2

and the unit's current state to a specification of a new level of activity for that unit.

Activation state of a connectionist system. A list of values displaying the level of activity for each of the system's **processing units**.

Affordances. The possible courses of action provided by an organism's perception of an object or situation. Introduced by J. J. Gibson, the concept provides a basis for understanding the fit between an organism and its environment without invoking the apparatus of cognitive processing. People imbibe liquids that are drinkable (they afford drinking); dogs chase squirrels (which afford chasing); etc. Given its opposition to cognitive processing mechanisms, this viewpoint is at odds with the basic approach of cognitive science.

Algorithm. A completely reliable routine or procedure that can be carried out in a finite number of steps to solve a problem. Algorithms are also called effective procedures. See also **Decision procedure**.

Ambiguity. When a word, phrase, or expression has more than one possible interpretation, it is said to be ambiguous. Ambiguity may arise from several possible sources. *Syntactic* ambiguity results when the same linguistic structure admits of more than one grammatical interpretation—for example, the various interpretations of the phrase "old men and women" (Were the women old also?) and the sentence "I greeted the woman with the flowers" (Did she have the flowers, or did I?). A special case of syntactic ambiguity occurs if the scope of a **quantifier** is not suitably fixed, as in the sentence "You can fool some of the people all of the time" (Is the same group always gullible?). In other cases involving *semantic* ambiguity, grammatical structure is not in doubt but a sentence component may have more than one meaning, as in the sentence "I walked to the bank" (where "bank" may refer

3

either to a financial institution or to the edge of a river). Still other ambiguities are *pragmatic*, when the intended effect of an utterance is not evident from its use.

Analog vs. digital systems. An analog system is one in which the transition between the system's states is continuously variable rather than discrete (digital). This feature permits analog systems to represent continuous values, with no jumps from one value to the next. Moreover, there is a direct quantitative relationship between an analog representation and what it represents. To illustrate these two points, contrast an ordinary on/off light switch (digital) to a rotary dimmer (analog). The dimmer, unlike the digital switch, passes through an indefinite number of states between (maximal) "on" and "off," and these intermediate positions correspond directly to (and can represent) indefinitely many degrees of brightness. Modern computers typically employ digital technology because of its flexibility and resistance to large-scale magnification of small errors.

Analogy/analogical reasoning. A form of inference based upon some observed similarity between two or more things. For example, someone might reason as follows: "My gasoline-powered lawn mower stopped operating when it ran out of gas; therefore this electric-powered mower's stopping is due to its running out of 'gas'" (that is, perhaps it has become unplugged). Reasoning by analogy is fallacious when (i) there are more differences than similarities, (ii) there are few but crucial differences, or (iii) the conclusion is thought to be conclusive rather than probable. Analogical reasoning is sometimes regarded as a variant of **inductive argument**—an area of research that has received considerable attention from cognitive scientists.

Analytic/synthetic distinction. A distinction traditionally drawn between different kinds of hypotheses as

4

possible objects of knowledge. **David Hume**'s version separated knowledge of *relations between ideas* from *matters of fact*. In the former case, one idea includes or excludes another (for example, the notion of being a genius includes the notion of being unusually gifted); the latter type of knowledge applies when two ideas are not definitionally related (for example, the weight and hair color of a person who happens to be a genius are not included in the notion of a genius). Similarly, **Immanuel Kant**'s version of the analytic/synthetic distinction separated knowledge of *conceptual connections* (one concept is contained in another) from knowledge that is *informative about the world*. Kant also asserted the existence of **synthetic a priori knowledge**: knowledge that is both informative about the world and also knowable independently of experience. In contrast, contemporary theories of knowledge tend to apply the category "analytic" only to **a priori** sentences, and the category "a posteriori" only to sentences that are synthetic. The entire analytic/synthetic distinction has been challenged in an influential critique by **Quine**.

Analytical Engine. A mechanical computer, designed (but never built to completion) by **Charles Babbage** during the early nineteenth century. Babbage's design contained the core ideas of modern computing: It was programmable (via punched cards); its programs could incorporate **condition-action rules**; it contained a memory store (**RAM**) and a "mill" for performing arithmetic and logical operations.

Anaphora. Reference to an entity previously picked out by one or another term in a discourse. Anaphoric reference may be accomplished via pronouns: "Linda saw Sally just before bumping into *her*" (Sally); or by ellipsis: "Ted likes beer and *so do I*" (that is, both Ted and I like beer). **Natural language processing** systems must be able to deal with this phenomenon.

Aphasia. A loss or impairment of language abilities, caused by brain damage. The language difficulties may vary, depending upon the type of brain damage sustained. Patients may encounter problems in speaking or may lose the capacity for various types of comprehension (for example, they may grasp literal meaning but fail to understand metaphors, or they may be unable to perceive sounds as words).

Arc. See **Link**.

ARCH-LEARNER. An artificial intelligence program developed by Patrick Henry Winston in 1970 as his doctoral project at MIT. Winston's program investigated concept acquisition (**categorization**) by **inductive argument** from a series of examples—some arches, and others nonarches but near misses. ARCH-LEARNER illustrates the **blocks world** approach to problem-solving.

Aristotle (384–322 B.C.). A student of **Plato** who became one of the most important philosophers in history. Aristotle was the first formal logician and the first systematic biologist, a great metaphysician and epistemologist. His work spans the entire range of human knowledge, including such diverse topics as ethics, psychology, politics, poetry, and aesthetics. See also **Logic, Syllogism**.

Artificial intelligence (AI). The branch of computer science that investigates the extent to which the mental powers of human beings can be reproduced by means of machines. AI research is a major contributor to the interdisciplinary field of cognitive science. See also **Connectionism, Symbolic AI, Strong AI, Weak AI**.

Artificial language. Any system of notation and its rules of use that has been deliberately constructed, often for special purposes other than ordinary communication between the members of a language-using community. Examples include **formal language** systems in pure mathematics (as uninterpreted systems) or programming languages in computer science (as interpreted systems) or Esperanto (a general-purpose human language invented to facilitate international communication). Certain special cases (such as Morse code) can be viewed as falling between natural and artificial language. Contrast **Natural language**.

Assemblers. Special-purpose computer programs that translate **assembly language** programs into **machine language**. The translation is required because machine language is the language to which a computer actually responds, but it is not mnemonic or intuitive to programmers who use assembly language. See also **Compilers**, **Interpreters**.

Assembly language. A relatively low-level **programming language** that reflects directly the operations that a computer actually carries out—for instance, moving a numeric value from one place in memory to another; checking the contents of a particular memory location; adding one number to another. Due to the high degree of correspondence between assembly language instructions and the computer's operations, programs written in assembly language typically run faster than those written in higher-level programming languages, although they are also more likely to contain errors. Assembly language programs are also machine-specific, meaning that they are not directly portable from one type of computer to another.

Associationism. The psychological doctrine that learning involves making connections. Early associationists maintained that the connections are made among *ideas* (sometimes viewed as the "atoms" or most fundamental units of experience), whereas **behaviorists** spoke of connections between observable stimuli and observable responses.

Associative network. See **Semantic network**.

Atomic formula. A formula that contains no quantifiers (all, some) and no **logical connectives** (not, and, if-then, or). Atomic formulas are the smallest possible **well-formed formulas**.

Attention. Intuitively, a concentration of mental energy on a particular task. Less metaphorically, the allocation of conscious processing resources to the performance of some cognitive task. Attention is a constraint that stems from a system's having limited conscious processing resources; typically, therefore, only a few tasks can be attended to simultaneously. Attention is also a crucial factor in perceptual processing, determining whether early perceptual information is retained. See also **Automatic vs. controlled processes, Chunking**.

Attribute/value notation. See **Slot/filler notation**.

Augmented transition network (ATN). See **Transition network**.

Austin, John Langshaw (1911–1960). British professor of philosophy at Oxford, noted for his analysis of the pragmatic dimensions of language. He focused attention on "how to do things with words," with special emphasis on **performative utterances** such as marrying, baptizing, promising, chastening, apologizing, and the like. Austin elaborated an important theory of **speech acts**.

Automatic vs. controlled processes. Automatic processes are those that require little or no **attention**, whereas controlled processes are attention-dependent. Controlled activities that initially require significant attention (such as mastering a particular dance step) can, through practice, become more or less automatic. When that happens, performance ceases to be so tightly constrained by the number of tasks being performed (for example, many people can carry out the complex tasks of automatically operating a cellular telephone while driving in congested traffic). See also **Chunking**.

Automaton. A theoretical device, often called a machine, whose behavior at any point is determined by an associated instruction set, an input, and the machine's internal state at the moment when it is called upon to apply an instruction. Some automata are also provided with memory capabilities, which may be limited in size or mode of access; these constraints on memory determine the automaton's type. In cognitive science, automata are particularly useful in theorizing about the production and analysis of linguistic structures. Although automata theory deals with machines in the abstract, it underlies real-world computers. For an extended description of one type of automaton see the entry for **Turing machine**.

B

Babbage, Charles (1792–1871). English mathematician and metalworker who designed the world's first programmable computer, a mechanical device which he called the **Analytical Engine**. Although the physical tolerances required by the Analytical Engine were not attainable in Babbage's day, analysts of the machine's design have concluded that it would have worked.

Backtracking. A technique often used in **natural language processing**—the syntactical analysis of linguistic structures. As an analysis proceeds, say, by considering in succession each of the terms in a sentence, a point may be reached at which several alternative grammatical analyses appear possible. The analyzer provisionally commits itself to one of them, but keeps track of the alternative possibilities, with the option of returning (backtracking) to those alternatives if the provisional commitment fails to produce a satisfactory result.

Backward chaining. A problem-solving strategy that starts with a goal and looks for an initial state plus a series of intermediate steps that will reach that goal. Given a goal, the backward chaining approach appeals to a set of **condition-action rules,** in order to generate the possible states from which the goal could have been derived. (The goal is represented as the action component, or right-hand side, of applicable rules, and possible prior states are represented by a rule's condition component, or left-hand side.) If more than one rule applies, a **conflict-resolution** technique may be employed. This process continues until the initial state is reached. Backward chaining, often used in **expert systems,** is useful for showing how the system reached a particular conclusion; this was a noteworthy feature of the expert system known as **MYCIN.** The backward chaining approach is sometimes described as top-down or goal-driven. See also **Bottom-up/top-down processing.** Contrast **Forward chaining.**

Backward error propagation (Backprop). See **Delta rule, generalized.**

Bars. Thin elongated areas that are identified in an early stage of visual image processing. They form part of a **primal sketch.**

Bayesianism. A theory of knowledge maintaining that **Bayes' theorem** captures the fundamental principle of scientific reasoning.

Bayes' theorem. $P(h/e)$—the probability of hypothesis h, given evidence e—equals the product of the probability of evidence e, given hypothesis h, multiplied by the probability of hypothesis h divided by the probability of evidence e. That is, $P(h/e) = P(e/h) \times P(h)/P(e)$, where $P(h)$ and $P(e)$ are known as unconditional (or absolute) probabilities insofar as they are not formalized relative to specific conditions. In order for the theorem (in this or more complex forms) to be applied, it is necessary to fix the values of the probabilities on the right-hand side to calculate the value of the probability on the left-hand side. The fashion in which this is supposed to be done is what divides various species of **Bayesianism**.

Behaviorism. An influential psychological movement dedicated to abolishing all reference to unobservable properties—especially internal mental states—as factors in bringing about behavior. Championed by John Watson and by B. F. Skinner, behaviorism was touted as a more scientific psychology than earlier studies of consciousness, which frequently relied upon **introspection**. A special case of **reductionism**, behaviorism has now fallen on hard times because, in contrast to behaviorism's disavowal of internal processes, an interest in cognition has become primary within psychology. In philosophy, behaviorist movement was also a significant force in philosophy, especially during the 1950s, due in large measure to the publication of **Gilbert Ryle**'s *The Concept of Mind*. However, rather than disavowing the existence of internal mental states, Ryle attempted to provide ways of analyzing them in terms of observable behavior.

Belief. The acceptance of a proposition; this might take the form of adding the proposition to a data base or knowledge base, or allowing a cognitive entity to act on the acceptance of this belief (for example, your acquiring the belief that it is raining may influence your choice of clothing). Such accepted propositions may be justified or unjustified and may or may not conflict with other beliefs that are held. Belief is typically the weakest form of epistemological **propositional attitudes**, and contrasts to the much stronger state of **knowledge**. An individual, however, may mistake belief for knowledge, and claim incorrectly to know something that in fact is only believed.

Best-first search. A **heuristic search** technique (using rules of thumb rather than fail-safe recipes) that combines the strategies of **breadth-first** and **depth-first** search. In looking for a path from an initial state to a goal state, the best-first approach at each point chooses the most promising next move(s). Typically, the process, after selecting a particular possibility, will follow it several moves ahead. But as this line of search continues, it may begin to look less and less promising, and is abandoned (perhaps temporarily) for earlier possibilities that have not yet been explored. These newer alternatives, however, may eventually become less promising than the path abandoned earlier, at which point the search may return to the latter point. Promising possibilities are calculated by a heuristic function.

Binary number system. A number system based on powers of two rather than the more familiar decimal system, which is based on powers of ten. Whereas the decimal system uses the digits 0–9, the binary system makes use only of 0 and 1. In the decimal system, columns of a decimal number can be interpreted from right to left as 10^0, 10^1, 10^2, 10^3, etc. Thus the decimal number 1101 can be evaluated (from right to left) as: $(1 \times 10^0) + (0 \times 10^1) + (1 \times 10^2) + (1 \times 10^3) = 1 + 0 + 100 + 1000 = 1101$. Analogously, the columns in a binary number, reading from right to left, represent 2^0, 2^1, 2^2, 2^3, etc. Thus, the decimal value of the binary number 1101, again proceeding from right to left, would be calculated as follows: $(1 \times 2^0) + (0 \times 2^1) + (1 \times 2^2) + (1 \times 2^3) = 1 + 0 + 4 + 8 = 13$. Although translations between binary and decimal notation are always possible, the binary system is used in digital computers, letting 1 signal the presence of a voltage, and 0 signaling its absence (or high and low voltages respectively).

Binary search. An efficient strategy for finding a target in an ordered series. The search begins by finding the midpoint of the series (or an approximation thereof if no exact midpoint exists); if the midpoint matches the target, the search is over. If there is no match, the series half containing the target is kept, and the other half discarded. The process next operates on the retained half just as it operated on the original series, continuing in the same way until either the target is found or no further items remain to be examined.

Binary vector. An ordered series of 0s and 1s (for example 01101). Such a series can be used to depict activity levels at various points in a **connectionist** system, and thereby represent a variety of phenomena by displaying patterns of activation. See also **Vector completion**.

Binocular disparity. The slight difference between the left and right retinal images, resulting from slightly different angles of vision between each of the eyes and an object of perception. The disparity provides important information to the visual processing system in calculating distance.

Bit (binary digit). The smallest informational unit in a computer system. Since the binary digit can be either 0 or 1, a single bit can represent either one of two states; a string of N bits can represent 2^N possible states. Bits are typically organized into larger units known as **bytes**. See also **Binary number system**.

Blackboard architecture. A type of structure for artificial intelligence systems, first introduced in the speech-recognition system **Hearsay-II**. The "blackboard" in this approach is a central information store, to which a number of independent program units called knowledge sources have access. Each knowledge source is assigned a specific task, for example identifying a particular subunit of speech (phonemes, syllables, words, etc.). It monitors the blackboard, looking for material relevant to its particular task, and, when appropriate, contributing its specialized expertise to propose or modify a hypothesis. In

Hearsay-II, blackboard hypotheses address different levels of linguistic analysis (e.g., phonemes, words, phrases); the final goal of this technique is to develop a high-level hypothesis that contains a solution to the recognition problem at hand.

Blind search. A strategy that, when considering a set of next moves toward a goal, does not discriminate between more promising and less promising possibilities; instead, all possibilities are accorded equal weight, in contrast to **heuristic search**. Examples are **breadth-first search** and **depth-first search**. See also **British Museum algorithm**.

Blindsight. A phenomenon that can occur as a result of damage to the visual cortex. A blindsighted patient reports complete lack of vision in a major portion of the visual field; however, if a stimulus is presented in that area and the patient is asked to guess when and where the stimulus occurs, the number of correct answers exceeds what would be obtained by chance.

Blobs. Small enclosed areas that are identified in an early stage of visual image processing. They form part of a **primal sketch**.

Blocks world. An imaginary realm (**micro-world**) consisting of a flat surface and various blocks that come in different shapes and sizes. Blocks worlds can be used by artificial intelligence programs to investigate the principles of object recognition, inference, and communication, along with the associated requirements of **knowledge representation**. An important underlying assumption of the blocks world approach is that principles useful for understanding intelligence in this limited domain can be generalized to larger domains as well. The best-known blocks world investigation is probably **SHRDLU**.

Bloomfield, Leonard (1887–1949). American linguist who pioneered techniques for studying unfamiliar languages. Bloomfield adopted a **behaviorist** approach to language, rejecting internal cognitive processing mechanisms—a view against which cognitive science is a reaction.

Boolean functions (Truth value functions). The functions of elementary logic, as represented by **logical connectives** (not, and, or, etc.). Each Boolean function, when applied to truth values of component statements, yields the truth value (either TRUE or FALSE) for the entire compound statement. For an array of examples, see **Truth table**.

BORIS (Better Organized Reasoning and Inference System). An artificial intelligence program written by Michael Dyer in 1980 at Yale University. It paid particular attention to the role that emotion plays in understanding stories and attempted to model human beliefs in such a way that they could be applied across different story contexts. BORIS answered questions about events resembling what might be found on television soap operas and often made likely conjectures about the characters by applying commonsense knowledge of human beings.

Bottom-up/top-down parsing. Two approaches aimed at analyzing sentence structures by reference to a set of grammatical rules, but (as the names suggest) one strategy is essentially the reverse of the other. Consider the sentence "Pat ate some strawberries," along with the following **grammar** (the → symbol means "consists of"):

> *Sentence → Noun Phrase + Verb Phrase*
> *Noun Phrase → Noun, or Article + Noun*
> *Verb Phrase → Verb + Noun Phrase*

Suppose that an associated dictionary contains the following lexical entries, with associated word categories:

Pat: *Noun*
strawberries: *Noun*
ate: *Verb*
some: *Article*

The dictionary shows our sample sentence ("Pat ate some strawberries") to be made up of *Noun* + *Verb* + *Article* + *Noun*. A bottom-up parse builds up from these units, attempting to find the higher-level structures that they compose (ultimately, *Sentence*); this can be accomplished by reading the grammatical rules from right to left. In the present example, this procedure identifies *Article* + *Noun* as composing a *Noun Phrase*; hence, the original *Noun* + *Verb* + *Article* + *Noun* can be rewritten as a higher-level structure *Noun* + *Verb* + *Noun Phrase*. Successive (right-to-left) applications of the same rules eventually yield the top-level structure *Sentence*; hence, "Pat ate some strawberries" is acceptable according to this grammar.

In contrast, top-down parsing proceeds by starting with the highest level structure—*Sentence*—and attempts to decompose that structure in such a way as to yield the sentence under consideration. Thus, starting with *Sentence* and applying the rules now from left to right yields *Noun Phrase* + *Verb Phrase*, etc. Continuing to decompose these latter units according to the rules eventually yields "Pat ate some strawberries"; its derivability from the highest structure according to the rules shows it to be grammatically acceptable. (Note that other sentences—for example, "Strawberries ate some strawberries"—can also be derived. They may be nonsensical but they still conform to the given grammar. Grammatical is not equivalent to meaningful.)

These two parsing techniques may differ in efficiency, depending upon the grammar and the particular sentence being scrutinized. Sometimes the bottom-up and top-down approaches are combined. See also **Bottom-up/top down processing**.

Bottom-up/top-down processing. Bottom-up processing employs a set of principles (such as **condition-action rules**) to operate on low-level data in order to arrive at higher-level structures, whereas top-down processing does just the opposite. The distinction is made in a variety of artificial intelligence projects—for example, in linguistic analysis, reasoning, and visual processing. To illustrate with the case of vision: a bottom-up approach might operate on low-level retinal information, with object recognition emerging only after a series of processing stages; in contrast, a top-down approach might use information about the structure of objects to generate confirmable expectations about retinal data. Often the two approaches are combined. Bottom-up processing is sometimes referred to as data-driven, and top-down processing as expectation-driven or goal-driven. See also **Bottom-up/top-down parsing**.

Brain/mind. Any plausible account of their relationship must start with the fact that the brain's physical structures are lawfully related to mental functioning. **Physicalism** in various guises argues that this relationship suggests the reducibility of mental states to brain states, whereas **dualism** maintains that the connection between brain and mind is one of cause and effect, not identity. According to one computational conception stemming from traditional artificial intelligence research (**symbolic AI**), the mind's operations arise out of rule-governed manipulation of symbols by the brain, on analogy with a computer program's controlling a computer's activities. **Connectionism**, however, proposes an alternative conception of the mind, in which symbol manipulation is discarded in favor of patterns of connections among neurons—connections that can also be modeled on computers. See also **Eliminative materialism**, **Functionalism**,

Mentality, Minds, Minds as semiotic systems, Representational Theory of the Mind, Syntactical Theory of the Mind, Token identity theory, Type identity theory.

Branching. Occurs at points in a computer **program** where sequential processing is abandoned and control is passed to some other location in the program. The most important use of this technique is called conditional branching, where two or more possible courses of action are encountered. The alternative that is actually selected depends upon which condition obtains when the choice-point is reached. Conditional branch points are represented by **condition-action rules**.

Breadth-first search vs. depth-first search. Breadth-first search is a technique whereby all the items at one level of analysis (as in one generation of a family **tree**) are looked at before proceeding to a deeper level. In contrast, depth-first search follows one path down through all possible levels, before returning to the top level and repeating the process for another path. The efficacy of either technique in a particular instance depends upon where in a **search space** the target happens to be located. Although a breadth-first search will eventually discover its target, it quickly runs the risk of **combinatorial explosion**, since each level (in a tree) is generally larger (and often *much* larger) than the preceding one. On the other hand, depth-first search runs the risk of pursuing a very large number of deep and unsuccessful paths. A compromise between the two strategies is **Best-first search**.

Brentano, Franz (1838–1917). German philosopher and psychologist whose original ideas on the nature of consciousness place him at the forefront of theorists of cognition. Brentano argued that psychology could be both subjective and empirical: subjective because it seeks to classify mental phenomena and their interrelationships, and empirical insofar as it stresses the relationship between psychological states and their (external) referents. He proposed that **intentionality** is the hallmark of mentality: mental states point to or *represent* other things. Since, according to Brentano, intentionality is present in mental phenomena but not in physical objects, he concluded that mind cannot be reduced to matter—a conclusion rejected by **physicalism**.

British Museum algorithm. This idea is sometimes picturesquely put as follows: "If a million monkeys typed on a million typewriters for an indefinite length of time, they would eventually produce all of the books in the British Museum." Applied to cognitive science, the reference is to problem-solving strategies that are essentially random, generating and testing every possible solution; it is, therefore, an example of **blind search** vs. **heuristic search**. As the phrase "indefinite length of time" suggests, such a strategy may never succeed in practice, and except in the case of relatively simple problems it is susceptible to **combinatorial explosion**.

Bruner, Jerome Seymour (b. 1915). American psychologist and author of many books, including the classic 1956 work *A Study of Thinking* (with Jacqueline J. Goodnow and George A. Austin). This work investigated strategies used in concept-formation (**categorization**) and broke with **behaviorist** methodology by taking seriously subjects' **protocols** as a window into cognitive processing.

Bytes. Informational units consisting of eight **bits**; they are typically used to measure the amount of memory or disk storage capacity in a computer system—most commonly in thousands of units (kilobytes) or millions (megabytes). A computer system's bytes may be organized into larger units called **words**.

C

Case grammar. A **grammar** based on the idea that there are fairly strong **semantic** constraints on the possible relationships (cases) that can exist between various grammatical units, for example between noun phrases and verbs. Moreover, these relationships may be independent of syntactic position. Consider, for example, the following two sentences: (1) "The driver killed the deer with the car" and (2) "The car killed the deer." In both (1) and (2), the phrase "the car" is the Instrument by which a Result (the deer's death) was achieved; the phrase "the deer" in both sentences is the Object acted on; and in (1) "the driver" is the Agent. Case information, stored with the lexical entry for each term in a computer's "dictionary," represents an important approach to **natural language processing**. Although case categories vary from one case grammar to another, the number of cases employed is often close to six. See also **Conceptual dependency**.

Categorization. Classification of information into groups or **concepts**. Categorization may be viewed as an instance of reasoning by **inductive argument**. Traditionally, conceptual categories were regarded as being sharply defined through a set of necessary and sufficient conditions for category membership. More recently, it has been recognized that category boundaries are not always sharp and that some members of a given category tend to be regarded as more typical than other members (for example, a robin is judged to be a more typical bird than is a chicken). Categorization tasks in a variety of experimental contexts provide a rich source of data for theorizing about conceptual structures. In a standard experiment, subjects are presented with various items to classify, and their **reaction times** yield clues as to the underlying classification system. See also **Family Resemblance**, **Generalization**, **Prototype**.

Central processing unit. See **CPU**.

Ceteris paribus clauses. Clauses that assert that something is the case, *other things being equal*. They are typically embedded in incomplete descriptions of the factors whose presence or absence bring about an outcome. Thus, ceteris paribus, striking a match will cause it to light (but not if the match is wet, if there is insufficient oxygen present, or if it is struck in a peculiar fashion).

Chinese Room. An example introduced by **John Searle** to illustrate his thesis that the **Turing test** is an inadequate criterion for the presence of genuine cognition. The Chinese Room consists of an enclosure around a person who knows no Chinese but who is equipped with an elaborate set of rules for manipulating apparently meaningless symbols. These symbols are received from the outside and manipulated according to the rules, with the resulting new combinations being returned to the outside. Unknown to the individual inside the Room, input symbols are actually questions in Chinese about a story, and output configurations are answers to those questions. Outsiders naturally but falsely conclude that the person inside the Room is fluent in Chinese. Likening the Chinese Room manipulation of "meaningless" symbols to the programmed operations of a computer, Searle maintains that such operations cannot yield **intentionality**: a computer possesses no more understanding than does the person inside the Room. This argument has been the subject of a voluminous literature.

Chomsky, Noam Avram (b. 1928). American linguist and professor of linguistics at MIT who has been among the most influential figures within the field. Applying formal models to the study of language, he has advanced a variety of theories concerning how languages should best be understood. Among the fundamental theses about the nature of language that Chomsky has advocated is the idea that some linguistic capacities are innate, and that all natural languages share certain common properties or **linguistic universals**. See also **Creativity in lan-**

guage, **Chomsky hierarchy**, **Poverty of stimulus**, **Universal grammar**.

Chomsky hierarchy. An ordering of types of **grammars** reflecting the spectrum of **formal languages** that each is capable of generating. In this ordering scheme, languages generated by the less powerful grammars are subsets of those generated by the more powerful ones. The hierarchy has four levels, designated 0, 1, 2, and 3, with level 0 representing the most powerful grammar and level 3 the least powerful. (For examples, see **Context-free grammars**, **Context-sensitive grammars**.) Each level in the Chomsky hierarchy corresponds exactly to a particular type of **automaton**.

Chunking. Organization of information into groups or chunks—which may themselves consist of smaller chunks. Normally, for example, one does not hear speech as consisting of individual words; instead, the words are chunked into larger units (such as phrases). In many instances, chunking can be developed through practice; experienced chess players, unlike beginners, see chess pieces as organized into meaningful configurations, and can often recreate a board's pattern of pieces from memory. A number of studies indicate that the capacity of human **working memory** is generally limited to somewhere between four and seven units. However, if each unit is a chunk, perhaps consisting of further chunks, larger amounts of information can be processed than would otherwise be possible.

Church, Alonzo (b. 1903). American logician and professor of philosophy emeritus at UCLA who discovered far-reaching results about the nature of formal systems. See also **Church's theorem**, **Church—Turing thesis**.

Church's theorem. A result in logic stating that in the more powerful logical systems there is no sure-fire method for determining an argument's validity. More technically, there is no mechanical routine (**decision procedure**) for establishing the validity of arguments in quantificational **logic** containing relations and multiple **quantifiers**. Although arguments couched in **First Order Predicate Calculus** are decidable via **truth tables**, logics of any higher order are not.

Church–Turing thesis. Formulated independently by Alonzo Church and Alan Turing in the 1930s, this is a conjecture proposing that an **algorithm** exists to solve a given problem only if there is a **Turing machine** that can compute the solution to that problem. This gives some precision to the idea of an algorithm, because Turing machines can be precisely characterized. Although the Church–Turing thesis is not formally provable, it is widely accepted. A psychological version of it maintains that the limits of human thought coincide with the limits of what can be computed.

Churchland, Patricia Smith (b. 1943). Currently a MacArthur Fellow, and also professor of philosophy at the University of California, San Diego, and adjunct professor at the Salk Institute. Patricia Smith Churchland's work in cognitive science has devoted particular attention to research in neurobiology and has introduced to the study of mind an empirically based approach that she calls neurophilosophy—linking traditional philosophical inquiry with empirical research. She has vigorously opposed **functionalism** and the **language of thought** hypothesis, often in collaboration with Paul Churchland. For two of her major contributions, see the Bibliography.

Churchland, Paul M. (b. 1942). Professor of philosophy at the University of California, San Diego. Paul Churchland has promoted one computational approach to the study of mind, emphasizing that the brain's processing of information cannot be properly understood by reference to the categories proposed by **folk psychology**.

According to Churchland, an organism's capacity for representation derives not from entertaining internal propositions or sentences in **mentalese** but from patterns of neural activity along the lines proposed by **connectionism**. He has frequently collaborated with Patricia Smith Churchland.

Closed-world assumption. An assumption often incorporated into artificial intelligence systems; it treats as false every proposition that cannot be proved true by the system. On this approach, therefore, "false" equates to "not known to be true." Suppose, for example, that an artificial intelligence system (embodying the closed-world assumption) contains various facts about family relationships, but none about food preferences. Such a system would treat the sentence "Grandma likes broccoli" as false. Although this might seem extreme, the technique prevents the system from making unwarranted assertions.

Cognition. Any instance of a mental operation that displays **intentionality**. Examples include perception, recognition, inference, memory, and problem-solving. In cognitive science, one approach to cognition has emphasized the importance of rule-governed symbolic manipulation by the brain (akin to a programmed computer's manipulation of symbolic structures, as in **symbolic AI**), while a second has sought to show how cognitive activity can arise from patterns of connection among neurons (as in **connectionism**). Yet another approach depicts **minds as semiotic systems**. See also **Brain/mind**.

Cognitive architecture. The interconnected mental components required to process mental representations in order to yield cognitive processes and intelligent behavior. Examples include **short-term memory**, **long-term memory**, and **production systems**. The term "architecture" is meant to imply that these components are essentially permanent; moreover, features such as memory size or the speed of memory operations can be important determiners of algorithms that a given system is capable of carrying out. Although theories of cognitive architecture are constrained by tasks that biological systems can actually accomplish, descriptions of architecture generally abstract from specific biological underpinnings. Thus, theories of cognitive architecture may be modeled in nonbiological systems such as artificial intelligence devices.

Cognitive penetrability. A criterion that has been proposed by **Zenon Pylyshyn** for determining whether an agent's behavior or internal processes can be explained in terms of his or her goals and beliefs or whether the explanation must appeal to a "lower" level that is biologically fixed—such as the amount of memory available or the way in which memory is accessed. The criterion works as follows: If the phenomenon in question can be modified in response to changes in the agent's goals or beliefs, then that phenomenon is said to be cognitively penetrable and thus explainable by reference to beliefs and goals. Otherwise, the structure is cognitively impenetrable and must be accounted for by system components that are "built in" and unmodifiable. For example, the conversion of a retinal stimulus into a signal transmitted to the brain is cognitively impenetrable because this process is not affected by information possessed by an organism. In contrast, the interpretation of perceptual information is cognitively penetrable because it is at least partly a function of an organism's beliefs and expectations (consider a hunter who mistakes a comrade for an animal).

Cognitive psychology. An approach to the study of mental phenomena in terms of **information processing** models, usually on analogy with a computer. Unlike **behaviorism**, against which it is a reaction, cognitive psychology postulates a number of internal mechanisms and processes that operate on information, both from the outside (as in perception) and from within (as in reasoning). These mechanisms may be concerned with perception (recognizing an object or estimating the distance of an object); language (determining grammatical structures or extracting meaning from speech); reasoning (solving an equation), etc. Although the postulated mechanisms (in humans and animals, anyway) are presumed ultimately to be biological, cognitive psychology treats them at a higher level of abstraction, thereby leaving open the possibility of cognition in machines and other nonhuman entities. Thus, instead of describing mentality in biological terms, cognitive psychology employs concepts such as **long-term memory**, **short-term memory**, **set effect**, and **semantic network**.

Cognitive science. The interdisciplinary study of the nature of cognition in human beings, other animals, and machines (if such a thing is possible). At first, this approach was marked by its emphasis on **information processing** concepts, and its attention to the **Representational Theory of the Mind**; computer programs were taken to suggest the right level for theorizing about cognition. More recently, a new approach has been gaining favor. **Connectionism**, instead of focusing on computer programs, focuses on a "lower" level where programs are implemented. In biological organisms this refers to interconnected neurons in the brain; in computer systems, it refers to interconnected **processing units**. In either case, however, the major contributing disciplines to cognitive science include philosophy, psychology, computer science (notably, artificial intelligence), linguistics, and the neurosciences.

Combinatorial explosion. The rapidly increasing set of possibilities that are generated by a process in which one step leads to multiple possible successors, each of which leads to multiple possible successors, etc. For example, the possible number of first moves in a game of chess is relatively small (20, to be exact) but as the game progresses, any given move creates a new set of possible responses, and the total number of different possible move sequences in a chess game is astronomical. No chess-playing strategy, therefore, can plausibly operate by looking ahead at all possible moves and countermoves. The problem of combinatorial explosion presents a challenge for cognitive science, insofar as cognitive processes must be explained in ways that avoid it. The design of artificial intelligence systems is also constrained by this requirement.

Commisurotomy. Commonly known as the split-brain operation, commisurotomy is the surgical severing of the corpus callosum—the primary connecting link between the brain's left and right hemispheres. The procedure is sometimes done to relieve severe cases of epilepsy. Under many ordinary circumstances, it results in no obvious behavioral deficits; however, in certain experimental settings, commisurotomized patients display behavior that suggests **hemispheric specialization**. This raises the question of how (and where) different mental capacities are represented in the brain. Moreover, the apparent independent functioning of the two halves of a commisurotomized patient's brain has been taken by some thinkers to suggest that everyone's brain may house two (or more) "selves."

Commonsense knowledge. Knowledge that everyone is supposed to possess (especially by the time of adulthood) and is often brought to bear on the experiences of daily life. Examples include knowledge that heavy objects typically fall when dropped, knowledge that alcohol contributes to traffic accidents, etc. Precisely what knowledge properly qualifies as common sense, however, is subject to dispute, and some such knowledge is culturally dependent (for example, that belching at the dinner table is impolite). Although commonsense knowledge underlies much human reasoning, it has proven fiendishly difficult to represent in artificial intelligence systems. **Hubert Dreyfus** has argued that some commonsense knowledge—for example, knowledge of how to ride a bicycle—*cannot* be represented in a computer system because it cannot be reduced to a series of rules. See also **Frame problem**.

Competence/performance distinction. A distinction in linguistics introduced by Noam Chomsky, referring (respectively) to the formal **grammar** describing a language and a native speaker's application of that grammar. A speaker's ungrammatical sentences can then be accounted for by reference to errors in applying the relevant rules. Even the most fluent native speakers occasionally produce ungrammatical utterances, so competence represents an idealization.

Compilers. Devices for translating computer programs written in a high-level **programming language** (such as Pascal or C++) into the low-level language (**machine language**) on which computers actually run. In performing its translation, a compiler checks to ensure that the high-level program is grammatically correct—in other words, that it conforms to the constructs permitted in its programming language. A compiler is itself actually a computer program that takes a high-level program as its input (**source code**) and produces a translated, low-level program (**object code**) as its output. (Each high-level language requires a compiler designed specifically for that language.) This "translation" approach is widely used because machine language is very difficult to understand, whereas higher-level languages are much easier for computer programmers to work with. See also **Assemblers**, **Interpreters**.

Completeness. The property of a formal system such that every true statement expressible in that system is provable by the rules of that system. Alternatively, a system of logic is said to be complete when every true formula of that system occurs as a theorem of that system. See also **Gödel's incompleteness theorem**, **Soundness**.

Compositionality. A principle of semantics which maintains that the meaning of a sentence is determined by the meanings of its constituent parts. Compositional semantics seeks to specify precisely the nature of this relationship between whole and parts.

Computability. A property defining the class of problems that can be solved by applying algorithms to formal systems. The **Church–Turing thesis** holds that an **algorithm** in any formal system can be computed by some **Turing machine**, which implies that the boundaries of computability are the same as those of problems that can be solved by Turing machines. A parallel thesis about the nature of thought maintains that all thinking is computation simply because computability defines the boundaries of thought.

Computation. An information-preserving, systematic transformation of input to output. In **symbolic AI** systems, this is accomplished by way of an explicit set of rules embodied in a computer program; in **connectionist** systems, it arises out of patterns of activity among various processing units. Although in the latter case computation may be *describable* in terms of a set of rules, it does not follow that the process of computation actually *invokes* those rules. (For example, a calculator is wired to carry out the functions of arithmetic without containing a set of internal rules that it refers to as a guide. And human beings speak pretty much according to rules of grammar, although few people could cite many of the rules that describe grammatical speech.)

Computational linguistics. The study of language in terms of **algorithms**. Examples include speech-recognition systems (such as **Hearsay-II**), automatic translators, and **parsing** mechanisms.

Computational theory of mind. See **Connectionism, Symbolic AI**.

Concepts. Abstractions that classify individual objects or events together on the basis of some feature or set of features. On the traditional notion of concepts, features meant a set of necessary and sufficient conditions for the application of the concept: a given concept applied just to those things that had the specified properties. More recently, it has been proposed that at least many concepts are fuzzy and cannot be applied on the basis of precisely specifiable conditions. "Game" is such a concept. Games may involve teams, or just a single player (as in solitaire); they may involve points, winners, and losers (as in basketball), or winners and losers without points (as in chess), or none of the above (as in tag), etc. See also **Categorization, Family Resemblance, Generalization, Prototype**.

Conceptual dependency (CD). Pioneered by **Roger Schank**, CD is essentially a **semantic network** system for representing the meanings of sentences. One of its central insights is that people tend to extract the meanings from sentences they encounter, remembering these rather than specific sentence forms. Moreover, a variety of different sentences may have essentially the same meaning, and reducing them all to a single representation yields a considerable savings in memory resources. Not only does the conceptual dependency approach claim to provide a model of how humans represent meaning, it also provides a vehicle for meaning representation in artificial intelligence systems. CD theory employs some of the core ideas of **case grammar** but adds several basic categories of actions (such as ingesting food or drink, changing location, or changing ownership). See also **Interlingua**.

Condition-action rules. Instructions of the form "If . . . then——," where what occurs on the left-hand side (". . .") indicates the condition to be tested for, and what follows "then" ("——") indicates the action to be taken provided that the condition tested for has been met. Condition-action rules are very important in **algorithms** and computer **programs**, where they serve as instructions for conditional **branching**.

Conditionals. Sentences of the form "If . . . then ——", where the ". . ." component is known as the antecedent and the "——" component as the consequent. The simplest kind of conditional is the *material* or truth-functional conditional, whose truth or falsity depends exclusively upon the truth values of its components. When either its antecedent is false or its consequent is true, a sentence of this kind is said to be true. Thus the sentences "If this stick of dynamite is ignited, then it will explode" and "If this stick of dynamite is ignited, then it will not explode"—taken as material conditionals— might both be true as long as their antecedents are false. A second kind of conditional, important in planning strategies, is the *subjunctive* (or *counterfactual*) conditional, which characterizes how things would be if the antecedent were true. In this case, the subjunctive sentences "If this stick of dynamite were ignited, then it would explode" and "If this stick of dynamite were ignited, then it would not explode" cannot both be true, since they characterize different outcomes, assuming that their antecedents are true.

Conflict resolution. A process required in **production systems** when an input is encountered to which more than one instruction (**condition-action rule**) applies. In such cases, it is necessary to decide which of the applicable rules shall prevail. A variety of conflict-resolution techniques is possible, for example "Follow the first rule that applies," or (more usefully) "Follow the most specific rule that applies."

Conjunction fallacy. A violation of the following principle of probability: A conjunction cannot have a higher probability than any of its conjuncts. Extensive studies by Tversky and Kahneman (for example, Tversky and Kahneman, 1983) have demonstrated that conjunction fallacies are often committed (even by sophisticated reasoners) in situations involving probability estimates. For example, suppose that subjects are given a highly incomplete biographical sketch of Sandy, who is described as "compulsive, mathematical, and lazy." They are then asked to decide which of the following is most likely: (1) Sandy is an accountant who likes jazz; (2) Sandy likes jazz. Typically, subjects assign (1) a higher probability than (2), in violation of the aforementioned principle of probability. Thus, human reasoning does not always proceed along the idealized lines of probability theory and a task for cognitive science is to develop accounts of reasoning that address this fact.

Connection machine. A **parallel processing** computer system, designed by W. Daniel Hillis. The Hillis machine can perform 65,535 simultaneous calculations, with memory access estimated at approximately 10^{11} **bits** per second. Much larger machines of this type are currently under development.

Connectionism (also called **Parallel Distributed Processing** or **PDP**). An artificial intelligence approach to understanding cognition, derived from viewing the brain as a network of interconnected neurons. Connectionist models consist of interconnected processing units or nodes. Instead of being under the control of some "executive," each processing unit behaves according to the input it receives (either from sensory input devices or other processing units). It performs a simple computation on the input and transmits the result to its neighbors. Many such units may carry out their computations simultaneously; thus connectionist systems are **parallel processing** devices. Moreover, knowledge in a connectionist system is distributed, because it is represented by *patterns* of network activation across multiple processing units instead of by locating individual items of knowledge in individual nodes. (From these two latter points comes the name *parallel distributed processing*.) PDP systems represent a promising approach to modeling learning mechanisms because their patterns of activity may be easily modified in the light of experience, resulting in new behaviors of the system as a whole. With powerful systems such as the **connection machine** already operational, and much more powerful systems now under development, connectionism is becoming a dominant research program in cognitive science today. Among the most important books in this area is a two-volume set of studies edited by Rumelhart et al. (1986). See also **Processing units in connectionist systems**.

Connectionist systems. See **Connectionism**.

Connective, logical. See **Logical connective**.

Consciousness. An ability to experience or perceive the environment, or to represent an actual or possible state of affairs (for example, through imagination). In general, consciousness is expressible, either through verbal or nonverbal behavior. Since it may admit of various degrees, a person (animal, machine) might be aware of some phenomena but not aware of other phenomena. In traditional modern philosophy, consciousness has been considered the fundamental hallmark of any **mind**. For biological creatures, the range of possible consciousness appears to be determined by neurophysiological capacities under the influence of environmental histories. Consciousness should be distinguished from *self*-consciousness, which is an awareness of awareness (or of one's own self). Self-consciousness, like consciousness, exhibits different degrees.

Constraint satisfaction. An approach to problem-solving in which the solution is taken to be whatever maximally satisfies a set of mutually restricted hypotheses (constraints). In the analysis of visual input, for example, adjacent points in a retinal image are generally assumed to correspond to approximately the same visual depth; the constraints in this case are hypotheses concerning adjacent retinal elements. The constraint-satisfaction approach is well-suited to **connectionism**, with connections among units representing constraints (perhaps with varying levels of influence).

Context of discovery/context of justification. A distinction (first recognized by **Aristotle**) between the invention or discovery of an idea (hypothesis, theory) and its acceptance or evaluation. It has widely been assumed that invention or discovery is exclusively psychological and that the principles of logic do not apply, whereas acceptance or evaluation is assumed to be a logical activity in which psychological considerations have no weight. Although various **heuristic** discovery techniques have been proposed, it is a matter of debate whether any non-heuristic general principles of discovery exist.

Context-free grammars. The rules of a **grammar** typically take the form "$X \rightarrow YZ$," indicating how one syntactical component (represented by the X on the left side) may be broken down into smaller units (represented by the YZ on the right side). In a context-free grammar, the rules are restricted as follows: Only one symbol may appear on the left side of a grammatical rule (although more than one rule may occur with the same symbol appearing on the left side). Context-free grammars occupy Level 2 in the **Chomsky hierarchy**. Although sufficiently powerful to describe many of the structures that appear in natural languages, there are some sequences of symbols that they cannot generate.

Context-sensitive grammars. The rules of a **grammar** are typically presented in the form "X→YZ," indicating how one syntactical component (represented by the X on the left side) may be broken down into smaller units (represented by the YZ on the right side). Context-sensitive grammars permit more than one symbol to occur on the left side of a given rule. Thus, the analysis of a given symbol may depend not only upon what the symbol is but also upon what precedes or follows it (its context). Context-sensitive grammars are at Level 1 in the **Chomsky hierarchy**. Many natural languages (English included) exhibit context-sensitive constructions.

Control structures. Strategies for determining which part of a computer **program** will execute at a given time. A variety of strategies is possible. For example, a program may run sequentially from start to finish; or it may pass control to a module or **subroutine** (with control returned to the point of departure as the subroutine is completed). Neither of these approaches seems to supply a realistic model of human cognition. More plausible approaches are **production systems** and **blackboard architecture**.

Controlled processes. See **Automatic vs. controlled processes**.

Conversational implicatures. First discussed by H. P. Grice, conversational implicatures are consequences that are suggested, rather than strictly implied, by what a speaker says in a particular conversational setting. The suggestions are interpretable because discourse typically is cooperative and somewhat structured. Thus, for example, if A says "I'm hungry" and B replies "There's a good restaurant near my house," B is said to implicate that the restaurant isn't too far away, that it is open, that A's hunger can be assuaged by going there, etc. Conversational implicatures are an important source of information that cannot be extracted directly from analysis of sentence content. As such, they pose a challenge to machine understanding of discourse. For an extended study of implicatures see Grice (1989), especially Chapter 2.

Corpus callosum. The network of fibers that connects the brain's left and right hemispheres. See also **Commisurotomy**.

Count nouns vs. mass nouns. Count nouns in their singular form require an article (such as *a*, *an*, *the*), whereas mass nouns can appear in their singular form without an article. As the names suggest, count nouns indicate items that can be enumerated, whereas mass nouns represent things whose quantity is indefinitely expressed through modifiers like *some* or *many* or *much*. Examples of count nouns are *table*, *person*, and *unicorn*; examples of mass nouns are *water*, *gold*, and *fuel*.

Counterfactuals. See **Conditionals**.

CPU (Central Processing Unit). The computer component that maintains physical control over a computer's actions. It consists of an arithmetic-logic unit (sometimes abbreviated ALU), which performs basic operations; a control unit, which coordinates demands made on the CPU by various sources (keyboard, printer, running program, etc.); and small (temporary) memories known as registers. It is possible to harness multiple CPUs together so that multiple operations are performed simultaneously—an approach used by **connectionism**.

Creativity in language. A phenomenon, emphasized by **Noam Chomsky**, referring to the fact that native speakers can produce and understand an indefinitely large number of sentences that they have never encountered before. Moreover, this phenomenon is exhibited by children at a fairly young age. Chomsky and others have argued that the ability to understand and produce indefinitely many novel sentences is based on an internalized grammar. Furthermore, since the grammar is not derivable from the linguistic data that a child encounters, the hypothesis of a **universal grammar** (common to every human speaker on the face of the earth) is required.

CT (computerized tomography) scans. A technique for obtaining three-dimensional images of the interior of a body. Computerized tomography depends upon the use of focused X-rays, the source of which rotates around the subject. From measurements of the amount of radiation that passes through the body, an image (or "slice") of that body is constructed, and repeated passes can provide a basis for putting together fair approximations of three-dimensional bodily images.

Cybernetics. Pioneered by Norbert Wiener, cybernetics is the scientific study of systems whose behavior is regulated by **feedback** mechanisms, which permit the output of a device to affect the processes that produced its output. Wiener argued that cybernetic machines could be regarded as striving for and maintaining goals; he further proposed that purposive human behavior could be explained with the concepts of cybernetics.

CYRUS. An artificial intelligence project developed at Yale University in the late 1970s by Janet Kolodner. CYRUS stands for Computerized Yale Retrieval and Updating System; the aptness of this acronym stems from the fact that the system was fed daily news stories about then secretary of state Cyrus Vance and could answer questions (framed in English) about him. As new information was provided to CYRUS, the program reorganized itself in such a way that further questions could then be answered. By making "educated guesses" CYRUS was also able to answer some questions on topics about which it had no direct information.

D

Data domain. The sets of observations and experiments that can be made or conducted in relation to a fixed set of technological instruments at one time. The introduction of the telescope, the microscope, and the electron microscope are appropriate illustrations, but more recent examples include **CT scans**, **PET imaging**, and **MRI** in relation to cognitive inquiries.

Data-driven processing. See **Bottom-up/top-down processing**.

Decidability. See **Decision procedure**.

Decision procedure (also called **Effective procedure**). A routine or procedure that can be carried out in a finite sequence that in every case yields a definite answer (*Yes* or *No*) to a question within a specific domain of inquiry. The task of discovering a decision procedure for a given class of problems is known as the decision problem. Once a decision procedure has been found (in cases where one exists) the problem is solvable and those questions are decidable. Contrast **Undecidability**.

Declarative representation. A method for storing information in a computer system by providing it with a set of explicit facts (declarative statements), in contrast to **procedural representation**, which stores knowledge implicitly as a set of actions to be taken in order to arrive at new facts. An example of declarative representation is the **semantic network**, whereas procedural representation is exhibited in a **production system**. Artificial intelligence systems commonly employ both types of representation, although the declarative / procedural distinction is not always perfectly sharp. Declarative representation is akin to *knowing that*: possessing a set of facts. See also **Knowing how vs. knowing that**.

Deductive arguments. Arguments that are intended to be conclusive, in the sense that their conclusions cannot be false when their premises are true (in contrast to **inductive arguments**). For example, when the premises "All beans are vegetables" and "Garbanzos are beans" are true, the conclusion "Garbanzos are vegetables" cannot be false. Such arguments are *valid* and their conclusions follow from them. Note that a valid argument may have a false conclusion when its premises are false. When all the premises of a valid deductive argument are true, however, the argument is described as *sound*. The conclusion of a sound argument cannot be false, but it can be difficult—sometimes very difficult—to separate sound arguments from merely valid ones. A valid deductive argument remains valid if other premises are added to it.

Deep structure. A level of analysis employed in a **transformational grammar** and contrasted to **surface structure** (the distinction was introduced by **Noam Chomsky**). The relationship between the two levels is revealed by the transformational grammar, which proposes a derivation of surface structure from deep structure. As the term "deep structure" suggests, this level of analysis does not closely correspond to the structure of an actual sentence, but it permits a number of generalizations to be made about underlying hidden similarities among sentences whose apparent structures differ from each other.

Default values. Those values assumed by a system to be true unless an alternative is expressly provided. Default values (or defaults) are sometimes assigned in a computer program through an explicit process known as initialization, although in other cases they are provided by the programming language itself. Various structures in a computer program—including variables, **semantic networks**, and **frames**—commonly make use of defaults.

Defeasibility. A property possessed by the conclusion of an argument when further information may cause it to be withdrawn. For example, it would be quite natural to conclude that Chris has a doctorate, given the information that Chris is a professor. Nevertheless, a dean's documented report that Chris never finished graduate school would cause this natural conclusion to be withdrawn; thus, the original conclusion is said to be defeasible. (With some additional filling in, the whole story might still be quite intelligible. For example, Chris might have published some brilliant articles, resulting in an offer of a professorship without regard to the completion of the Ph.D.). An important challenge for cognitive science is to understand how defeasible conclusions are reached. This is part and parcel of understanding how **commonsense knowledge** is represented. Defeasible systems of reasoning are referred to as nonmonotonic. See also **Inductive arguments**, **Monotonicity**.

Definitions. Linguistic entities that have two parts: a *definiendum*, which consists of the word, phrase, or expression to be defined, and a *definiens*, which is some word, phrase, or expression by means of which it is defined. A standard symbol for displaying a definition is ". . . $=_{df}$ ——," to be interpreted as ". . ." means by definition "——." It has been observed, however, that not every word in a language can be defined without introducing either (1) an infinite regress (whereby new words are introduced to explain the meaning of old words, and newer words to explain their meaning in turn, ad infinitum) or (2) a vicious circularity (where a word is explained by means of other words that are ultimately explained by reference to the original word). One way out of this difficulty in the case of a natural language involves the use of **ostensive definition** (explaining a concept by means of examples). But for a **language of thought** such as might be used by the brain, the problem of **original meaning** must admit of some other solution. See also **Symbol grounding problem**.

Delta rule. A measure of the amount of learning in a system, as indicated by the difference (delta) between the system's actual output and the system's desired output. See also **Delta rule, generalized**.

Delta rule, generalized. An extension of the **delta rule**, for use in **connectionist** systems with three or more layers of **processing units**. The generalized delta rule is employed in training a system to carry out new tasks. This is accomplished in two steps. First, the system is provided with an input, and its resulting outputs are compared with their desired values. Any difference between the two values is treated as an error, which is sent back (back-propagated) through the network, causing appropriate alterations in connection strengths among the processing units. The process is then repeated until the differences between actual and desired output are eliminated.

Demons. Narrowly circumscribed rules occurring in some computer programs. They "watch for" and are activated by a prespecified condition, and cause the system to adjust itself appropriately in response. Demons are common in **expert systems** and play an important role in the **society of mind** approach to **cognition**.

DENDRAL. An early **expert system**, developed at Stanford University beginning in the 1960s under the direction of **Edward Feigenbaum** and others. The system had the ability to analyze chemical compounds and was also used to explore issues in scientific hypothesis construction and validation.

Dennett, Daniel C. (b. 1942). American philosopher, currently distinguished arts and sciences professor and director of the Center for Cognitive Studies at Tufts University. Dennett has written widely on the relationship between artificial intelligence and human cognition (see Bibliography). His recent and highly regarded *Consciousness Explained* outlines a theory of the mind as a **Von Neumann machine** that runs on the parallel processing architecture of the brain. See also **Intentional stance**.

Depth-first search. See **Breadth-first search vs. depth-first search**.

Descartes, René (1596–1650). French mathematician and philosopher, often referred to as the father of modern philosophy. Descartes shifted attention from the objective (external) world to the subjective (internal) mind; the latter thus became the point of departure for psychological theorizing. He employed a method now referred to as Cartesian doubt, the idea being that any proposition incapable of being doubted could be taken as certain and true. In this way, Descartes forged an alliance between psychology and epistemology. He also presented arguments in support of **dualism**, claiming that while bodily processes could be explained by mechanical means, the processes of the mind could not. Moreover, by separating mind from body, Descartes provided a basis for the religious doctrine of immortality.

Determiners. Words such as "all," "some," "the," and "a" that make up a syntactic category whose members' role is to introduce common nouns.

Determinism / free will. The controversy over determinism and free will concerns whether or not human behavior is caused and, if so, whether or not it makes sense for people to be held morally responsible for their actions. There are three traditional viewpoints on this matter. The *hard determinist* position holds that all behavior is caused and that, consequently, it never makes sense to hold anyone morally responsible for his or her behavior.

This view is often supported by contending that, since no one could ever have done otherwise, praise and blame do not apply. The *soft determinist* position maintains that even though all behavior is indeed caused, people may nonetheless sometimes be held responsible for what they do; namely, when their actions are caused by their own internal psychological states (such as beliefs, desires, or perceptions). On this view, a "free" action is internally caused, not uncaused. In contrast, the *libertarian* position asserts that people are morally responsible for their behavior only when it is freely chosen, which is taken to require an *absence* of causation. Determinist views (both hard and soft) are naturally associated with **physicalism**, whereas the libertarian position is often associated with **dualism**.

Digital Systems. See **Analog vs. digital systems**.

Dispositions. Tendencies to display specific outcome responses under suitable conditions—specifiable via subjunctive **conditionals**. For example, if sugar were put in water it would dissolve (it is so disposed), and if glass were pounded with a hammer it would break. Many psychological states appear to have a dispositional core: for example, a person's knowledge of a particular fact may only be displayed on occasion, as may particular goals and intentions. When a distinction is drawn between observable and unobservable properties, dispositions tend to be viewed as unobservable properties whose observable manifestations are not assumed to exhaust their content. See also **Observational / theoretical distinction**.

DOCTOR Program. See **ELIZA**.

Dreyfus, Hubert (b. 1929). Professor of philosophy at the University of California, Berkeley, and a prominent critic of artificial intelligence. Dreyfus argues that much of human activity, including **commonsense knowledge**, is not explainable by **algorithms**, and that the success of artificial intelligence systems in dealing with **micro-**

worlds does not generalize well to larger problems. His views are developed in Dreyfus (1979).

Dualism. The theory that reality ultimately consists of two kinds of substance, usually identified as physical vs. nonphysical, although other dualistic categories are possible. In cognitive science, dualism is usually taken to mean that the **mind** is nonphysical—a view that few cognitive scientists endorse. Although mind / body dualism was introduced by the ancient Greeks, it is most often associated with **Descartes**, whose version of the theory is thus known as Cartesian dualism. Cartesian dualism maintains not only that mind and body are separate substances, but also that the two substances causally interact. This presents a notorious problem because the nature of the interaction has never been adequately explained.

E

Ecological psychology. An approach to the study of cognition which maintains that mental phenomena represent and predict the flow of external events in continuous interaction with the environment. This view stands in contrast to cognitive psychology, which tends to view the environment in more static terms, with organisms encoding momentary "snapshots" (such as retinal images) of the external world and subsequently subjecting them to internal processing. A prominent exponent of the ecological approach is **J. J. Gibson**.

Edges. Lines of contrast between light and dark that are identified in an early stage of visual processing. As components of the **primal sketch**, they provide an important clue to location of boundaries between objects.

Effective procedure. See **Decision procedure.**

Eliminative materialism. The theory that the ordinary concepts of ordinary **folk psychology** (such as beliefs, desires, goals) do not accurately represent the correct categories of cognition and that a neuroscientific account of mentality will therefore not match up in any straightforward way with those familiar but incorrect ordinary categories. On this view, the old commonsense psychological framework cannot be reduced to a neurophysiological account, but instead must be abandoned with the development of neuroscience.

ELIZA. A well-known early artificial intelligence program designed in 1966 by **Joseph Weizenbaum**. The program mimics a nondirective (Rogerian) psychotherapist and was written to show how certain problems in **natural language processing** might be handled by means of relatively simple principles. Weizenbaum's classic demonstration dialog began as follows (the human's input is lowercase, and the computer's response is capitalized):

> Men are all alike.
> IN WHAT WAY?
> They're always bugging us about something or other.
> CAN YOU THINK OF A SPECIFIC EXAMPLE?
> Well, my boyfriend made me come here.
> YOUR BOYFRIEND MADE YOU COME HERE?
> He says I'm depressed much of the time.
> I'M SORRY TO HEAR YOU ARE DEPRESSED.

Within limited conversational domains, ELIZA's responses to input appear to be intelligent; hence, ELIZA, like **SHRDLU**, is sometimes mentioned in connection with the **Turing test**. ELIZA's restricted scope, however, does not begin to meet the wide-open questioning that

Turing's test envisaged. For further discussion of ELIZA see Weizenbaum (1976).

Empirical testability. A hypothesis or theory is said to be empirically testable when there are processes or procedures—observational or experimental—by means of which evidence relevant to determining the truth or falsity of that hypothesis or theory can be obtained. If the evidence that could be obtained under suitable conditions would provide conclusive grounds for accepting that hypothesis or theory as true, the hypothesis or theory is said to be verifiable. If the evidence that could be obtained under suitable conditions would provide conclusive grounds for rejecting that hypothesis or theory as false, the hypothesis or theory is said to be falsifiable. In the absence of conclusive evidence for their truth or falsity, hypotheses and theories can merely be confirmed and disconfirmed by means of fallible and incomplete evidence.

Empiricism. The view that knowledge is entirely derived from experience; hence, that there is no a priori knowledge if that knowledge is supposed to be innate, or independent of experience. Empiricism allows the possibility of **analytic** knowledge in the form of sentences whose truth or falsity follows from the adoption of a language alone, provided that knowledge of the language can be accounted for in a manner consistent with empiricist principles. Various versions of empiricism tend to be distinguished on the basis of whether they affirm or deny an infallible foundation of knowledge based on experience. Contrast **Rationalism**.

ENIAC (Electronic Numerical Integrator and Computer). The world's first programmable electronic digital computer. Built at the University of Pennsylvania in 1946 at a cost of $500,000, ENIAC contained 18,000 vacuum tubes embedded in 30 subunits which, when lined up side by side, covered 80 linear feet of floor space. Programming the ENIAC was accomplished through a combination of 6,000 switch settings and numerous cable routings; input data were entered on punched cards. The ENIAC represented a considerable improvement in speed over its precursors, although a 20-second computation required two days of programming.

Episodic memory. Memory of personally experienced events, as contrasted to **semantic memory**, which involves vocabulary and general facts about the world. Arguments that the episodic/semantic distinction has a physical basis draw heavily from physiological measures (such as measures of blood flow in the brain and the effects of frontal lobe lesions), but interpretation of this evidence is not univocal.

Epistemology (the theory of knowledge). The study of the sources, nature, and limits of knowledge, and related concepts such as justification and belief.

Equipotentiality. The doctrine that a variety of the brain's structures are capable of supporting the same functions. On this view, therefore, many neurological structures are not limited to the performance of a single function. See also **Plasticity**.

Expectation-driven processing. See **Bottom-up/top-down processing**.

Experiential findings. Observations and experiments whose outcomes can be described by means of observational language. Experiential findings in general cannot exhaust the content of hypotheses and theories expressed by means of theoretical language and subjected to empirical tests, whose content goes beyond their observational and experimental consequences. Thus, what **W. V. O. Quine**, among others, has called the "underdetermination of theories by evidence" refers to the incapacity of experiential findings to exhaust the content of a theory. But instrumentalists, who tend to view theories as devices for prediction rather than as grounds for explanation, sometimes maintain that there is nothing more to a theory than its experiential consequences—a claim that scientific realists deny. See also **Observational/theoretical distinction**.

Expert system. An artificial intelligence system that displays the domain-specific knowledge capacities of a human expert. An expert system contains three main components: a *knowledge base* gathered from human experts by a process called knowledge engineering; a set of *decision rules* specifying what action to take under various conditions; and an *inference engine* that applies appropriate rules to the knowledge base. A common architecture for expert systems is the **production system** approach; it was used in the well-known systems **MYCIN** and **XCON**.

Explicit vs. implicit memory. Explicit memory involves conscious recollection of a previous experience, whereas implicit memory utilizes previous experiences but without conscious recollection. Evidence for the latter type of memory comes from experiments that, for example, present subjects with a list of words to study, and subsequently present a word completion task ("Fill in the missing letters in the word TAB__ __"). In such a case, subjects tend to draw from the recently studied list, even if other words would fit the presented schema (here, *table*, *taboo*, and *tabor* would all theoretically fit).

Extensional logic. Any system of logic in which only the referents (denotations, extensions) of terms contribute to the truth values of sentences in which they appear. In such a system, the truth or falsity of a compound sentence is strictly a function of the truth value of its constituent parts. Thus, for example, a sentence of the form "P and Q" is true when both P and Q are true, and false otherwise. For related discussion, see **Conditional**. Contrast **Intensional logic**.

F

Family resemblance. An idea deriving from Wittgenstein (1968) which holds that membership in a category is not determined by a precise set of necessary and sufficient conditions; instead, a category's members often display various overlapping features (in varying degrees), as members of a family characteristically do. See also **Categorization**, **Concepts**, **Prototype**.

Fan effect. A phenomenon that characterizes slower memory retrieval when the fact being retrieved is associated with a large number of related items. To illustrate, if you have memorized many facts about A and fewer facts about B, then it will typically take longer for you to verify a given fact about A than about B. This phenomenon is captured in **semantic network** representations of memory by reference to **activation** spreading from a given point in the memory network to related points, with both speed and strength of activation being reduced as the number of network connections increases. Fan effect refers to the inverse relationship between number of associations and **reaction time**. See also **Spreading activation**.

Feature analysis. An approach that can be used in systems designed for **recognition** tasks, such as visual recognition of objects. The target is analyzed in terms of key properties, that are then matched against descriptions stored by the system. To take a simplified example, the letter H might be described as two essentially parallel and more or less vertical lines, connected by a third line that is essentially horizontal. An important advantage of this approach is that a single description makes allowance for a variety of typographical styles, as contrasted to **template matching**, which is less accurate and requires significantly greater memory resources.

Feedback. The property of a system whereby a component responds to the consequences of its own behavior. A familiar example is the household thermostat; together the thermostat and the furnace it controls comprise a self-adjusting system. This type of system employs negative feedback; the controlling device operates so as to *compensate* for its consequences, thereby maintaining a relatively stable state (relatively constant room temperature in this case). Positive feedback, in contrast, has the opposite effect, continuing to *magnify* the consequences of the controller's behavior. Many biological systems employ feedback (such as systems of muscular control, hunger, and thirst). See also **Cybernetics**.

Feigenbaum, Edward A. (b. 1936). Professor of computer science at Stanford who has done pioneering work on expert systems, including the early **DENDRAL** project. Feigenbaum has published a variety of books, including *The Handbook of Artificial Intelligence*, a multivolume work of which he is a co-editor.

Finite-state automaton. An abstract computer (**automaton**) that is not provided with any memory. It corresponds to a **finite-state grammar** in that both are capable of generating exactly the same strings of symbols.

Finite-state grammar. A **grammar** whose rules are restricted as follows: The right-hand side of each rule contains at most one **nonterminal symbol** (some type of phrase) in addition to any number of **terminal symbols** (word types). This type of grammar embodies the view that sentences are produced from left to right, with each sentence element limiting the choices that may come next. For example, if the initial element is the word "these," the next term could be "people," "days," or "automobiles" but not "water," "student," or "sky." Once this choice is made, the following term (probably a verb) would be constrained by what preceded it (in this illustration, a plural form would be required). Finite-state grammars are the least powerful grammars in the **Chomsky hierarchy** and are incapable of generating some sentence structures in English.

First Order Predicate Calculus (FOPC). A **formal language** system capable of representing various patterns of **deductive argument**. It permits statements to be formulated not only about named individuals, but also about groups of individuals through the application of the existential and universal **quantifier** (interpreted as "some" and "all," respectively). "First order" refers to the restriction that quantifiers may be applied only to individuals and not to properties possessed by individuals. Notations in artificial intelligence programs often reflect the structures of FOPC.

Flowcharts. Schematic diagrams that depict the logical structure of a computer **algorithm** or **program**.

Fodor, Jerry A. (b. 1935). American philosopher and psychologist affiliated with the City University of New York and with Rutgers University. Fodor proposed the controversial **language of thought** hypothesis, which claims that everyone has an innate language whose expressive power is equivalent to any natural language that may later be acquired. He also proposed the modularity of mind thesis, according to which various mental operations such as parsing a sentence (determining its grammatical structure) are carried out by specialized "hard-wired" units of the brain. Fodor has written widely on the topics of language, mind, and computers.

Folk psychology. The psychology of ordinary people that is based on the ascription of motives, beliefs, and ethics. It reflects our everyday view that individual

51

behavior can be explained by reference to those states, for example: "Jane left the party early because she was tired"; "Bill's belief that the end of the world was imminent prompted him to give all his money away and to seek refuge in a cave." If folk psychology is at least roughly correct, then adequate scientific explanations of human behavior will continue to be fashioned by means of these explanatory categories, even though there may come to be refinements in our understanding of their nature in the light of scientific progress. Opponents of folk psychology, however, argue that these categories will gradually evaporate with the growth of scientific knowledge, eventually yielding a completely new kind of explanation for human behavior—possibly one that envisions humans as special kinds of neurophysiologically based computing machines. Among the most important critics of folk psychology are **Patricia Churchland**, **Paul Churchland**, and **Stephen Stich**.

Formal language. A specification of a set of **well-formed formulas**, by stipulating: (1) a set of primitive (undefined) symbols and (2) a set of formation rules that specify what combinations of symbols are permissible (grammatical). As such, symbol strings in a formal system remain uninterpreted; however, it is possible to assign interpretations to the system's components, in which case the language acquires a **semantics**.

Formal system. A specification of a **formal language** and its theorems (purported truths), and often also including a **semantics** for the language. Results such as **Church's thesis** and **Gödel's incompleteness theorem** are about the properties of formal systems.

Forward chaining. A problem-solving strategy that, given an initial state, tries to find series of intermediate steps that will reach a desired goal. Starting with a problem's "given" or initial conditions, forward chaining proceeds by appealing to a set of **condition-action rules** in order to generate the possible first moves that could be made. (The initial condition is matched against the condition component, or left-hand side, of an applicable rule, and the next-move state is represented by the rule's action component.) If more than one rule applies, a **conflict-resolution** strategy may be employed. Assuming that the newly generated state is not yet the goal, the rules are then applied to the new state, yielding yet another state. The process continues until the goal is reached. Forward chaining uses data-driven or **bottom-up processing**. Contrast **Backward chaining**.

Frame problem. The problem of representing knowledge in a system so as to capture what will and what will not change about a situation or state of affairs across time. For example, if you flip an appropriate switch the light will normally turn on, but the windows will not open and the ceiling will not collapse. Although this seems obvious, it is not at all obvious how to represent such information in a computer system. Some theoreticians maintain that the problem concerns common sense rather than scientific knowledge, whereas others, with some justification, contend that scientific knowledge is required to resolve it. Among those who have dealt with this issue are **John McCarthy** and Pat Hayes.

Frames. Information structures that are frequently used in artificial intelligence programs. A frame organizes a variety of information about a particular type of object. For example, commonsense information about the human body's structure might be stored in units describing arms, legs, head, trunk, etc. The "arm" frame could indicate (1) major parts, such as forearm, wrist, and elbow; (2) the bodily parts to which the arm is attached (shoulder, hand); material composition (flesh, bone). Some of the information, such as that concerning length, could be provided as **default values**, possibly to be overridden in particular cases (say, if the arm is that of an infant). Frames, besides being useful for **knowledge representation** in artificial intelligence work, probably have some degree of psychological reality in humans. As hierarchical information organizers, they involve **chunking**. See also **Scripts**.

Function. An operator that can be applied to a pre-specified number of individuals (or arguments), returning an object as a result. For example, the function "+," applied to the numbers 5 and 2 (the function's arguments in this illustration), returns the value 7. And supposing that Fran is Fred's mother, the function "mother of," applied to Fred, would yield Fran. Functions may also be applied to functions. For example, "mother of (mother of Fred)" would return Fred's maternal grandmother, whereas "mother of (father of Fred)" would return Fred's paternal grandmother, whoever those individuals happened to be. Not only are functions an essential part of the **First Order Predicate Calculus**, they are also fundamental to many programming languages (**LISP** is an especially noteworthy example).

Functionalism. The view that mental states can be characterized in terms of their role in connecting inputs with outputs as well as connections to each other. There are at least two principal varieties of functionalism. The first is *machine state* functionalism, which maintains that human beings can be properly understood as special instances of computing machines and that mental activity involves physically embodied transitions from one computational state to another. This position was advocated by **Hilary Putnam** in some of his early work. The second is *causal role* functionalism, which maintains that the identity of a mental representation (symbol, sign) is determined by its causal role in influencing behavior. Machine state functionalism is not a widely held theory at present, but causal role functionalism is popular.

Fuzzy set. A category or set for which membership is not simply a matter of yes or no; rather, membership can be partial, as indicated for example on a scale from zero to one. Correspondingly, statements about fuzzy set membership, rather than simply taking the binary values TRUE and FALSE, are assigned truth values that exhibit probabilities from zero to one. These truth values do not represent uncertainty on the part of an evaluator, but instead reflect a property intrinsic to the statements themselves. Fuzzy sets provide an approach to **knowledge representation** for **categorization** tasks that do not neatly abide by necessary and sufficient conditions for category membership. See also **Prototype**.

G

General Problem Solver (GPS). An artificial intelligence project developed in 1957 by **Newell**, Shaw, and **Simon**. It was capable of solving a variety of problems in logic, mathematics, and chess, using the method of **means-ends analysis**. One of its well-known abilities involved the solution of cryptarithmetic problems, for example SEND + MORE = MONEY. The goal here is to figure out what number is represented by each letter, so that the sum works out correctly. (Once it is decided what number is represented by one occurrence of "E," the same value must be used for all the other occurrences of "E" as well.) The point of GPS was to uncover a broad set of techniques that humans use in problem-solving—techniques that were obtained from subjects through **protocols**. Thus, GPS was viewed by many in the artificial intelligence community as providing a model of human thinking.

55

Generalization. The forming of a conclusion about all members of a category on the basis of information about some specific category members—usually by **inductive argument**. See also **Categorization**, **Concepts**.

Generate and test strategy. See **British Museum algorithm**.

Gestalt principles of organization. A conception of organization based on the idea that a perceived whole is not just the sum of its parts; rather, the parts are organized into structures (see **Holism**) in principled ways. For example, items that are in close proximity to each other tend to be perceived as a unit (the letters in this sentence are seen as words that are separated by spaces). A variety of principles of organization were proposed by Gestalt psychologists such as Kurt Koffka and Wolfgang Köhler. Although the phenomena documented by Gestalt psychologists are incontrovertible, Gestalt principles have never been buttressed by a theory of neurophysiological underpinnings.

Gibson, James Jerome (1904–1979). American experimental psychologist whose influential studies of perception emphasized that much information is contained in a perceptual stimulus, thereby implying that much of what goes on in perceptual recognition does not require appeal to unconscious inferences or computational processes. See also **Ecological psychology**.

Goal-driven processing. See **Bottom-up/top-down processing**.

Gödel's incompleteness theorem. A landmark result published in 1931 by the Czech-born mathematician Kurt Gödel. The theorem states that any formal system powerful enough to generate the natural numbers will also permit the construction of true propositions that cannot be proved within that system (so long as that system is consistent). In this sense, such a system is incomplete. This result shattered a centuries-old assumption to the contrary. Some writers have taken Gödel's theorem to establish an unbridgeable gulf between the abilities of humans and computers, since the operations of computers ("logic machines") are constrained by the properties of the formal systems on which they are based. But in fact there is no reason to suppose that humans are not similarly constrained. An accessible presentation of Gödel's theorem and its proof is contained in Nagel and Newman (1958); a sustained meditation on Gödel's work in the context of cognitive science appears in Hofstadter (1979).

GOFAI (Good Old-Fashioned Artificial Intelligence). A term coined by John Haugeland to refer to theories embodying the following two claims: first, that intelligence arises out of the capacity to reason (both consciously and unconsciously) and, second, that the capacity for reason derives from the manipulation of internal symbols. See also **Information processing**, **Physical symbol system**.

Government-binding theory. An outgrowth of **transformational grammar** that employs just one transformational rule. To avoid the creation of unacceptable surface structures, various constraints on that rule's application must be introduced. The nature and number of those constraints is the subject of much contemporary debate.

Graceful degradation. The ability of a **connectionist system** to continue operating, although perhaps with diminished accuracy, in the face of damage to some of its components. Although the quality of information is reduced, the information is not entirely lost. (Similar items, for example, may tend to be confused.) This property of connectionist systems resembles what happens to biological organisms in the face of damage and thereby lends some support to connectionism as a model of cognition.

Grammar. In cognitive science this term generally means **syntax**, or set of formal rules that can be used to analyze or produce the sentences of a language. The specification of a grammar often is given via a series of rewrite rules that indicate how a structural component can be broken down into constituent parts. For example:

Sentence → *Noun Phrase* + *Verb Phrase*
Noun Phrase → *Noun*, or *Article* + *Noun*
Verb Phrase → *Verb* + *Noun Phrase*.

This means that a sentence consists of two main parts (here called *Noun Phrase* and *Verb Phrase*), with each of those parts composed of even smaller units, as indicated. The smallest structural units of a grammar are called **terminal symbols** (*Verb* is an example here). Grammars are of particular importance in **parsing**, and they raise for cognitive science the question of how (and what) grammar is represented in the mind.

Grandmother cell. A reference to the discredited idea that discrete memories or items of knowledge are represented in the brain by discrete neurological units. If such a representation scheme actually existed, then damage to a particular neurological component should be highly selective, for example resulting in a person's loss of the representation of "grandmother" while still retaining the concept "wife of grandfather," "female parent of parent," etc. This does not in fact occur, and arguably it does not make sense to suppose that it *could* occur.

Graph. A set of elements (**nodes**) and their interconnections (**links**, also called arcs). One important use of graphs in cognitive science is to depict the multifarious relations among concepts as they might be stored in human memory (see **semantic network** for an example). Pictorially, a graph consists of circles connected by arrows, although for artificial intelligence applications the pictorial representation must be converted into structures that can be implemented by a computer language. In computer programs, graphs provide a powerful basis for various **knowledge representation** strategies. A frequently encountered special case of the graph is the **tree**—essentially, a structure starting with a single element, which gives rise to additional elements, each of which gives rise to further elements (such as might be found on a hierarchical corporate organization chart with the president at the top, with various managers and other employees on lower levels).

Gray-level array. The retinal image, represented as a pattern of points of light (**pixels**) varying in degrees of intensity. In computational analyses of vision, different intensities can be assigned corresponding numerical values, which can then be operated on by appropriate **algorithms**. The gray-level array provides the original source of data from which the recognition of objects must eventually be derived. Computations performed on it give rise to another stage of early visual processing, the **primal sketch**.

H

HACKER. A program developed by Gerald Sussman in 1973 as his Ph.D. project at MIT. HACKER modeled the process of skill acquisition by developing plans for manipulating objects in a **blocks world**. A noteworthy feature of the program was its ability to debug strategies that had previously failed, thereby learning from and correcting its mistakes.

Halting problem. The problem that no general procedure exists by which to determine whether a particular **program** running on a particular **Turing machine** will eventually terminate. More formally, given a particular input i and a description of some Turing machine T, no algorithm exists to establish whether or not T will halt. This does not mean that it is impossible in every single case to determine whether a given Turing machine will halt; rather, there is no general procedure for settling the question for all cases.

HEARSAY-II. An artificial intelligence system designed to understand speech. For some details see **Blackboard architecture**.

Hebb, Donald O. (1904–1985). Canadian neuropsychologist whose 1949 book *The Organization of Behavior* contained ideas about learning that were later incorporated into **connectionist systems**. Hebb argued that patterns of behavior are gradually established through connections among sets of cells and that the strengths of connections between could be increased when both units were active. Although contemporary connectionist systems rely on a variety of rules for modifying the strength of connections between processing units, they owe their inspiration to Hebb's proposals.

Hemispheric specialization. Also called lateralization, this term refers to the hypothesis that the brain's left and right hemispheres perform essentially different functions. According to the specialization hypothesis, the brain's left hemisphere is associated with linguistic and analytical skills and the right hemisphere with spatial and nonverbal abilities. Although there is merit to this idea, evidence from patients who have undergone **commisurotomy** suggests that the functional capacities of each hemisphere differ in degree and are not divided with any precision. Moreover, patients who suffer damage to one hemisphere—especially if at an early age—often exhibit remarkably little loss of function because the brain's **plasticity** permits the remaining hemisphere to compensate for the damage. See also **Equipotentiality**.

Heuristics. Rules of thumb which, in the absence of **algorithms**, are useful generalizations for problem-solving tasks. Although heuristics do not guarantee solutions, they are often very helpful in dealing with problems that might not otherwise be resolved. Examples of heuristics are "Get your queen out early" (chess); "Try to place your mark in two opposite corners" (tic-tac-toe); "Follow a set of railroad tracks" (for pilots whose navigational systems break down); "Find a problem that you have solved before and which is similar to the new, unsolved one" (a general problem-solving strategy).

Heuristic search. A technique that, in considering possible next moves toward a goal, views some moves as more promising than others, according to a **heuristic** function. Contrast **Blind search**.

Hidden units. See **Processing units in connectionist systems**.

High-level/low-level languages. See **Programming language**.

Hofstadter, Douglas (b. 1945). Computer scientist at Indiana University, former author of *Scientific American's* "Metamagical Themas" column, and author of various works on cognitive science (see Bibliography), including the Pulitzer Prize-winning *Gödel, Escher, Bach*.

Holism. (a) The doctrine that a whole cannot be reduced to the sum of its parts—that is, that some things have significance that perhaps emerges from lower-level constituents but which cannot be adequately captured by focusing on those constituents alone. Examples include the alleged impossibility of reducing a meaningful sentence to syllables, rules, and grammars; or the notion that object recognition cannot be ultimately accounted in terms of discrete stimuli (see **Gestalt principles of organization**). This point of view challenges cognitive science's assumption that cognitive processes can be explained

61

mechanically in terms of underlying components. Hofstadter (1979) devotes considerable attention to the relationship between holism and the contrasting view of **reductionism**. (b) The doctrine that the brain as an integrated whole performs its intellectual tasks, in contrast to the **localization** theory, which maintains that specific mental functions are carried out by specific neurological structures.

Homunculus. Literally "little man," the idea of a homunculus is presupposed by theories of mind that tacitly invoke cognitive processes in order to explain cognitive processes. For example, visual perception is sometimes thought of as involving the production of pictorial images in the mind. But if this were an accurate account, then the internal pictures would presumably have to be looked at by some internal agent (homunculus)—yet no such agent is to be found. Moreover, the homunculus approach threatens to generate a vicious infinite regress, since the perceptions of a homunculus would also need to be accounted for (in terms of *its* internal homunculus?). On a more subtle level, theories of cognition that posit symbols that are "manipulated according to rules" must explain how symbolic processing can be done without appealing to a conscious agent that interprets symbols and consults rules. **Daniel Dennett** has written extensively on this issue.

Hume, David (1711–1776). Scottish philosopher, important for analyses of such notions as causation, induction, and the self and for his denial of the existence of natural (or nonlogical) necessities in nature. According to Hume, any idea must ultimately be traceable to some experience that gave rise to it. He denied that causes have to "bring about" their effects, insisting that the notion of causation was reducible to relations of resemblance and of regular association. Hume emphasized that, since we have no rational warrant to believe in the existence of natural necessities, we have no reason to believe that the future will resemble the past—a difficulty now known as the problem of induction. See also **Inductive arguments**.

I

Iconic memory. Very brief (approximately one-second) storage of visual information taken in during perception. The information preserved in iconic memory may provide a basis for processing that leads to the **primal sketch**.

Icons. One of three kinds of representative entity in a famous classification introduced by **C. S. Peirce**, icons (for example, statues or photographs) represent things by virtue of resembling them. The other two categories are **indices** and **symbols**.

Identity Theory. The doctrine that mental states are identical with physical states of the brain. See also **Token identity theory**, **Type identity theory**.

Imagery. See **Mental Imagery**.

Imitation game. See **Turing test**.

Implicatures. See **Conversational Implicatures**.

Implicit memory. See **Explicit vs. implicit memory**.

Incompleteness. See **Gödel's incompleteness theorem**.

Incorrigibility. Characterizes sentences that report the contents of sense experience when those sentences are supposed to be immune to the possibility of error. An incorrigible sentence is one that could not possibly be false, not as a matter of logic but as a matter of its epistemic standing. Traditional examples are "I am in pain" and "I seem to see something green." Earlier psychologists often treated reports obtained from **introspec-**

63

tion as incorrigible, a view that was emphatically discarded by **behaviorism**.

Indeterminacy of translation. The thesis that meanings in a language can never be translated with complete determinacy, because the evidence for a meaning never exhausts that meaning. Advanced by **W. V. O. Quine**, this thesis is a special case of the **underdetermination of theories** by empirical evidence.

Indices. One of three kinds of representative entity in a famous classification introduced by **C. S. Peirce**, indices (such as dark clouds signifying rain, or ashes indicating a fire) represent by virtue of being a cause or effect. The other two categories are **icons** and **symbols**.

Inductive arguments. Arguments that are inconclusive, in the sense that their conclusions can still be false even if their premises are true (in contrast to **deductive arguments**). For example, even when the premises "Almost all swans are white" and "Leda is a swan" are true, the conclusion "Leda is white," although thereby well supported, can still be false. Inductive arguments are *proper* when their premises provide sufficient evidence for their conclusions, and proper inductive arguments with true premises are *correct*. However, a proper argument may not remain proper if other premises are added. The major difficulty confronting inductive reasoning is distinguishing inductively proper argument forms from others that are merely fallacious. See also **Categorization, Concepts, Generalization**.

Inference engine. A component of an **expert system** that applies the system's decision rules to its knowledge base in order to arrive at its conclusions.

Inference to the best explanation . A form of reasoning introduced by **C. S. Peirce** (who called it "abductive inference"). Candidate hypotheses for "best explanation" that explain more of the available relevant evidence are deemed preferable to those that explain less. Hypotheses that are both preferable and explain enough of the available relevant evidence are considered acceptable. And those that are incompatible with the evidence are rejected as false. Although some hypotheses may in fact be false even when they are marked acceptable (which makes inference of this kind fallible), they still remain the most rational among those alternatives under consideration. A difficulty that confronts abductive inference is the need to ensure that every relevant alternative receives consideration as a hypothesis.

Information processing (IP). The input, output, storage, retrieval, and manipulation of symbols (representations) by means of **algorithms**. Although IP symbols are often taken to stand for (represent) various objects, any operations upon the symbols proceed by treating them as purely syntactic units, disregarding whatever "meaning" they might have. Moreover, the principles of information processing are assumed to be characterizable independently of whatever physical "stuff" an IP system might consist of; hence, such a system is theoretically constructible out of just about anything (biological mechanisms, computer parts, water pipes, etc.). See also **Representational Theory of the Mind.**

Information theory. Founded by Claude Shannon, information theory is a mathematical approach to the study of communication. It emphasizes informational quantities (the **bit** being the basic unit of measure) rather than informational content. Suppose, for example, that information is being gathered about a group of automobiles; the categories of interest are old vs. new, foreign vs. domestic, and compact vs. full or midsize. Each category can be represented by a binary number: old = 0 and new = 1; foreign = 0 and domestic = 1; compact = 0 and full/midsize = 1. In this simple scheme, the required

65

information about any car can be represented by *three bits*; thus, an old, domestic, midsize vehicle would receive the code 011. For a good introduction to information theory in the context of cognitive science, see Dretske (1981). See also **Information processing**.

Inheritance of properties. A feature, often incorporated into artificial intelligence systems, whereby information about class instances can be derived from (inherited from) information stored about the class itself. For example, consider a system that encodes information about species of birds. Some of that information is generic (for example, that birds have wings and feathers) and need not be stored separately for robins, pigeons, chickens, etc. Once a system is given the information that robins, etc., are birds, it can retrieve the generic information when necessary and apply it to particular cases. This technique therefore allows for correct inferences in some cases where a piece of information has not been directly provided. It also conserves memory resources. Inheritance of properties is commonly found in **frame**-based systems and in **semantic networks**.

Innateness hypothesis. See **Nativism**.

Intelligence. Historically, intelligence has been viewed as the capacity of cognitively endowed creatures to learn. When that ability or capacity is evaluated in relation to chronological age by employing standardized tests, the result is a numerical value known as intelligence quotient or IQ. (These tests have often been criticized on the grounds that they are culturally biased, or that they fail to take account of the *varieties* of intelligence—for example, musical intelligence, or the intelligence demonstrated by a consummate basketball player.) The occurrence of the term "intelligence" in the phrase "artificial intelligence" suggests that, even if machines are lacking in cognition, they might still be described as intelligent by virtue of their capacity to perform various complex tasks successfully and reliably—especially some of those tasks that have traditionally required human beings. See also **Strong AI, Weak AI**.

Intensional logic. Any system of logic in which the truth or falsity of expressions is not exclusively determined by their referents but rather depends upon the meanings of those expressions. In intensional systems, the meaning of an expression is tied, not just to the actual world, but also to a set of "possible worlds" (of which the actual world is just one). This permits the construction of various counterfactual statements (e.g., "If John Kennedy had not been assassinated, the Vietnam conflict would have ended much sooner") that are not available in **extensional logic**. Intensional logics, besides dealing with counterfactual situations, also provide for modal constructs involving "necessarily" and "possibly." Moreover, it has been demonstrated that the terms "knowledge" and "belief" may be analyzed as modal constructs, to which the apparatus of intensional logic may be brought to bear. See also **Conditionals**.

Intentional stance. A viewpoint (introduced by **Daniel Dennett**) for describing a system in terms of cognitive categories. Dennett argues that a system may be treated as an intentional system (with cognitive features such as motives and beliefs) whenever treating it *as if* it had those cognitive features is explanatorily and predictively useful—whether or not that system is biological. Using this position as a point of departure, Dennett has developed and defended a version of **functionalism**.

Intentionality. A property attributed to any mental state that is representative or "about" something—whether or not that something actually exists. Beliefs, for example, exhibit intentionality (such as the belief *that Madonna and Ross Perot are rich*, or the belief *that the tooth fairy leaves money in exchange for a tooth tucked under the pillow*). According to **Franz Brentano**, intentionality is uniquely characteristic of **minds** and not exhibited by any physical substance; however, this view is disputed by various versions of **physicalism**. Beliefs, memories, goals, desires, expectations, etc., all display intentionality, whereas sensations (such as itches and tickles) do not. Terms describing intentional states (that is, words such as "remembers," "believes," "wonders," etc.) create contexts marked by **referential opacity**.

Interference. Degradation of speed and/or accuracy of some cognitive processing tasks (such as recognition, retention) due to the presence of competing factors. For example, attending to a message may be difficult if another, similar message is being broadcast at the same time in the same voice (less so if the messages and the voices differ). For another illustration, see **Fan effect**.

Interlingua. A symbolic system for representing the meanings of natural language sentences; it appears in some systems that do **natural language processing** (see **Conceptual dependency** for one example). On this approach, sentences that are essentially similar in meaning would be represented in the same way, even if their surface forms differed significantly. For example, the sentences "A threw the ball to B"; "The ball was thrown by A to B"; and "B caught the ball that A threw" all express the same core idea that *the ball's location was transferred from A to B*. Using the italicized expression as a common interlingua for all three sentences, therefore, permits a simplified representation scheme. Moreover, a single interlingua for representing the meanings of sentences taken from any natural language would simplify computer-based translation of languages. For, instead of requiring rules that relate every language to every other, an interlingua-based translator would only require rules that provide for translations between a given language and the one interlingua. Then any two natural languages could be intertranslated by means of a single intermediate representation scheme—much as the hub of a wheel serves as a common connecting point for various spokes. The artificial language Esperanto has been proposed as an interlingua for international communication.

Interpreters. Automatic translators of high-level computer programs into the **machine language** on which computers actually run. Unlike **assemblers** and **compilers**, however, which must translate an entire program before it can execute, interpreters translate each line of the program as it executes. Languages (such as BASIC and **LISP**) that have traditionally used this technique typically result in programs that run considerably slower than those that are compiled or assembled. Thus, in some cases compilers have been provided for languages that historically used interpreters.

Introspection. Ascertaining (and perhaps describing) the contents and operations of the mind by direct inspection. During the late nineteenth century, introspection was often viewed as the proper means for obtaining reliable psychological data; subjects' descriptions were taken to yield mental contents and subjects' theories about their own thought processes were generally taken at face value. Lacking corroboration, however, data obtained in this way came to be regarded as scientifically suspect, and twentieth-century **behaviorism** discounted them altogether. In cognitive science, introspection has a role to play in the production of **protocols**, or subjects' reports; however, those reports are no longer taken as unchallengeable.

Inverted spectrum problem. Consider the ROYGBIV color spectrum (red, orange, yellow, green, blue, indigo, violet). Suppose that a given object, x, causes A to experience red and B to experience violet; another object, y, causes A to experience orange, and B to experience indigo; etc. Thus, the experienced spectra of A and B are inverted with respect to one another. Yet it appears that the verbal reports of A and B would be in agreement, since each has learned to apply the term "red" to objects like x, and "orange" to objects like y. Moreover, A's inner state when experiencing x would play the same functional role as B's despite differences in their **qualia** (the qualitative "feel" of their experiences). This scenario has been taken by some philosophers to constitute a reductio ad absurdum of **functionalism**, since functionalism would assign the same content to the functionally equivalent inner states of both A and B. See also **Absent qualia problem**.

IS-A hierarchy. A system of **knowledge representation** based on the idea that memory structures may be ordered in terms of classes and their members. For example, a robin IS-A bird which IS-A animal which IS-A living thing, etc. **Semantic networks** often use this system. One of its major advantages is that lower members of the hierarchy can exhibit **inheritance of properties**. The genesis of the IS-A hierarchy can be found in the later writings of Plato.

J

Johnson-Laird, Philip N. (b. 1936). British-born professor of psychology and cognitive science at Princeton University. He is best known for elaborating a theory of what are known as **mental models**. Often in collaboration with P. C. Wason, Johnson-Laird has also investigated the performance of subjects on various mental tasks, especially those involving deductive reasoning.

K

Kant, Immanuel (1724–1804). German philosopher, enormously influential for his work in epistemology and in moral theory. Kant said that he had been awakened from his "dogmatic slumber" by the work of **David Hume**, who had denied the existence of necessary causal connections relating future events to past events. Kant held that these connections were not properties of nature but rather features of our *experience* of nature, because the human mind imposes certain forms and categories upon everything that is experienced.

Knowledge. The traditional theory of knowledge holds that A knows that p if and only if (1) A believes that p, (2) A is justified in believing that p, and (3) p is true. Hence, based on this view, knowledge is justified true belief. But this conception has been called into question because it is possible to possess by sheer accident a belief that meets these conditions. Dretske (1981) has proposed an alternative account of knowledge, based on ideas derived from **information theory**. In any case, belief itself is never viewed as sufficient for knowledge. The importance of beliefs in practical contexts stems from the guidance that beliefs provide in the conduct of behavior. In theoretical contexts, beliefs figure importantly in the systematic explanation and prediction of events. See also **Belief**, **Commonsense knowledge**.

Knowledge representation. The encoding of knowledge in biological systems or computers. A variety of schemes for representing knowledge has been advanced, including the **First Order Predicate Calculus**, **frames**, **fuzzy sets**, **production systems**, **scripts**, and **semantic networks**. Important considerations in choosing among these alternatives for a particular application are accessibility and relevance of information. A theory of knowledge representation, when adequately elaborated, ought to provide a foundation for understanding when a particular mode of representation is most appropriate, along with the strengths and limitations of alternatives. Another issue concerns what systems of representation are found in

71

humans. Much of the artificial intelligence literature that discusses knowledge representation might better be regarded as addressing belief representation, insofar as knowledge is often described there as if it were nothing more than belief.

Knowing how vs. knowing that. Also referred to as *nonpropositional* vs. *propositional* knowledge, the distinction is between knowing that something is the case (for example, that Ronald Reagan was twice elected president) and knowing how to do something (how to count to a hundred, ride a bicycle, play chess, etc.). An issue for cognitive science concerns whether knowing how is reducible to knowing that; if not, it would appear that some forms of knowledge lie beyond what can be represented in a form suitable for computation.

Kripke, Saul (b. 1940). American philosopher, currently at Princeton University, who has produced seminal work on logic, metaphysics, and the philosophy of mind. Among his most fundamental contributions are a semantics for modal logic (logic that incorporates the notions of necessity and possibility) in terms of **possible worlds**, and a causal theory of how terms acquire their reference.

L

Language. See **Artificial Language, Natural Language**.

Language acquisition device (LAD). A hypothetical set of innate principles that enable a child to begin to understand and produce grammatical sentences in its native tongue. See also **Linguistic universals**.

Language of thought. A hypothetical innate coding scheme, rich enough to express every distinction that may ever be drawn in any natural language. In contemporary cognitive science, this idea was proposed by **Jerry Fodor**. Counterintuitive though it may sound, Fodor argues that such an innate language (sometimes called mentalese) is logically required for learning a natural language. The basic idea is that a child being exposed to its first natural language must begin to formulate hypotheses about what natural language expressions refer to; but in order to formulate such hypotheses, some antecedent language is required. To avoid an infinite regress, an innate language of thought must be postulated.

Lashley, Karl Spencer (1890–1958). American neuropsychologist who argued for the **equipotentiality** of brain structures and who challenged **behaviorism** by arguing that "serial behavior" (playing the piano, holding a conversation, etc.) cannot be satisfactorily accounted for by stimulus-response connections. Instead, Lashley maintained, such serial activity requires planning that (1) is hierarchical, with broad goals subsuming details; (2) is often independent of environmental causes; and (3) proceeds from within the brain of an organism.

Lateralization. See **Hemispheric specialization**.

Learning. (a) Any change in a thing's behavior patterns as a result of past experience. (b) A thing's self-adaptation for improved performance in response to new circumstances. Typically the improved performance is attributed to increases in knowledge, and the power to make use of that knowledge. (The knowledge may be either of the **knowing how** or **knowing that** variety.) A major research endeavor for cognitive science is the development of theories of learning for both biological organisms and computer systems. **Connectionism** provides one compelling approach.

Left brain/right brain. See **Hemispheric specialization**.

Linguistic universals. Any principles of grammar or

other underlying properties that affect every ordinary language by virtue of being possessed by every neurologically normal human being. Among the strongest candidates for linguistic universals are (1) the properties of **compositionality** of meaning—according to which the meaning of a linguistic whole is a function of the meaning of its constituent parts—as a **semantic** universal and (2) the **recursive** generability of sentences, as a **syntactic** universal (thus permitting the production of an infinite number of grammatical sentences from a finite set of rules). **Noam Chomsky** has suggested the existence of **universal grammars**, and **Jerry Fodor** has elaborated this notion by including conceptual primitives as additional components of our genetic legacy. See also **Nativism**.

Link. A labeled connection, pictorially represented as an arrow, between **nodes** in a **graph** or **tree**.

LISP (LISt Processing). A computer programming language commonly used in artificial intelligence projects. Because LISP is particularly well suited for constructing associations among various pieces of information, it is often the language of choice for programs that model **knowledge representation** structures such as **semantic networks** and **frames**. Although implementations of LISP typically employ an **interpreter**, program execution speed is improved on some systems by permitting LISP programs to be compiled; also, fast, special-purpose LISP machines have been built that carry out the interpreter's functions at the hardware level.

Localization. The view that discrete mental functions are supported by discrete neurological processes. Accordingly, damage to different areas of the brain would be expected to correspond one-to-one with different functional impairments. Contrast **Holism** (b), which stresses neurological integration over a wide range of cognitive tasks.

Logic. The study of arguments, which are usually separated into the categories of **deductive** and **inductive** (some writers would include **abduction** and **analogy**). The first system of logic was that of classical term logic, formalized by **Aristotle**, which investigates the validity of arguments that can be formulated by means of a restricted class of sentences having specific kinds of logical form. Classical term logic characterizes the conclusions that follow from one categorical premise (a case of immediate inference), and also the conclusions that follow from two premises (see **syllogism**). Until around the mid-nineteenth century, Aristotelian logic was widely viewed as exhaustive of the subject. Gottlob Frege, however, revolutionized the topic, and today Aristotelian logic is recognized to be only a special and relatively modest fragment of modern logic, which includes sentential or propositional logic (or the study of arguments when whole sentences are the basic units of analysis) and predicate logic (or the study of arguments whose sentences are analyzed on the basis of their internal structure). See also **Extensional logic**, **Intensional logic**.

Logical connective. A symbol that permits one **well-formed formula** (**WFF**) to be connected to another, thereby creating new wffs. The usual connectives as presented in logic texts are "*not-———*," "*. . . and ———*," "*. . . or ———*," "*if . . . then ———*," and "*. . . if and only if ———*," where "*. . .*" and "*———*" throughout can be replaced by arbitrary sentences. In **extensional logic** all of these connectives are truth-functional, where the meaning of any molecular sentence is completely determined by the truth-values of its atomic components. In **intensional logic**, additional connectives may be introduced to reflect not only logical but also causal and other kinds of relations.

Logic gates. Computer components that take one or more input signals and produce a single output (possibly null), the characteristic of which depends upon the type of gate and the characteristics of the input signals. The behavior of a given logic gate reflects a corresponding logical construct (*and*, *not*, *or*, etc.). For example, just as the conjunction "*p* and *q*" is true just when both *p* and *q* are individually true, an "AND gate" would produce an output just when two input signals are present; otherwise, no output would result. In this way, logical constructs that are fundamental to computer programming languages can be implemented physically by means of signals present or absent at particular points in a machine.

LOGO. A computer programming language designed in the 1960s by **Seymour Papert** and tailored especially for use by children. Users are introduced to LOGO with the aid of a Turtle, which may be a movable mechanical device or an animated figure on the computer screen; children learn to move the Turtle in various directions by issuing simple programming commands. In discussing LOGO-based pedagogy, Papert stresses the importance of what he calls the LOGO environment—an open-style, nonauthoritarian classroom that encourages individual exploration. See Papert (1980) for an accessible account.

Long-term memory (LTM). Large-capacity storage that can be accessed even after some considerable period of time. It appears to be organized as an associational structure (closely related concepts connected by short paths) that might be modeled by a **semantic network**. Retrieval of an item from long-term memory endows it with a higher degree of **activation** than it possessed prior to activation, thereby making it more immediately available for further use.

Lovelace, Lady Ada Augusta (1815–1852). Daughter of Lord Byron and companion of **Charles Babbage**, Lady Lovelace is generally regarded as the world's first computer programmer. She made a careful study of Babbage's plans for his **Analytical Engine**, suggested various programming techniques for it, and argued that, despite its capabilities, the Analytical Engine could not properly be regarded as thinking because its program dependence showed it to be utterly lacking in originality. The U.S. Defense Department's programming language Ada is named after her.

Low-level/high-level languages. See **Programming language**.

LUNAR. A **natural language processing** system developed by William Woods in the early 1970s. It answered questions framed in English about moon-rock samples and soil composition based on data from the Apollo 11 mission. The purpose of the system was to investigate the coupling of a natural language interface to a data base whose records were stored in a different, artificial language format. LUNAR employed an augmented **transition network**.

M

Machine language. The language to which a computer directly responds, as distinguished from higher-level languages (Pascal, BASIC, Fortran, etc.) which are commonly used by computer programmers. Represented by **binary numbers**, machine language versions of higher-level programs are produced by means of a **compiler** or **interpreter**. See also **Object code**.

Magic number seven. An approximate upper limit on the number of informational units an individual can consciously discriminate or process at a given time. Informational units may encompass a variety of stimuli, such as numbers flashed on a screen, or linguistic entities such as syllables, words, or phrases. To some extent, however, this limit of seven can be bypassed through **chunking** smaller informational units into larger ones. Thus, although it may be possible to remember no more than seven rapidly presented meaningless syllables, it is quite easy to remember seven syllables if they are grouped into meaningful words.

MARGIE (Memory, Analysis, Response Generation in English). An artificial intelligence system for understanding written language that was fed into it, developed under the direction of **Roger Schank** at Yale University. MARGIE's approach to understanding used the **conceptual dependency** technique for representing sentence meanings and was the first system with the capacity to paraphrase, translate, and make inferences.

Marr, David (1945–1980). British-trained neurophysiologist who joined the Artificial Intelligence Laboratory at MIT in 1973 and developed an important computational approach to the analysis of vision. Marr emphasized that computer models of vision should be constrained by what is known about the brain's capacity to implement proposed **algorithms**.

Mass nouns. See **Count nouns vs. mass nouns**.

Materialism. See **Physicalism**.

McCarthy, John (b. 1927). Professor of computer science at Stanford University and one of the leading figures in artificial intelligence (He is said to have coined the term "artificial intelligence" at a 1956 Dartmouth College conference on computers). Some of McCarthy's most important work concerns programs incorporating common sense, programs that can exhibit nonmonotonic reasoning (see **Monotonicity**), and attempts to address the **frame problem**.

Meaning. The problem of meaning, often also referred to as the problem of representation or the problem of content, is among the central issues confronting cognitive science. Since different signs (words, sentences) can have the same meaning, the meaning of a sign (word, sentence) cannot be properly identified with its linguistic (or other) formulation. Moreover, to say that two or more linguistic units have the same meaning does not explain what it means for any of them to have any meaning at all. Among the various theories of meaning that have been proposed, the **language of thought** hypothesis maintains that every human being possesses an innate mental language, and that learning an ordinary language involves pairing up the words in that ordinary language with innate concepts in the language of thought. The **semantic network** model holds that words and sentences, especially, derive their meaning from their location within a network of conceptual relations by virtue of definitional and other inferential connections. Yet another account is the semiotic system conception, according to which the meaning of a sign is determined by its causal role in influencing mental states and behavior under various conditions (see **Minds as semiotic systems**). See also **Original meaning, Symbol grounding problem**.

Means-ends analysis. A problem-solving strategy first used by **General Problem Solver**. Means-ends analysis proceeds by matching a current state against the goal it is attempting to reach. If no difference exists, the goal has been found; otherwise, an attempt is made to reduce the difference between the current state and the goal by creating intermediate subgoals (which may in turn require further subgoals) until a performable next move is discovered.

Mechanism. The doctrine that all behavior (including that indicative of cognition) can be explained purely in terms of causally interacting mechanical processes. Put another way, all explanations according to mechanism are nonteleological, proceeding in terms of causes rather than reasons. In **Plato's** *Phaedo*, these two points of view are contrasted by Socrates, who is examining alternative explanations of how he ended up in prison. Socrates complains that (what we would now call) the mechanist would explain Socrates' being in prison by providing a physiological account of the arrangement of his bones, joints, and sinews—all the while ignoring the real reasons for his being there: his values, beliefs, and decisions. Mechanism is a fundamental tenet of **physicalism** and is opposed by **mentalism**.

Meinong, Alexius (1853–1920). Philosopher and psychologist who studied under **Franz Brentano** and whose theory of the objects of consciousness included those that do not exist but about which statements or thoughts can be directed (for example, female popes, gold mountains, and the present king of France).

Memory. The capacity for information storage, both in computer systems and biological systems. This general capacity is often described in terms of **long-term memory** and **short-term memory**. See also **Episodic memory, Iconic memory, Recall, Recognition, Semantic memory**.

Mental architecture. See **Cognitive architecture**.

Mental imagery. A form of mental representation that appears to be pictorial rather than propositional. An ongoing debate in cognitive science concerns the question whether mental images are somehow reducible to propositional format (descriptions). Construing images literally as pictures is problematic, because (1) no pictures literally exist in the brain; (2) if they did, a **homunculus** would presumably be required to view the pictures. See also **Mental rotation**.

Mental models. Representations both of the actual world and of possible situations constructed in the course of perceiving, reasoning, remembering, etc. These models reflect **semantic** information (meaning) as well as information about syntax. According to **Johnson-Laird**, mental models are basic instruments of human thought, especially of human reasoning. For example, a deductive argument is said to be valid only if its conclusion could not be false if its premises were true; psychologically, it is possible to discover that an argument is valid by imagining the situation described by the premises and attempting to imagine if the situation described by the conclusion could possibly be false. The mental model approach also predicts and explains cases of *invalid* reasoning. Mental models have been introduced to encompass perception and induction as well as other cognitive phenomena.

Mental rotation. The rotation of **mental imagery**. This topic became the source of major debate as a result of experiments performed in the 1970s by Roger Shepard and others. If experimental subjects are presented with two figures viewed from different angles and asked to judge whether the two are identical, judgment time directly reflects the number of degrees that one figure would have to be physically rotated in order to match the other's angle of presentation. A natural interpretation of this result is that subjects form an image of one figure and rotate it, comparing the rotated image with the other figure. The issue is well presented in Kosslyn (1980).

Mentalese. A term introduced by **Jerry Fodor** for the **language of thought**. See also **Meaning**, **Nativism**.

Mentalism. The doctrine that human cognitive abilities can be explained only by reference to a set of internal mental representations and rules that operate on them, as opposed to **mechanism**. The term "mentalism" is also used more narrowly in discussions of **Chomsky**'s account of linguistic abilities by reference to linguistic rules that are assumed to be internalized by every speaker.

Mentality. The hallmark of having a mind; to have a

mind is to exhibit mentality. Just what this amounts to, however, is the subject of vigorous debates. Some conceptions of mentality are inspired by drawing parallels with computers and hold that mind can arise from manipulations that are purely syntactical; not surprisingly, this approach is known as the **Syntactical Theory of the Mind**. Other conceptions of mentality deny that syntactical manipulation is sufficient, maintaining instead that any adequate account of mind must refer to the semantic features of mental representation (thereby introducing the notion of **intentionality**). This approach is known as the **Representational Theory of the Mind**. Still other conceptions envision minds as properties of the users of signs (see **Minds as semiotic systems**). A variety of theories of representation, meaning, or content have been advanced by Robert Cummins, Fred Dretske, and **Stephen Stich**, among others (see Bibliography). An adequate theory of mentality should explain why human beings, other animals, and computing machines do or do not possess it and the extent to which mental states make any difference to our behavior. See also **Chinese Room, Connectionism, Methodological solipsism, Minds as semiotic systems**.

Methodological solipsism. The position that psychological theorizing about the mind must restrict itself to the formal (syntactic) properties of representations or mental contents, ignoring the semantic properties of representations or contents, including any connections that obtain between them and their possible environmental causes. A key argument (by **Jerry Fodor**) for this view is that no satisfactory laws relating environmental causes to an organism's behavior can be specified until the environmental causes themselves can be characterized in a way that illuminates their relevant (causal) properties. But not only is this task not the business of psychology, it is a requirement that awaits the completion of the physical sciences. It follows from this view that the semantic aspects of mental representations (aspects such as truth and reference) cannot really be part of the study of **mentality**. Psychologists, therefore, should study the mind *as if* it had no access to a reality beyond its own mental representations; in so doing, psychologists would be adopting methodologically the position that solipsists (implausibly) take to be true in fact: that no world at all exists beyond one's own mental representations. See also **Problem of primitives**.

Micro-world. A domain whose contents (objects, features, relations) are highly restricted for investigation by an artificial intelligence system. Examples include **blocks worlds**; conversation in a psychotherapy setting (**ELIZA**); specialized medical diagnosis (**MYCIN**); and limited information handling as might be done by a particular individual (**CYRUS**). One point of debate is the extent to which principles used in the investigation of a micro-world can be generalized to larger cognitive tasks.

Miller, George Armitage (b. 1920). American psychologist whose 1956 article "The Magic Number Seven" is a classic in the field. That article suggested a built-in limitation in human information processing across a variety of domains. Miller is currently at Princeton University and has written a number of books on the psychology of language. See also **Magic number seven**.

Mind/body problem. The problem of characterizing the correct relationship between mental phenomena and bodily events (including those occurring in the brain). This problem arises because typical experiences (such as the taste of peanut butter, a mental image of an orange, or the thought that $2 + 2 = 4$) do not present themselves to us as physical phenomena; nor would a neurosurgeon discover anything orange in the brain of someone who was imagining an orange object. Such reflections lead naturally to **dualism**, which views the mind as nonphysical and separate from the body. But since dualism places the mind off limits to scientific investigation, alternative conceptions have emerged. These include **behaviorism** (which ties mental phenomena to observable behavior) and a large variety of **physicalist** theories relating the mind to the brain (see **Mind/brain**).

Mind/Brain. See **Brain/Mind.**

Minds. Minds are the possessors of **mentality**. According to syntactic conceptions of the mind, the capacity to process syntax is sufficient for something to have a mind. On stronger conceptions, this is not enough; the capacity to process syntax may be necessary but is not sufficient for something to have a mind. Within the philosophy of mind, there are three great problems: the nature of mind, or "What does it take for something to possess mentality?"; the mind/body problem, or "How are minds related to bodies?"; and the problem of other minds, or "How can I know whether anything besides myself possesses mentality?" An adequate theory of mind ought to have adequate answers to all three. See also **Brain/mind**, **Meaning**, **Mentality**, **Mind/body problem**, **Minds as semiotic systems**, **Other minds problem**.

Minds as semiotic systems. The conception of minds as semiotic systems is built on the theory of signs elaborated by **Charles S. Peirce**. Peirce distinguished three sorts of representative entities: *icons*, *indices*, and *symbols*. Icons (for example, statues or photographs) represent things by virtue of resembling them; indices (such as dark clouds signifying rain, or ashes indicating a fire) represent by virtue of being a cause or effect; and symbols (such as written words) represent as a consequence of conventional agreement. Peirce's own threefold distinction may be extended naturally so as to introduce minds of different kinds. Minds of Type I can utilize icons; minds of Type II can utilize icons and indices; and minds of Type III can utilize icons, indices; and symbols. A criterion of mentality that follows from the semiotic conception of mind is the capacity to make a mistake, since mistakes involve taking something to stand for something else (in some respect or other). This idea, elaborated by James H. Fetzer, generalizes and inverts Peirce's own view, which implied that sign users must be human beings (somebodies), thereby precluding the possibility that other animals or inanimate machines might have the capacity to use signs and thus qualify as endowed with mentality.

Minimax procedure. A technique used in game-playing (and often in artificial intelligence programs) by which a player attempts to maximize his or her own score while minimizing the score of an opponent. The technique operates by Player A's looking at possible next moves, and assigning a value to each alternative, then considering Player B's possible defensive countermoves, which are presumably aimed at minimizing A's score. This look-ahead evaluation, ideally represented as a **tree**, is developed for as many levels as is feasible. The optimal next move for player A is the one lying on a path to a later state (or goal) in which A's score is maximized and B's is minimized.

Minsky, Marvin Lee (b. 1927). One of the founding fathers of artificial intelligence, mentor to numerous AI students, and author of influential books on the mathematical foundations of computing, machine learning, robotics, linguistic analysis, and computational theories of the mind. Currently, Minsky is Donner Professor of Science at MIT. See also **Society of mind**.

MIPS (Millions of Instructions per Second). A common measure of the speed of computer systems.

Modal operators. The most common modal operators are "possibly" and "necessarily" as qualifiers of whole sentences; symbols for the operators are typically applied at the beginning of the sentence. Distinctions can also be drawn between different kinds of possibility and necessity. A sentence describes a *logical* possibility if the sentence's denial is not self-contradictory; it describes a *physical* possibility if its truth would not conflict with the laws of nature. Additional modal operators are "deontic" operators (denoting moral obligation), and "tense" operators (denoting times or temporal relations). "Knowledge" and "belief" also function in ways akin to standard modal operators. The study of modal operators falls within the purview of advanced logic.

Model-theoretic semantics. A mapping from the elements of a formal language to entities in a specified domain (or model or **possible world**) is known as an *interpretation* of that language. For example, an intransitive verb such as "smiles" may be assigned an interpretation consisting of a set of elements from the model (those individuals who at a given moment are smiling), and a transitive verb such as "loves" may be assigned an interpretation consisting of ordered pairs of individuals. Sentences are built up from basic terms according to syntactic rules, and the truth or falsity of a sentence is a function of the truth values of its constituents, as provided for in a set of truth rules. Since models concern relations between elements of a language and other things, the study of models falls within the scope of **semantics**. The model-theoretic approach, developed by **Johnson-Laird** (1983), also utilizes ideas from **procedural semantics**. An alternative account is provided by **semantic networks**.

Modularity. The doctrine that various forms of cognitive processing (visual recognition, speech, memory, etc.) involve distinct, functionally isolated components that perhaps also operate by means of fundamentally different principles—and which may lack **cognitive penetrability**. This view is opposed to the theory that a unified set of principles underlies all cognition (see John Anderson's

ACT system). Forms of the modularity thesis have been defended by **Noam Chomsky** and by **Jerry Fodor**.

Modus ponens/modus tollens. Two of the most useful principles of deductive inference. Modus ponens asserts "Given the sentences 'if p then q' and 'p,' infer 'q'" (this rule warrants the conclusion "Fido is a mammal" from "if something is a dog then it is a mammal" and "Fido is a dog"). Modus tollens asserts "Given 'if p then q' and 'not-q,' infer 'not-p'" (this rule warrants the conclusion "San Francisco is not a dog" from "If something is a dog then it is a mammal" and "San Francisco is not a mammal"). Both rules, like all other rules of deductive inference, are demonstrative (true premises guarantee true conclusions), nonampliative (the conclusion's content was already contained, implicitly or explicitly, in the premises), and additive (or monotonic; see **Monotonicity**).

Monotonicity. A property of valid deductive arguments in classical truth-functional logic by which the addition of further premises does not affect the strength of the logical relation between the premises and the conclusion (so long as any larger set contains the original premises). In contrast, an argument is said to be nonmonotonic when the addition of further premises can strengthen or weaken the evidential support provided to the conclusion by the original premises. Valid deductive arguments are monotonic, whereas inductive arguments are nonmonotonic.

Morpheme. The smallest unit of meaning in linguistic analysis. A morpheme may in some cases correspond to a word (as in "cow"); however, it may also be composed of a single letter (as when s is added to a noun to indicate plurality, or when ed is added to a verb to signify past tense).

Morphology. The study of how **morphemes** are constructed from **phonemes**, or units of sound.

MRI (magnetic resonance imaging). A technique for obtaining images of the interior of a body. Magnetic resonance imaging places the subject within a strong magnetic field, where energy in the form of radio waves is then introduced. Atoms of different kinds of tissue resonate in distinctive ways under the waves' influence, permitting a highly detailed, composite image to be constructed.

MYCIN. A well-known **expert system** developed at Stanford University in the 1970s by Edward Shortliffe. A **production system**, MYCIN diagnosed bacterial infections of the blood and suggested therapies. MYCIN employed approximately 500 **condition-action rules** and through the use of **backward chaining** was able to provide justifications for its responses to input queries.

N

Nativism. The **poverty of stimulus** argument advanced by **Noam Chomsky** maintains that linguistic ability must be innate, inborn, or "native" to human beings. Ramsey and **Stich** have suggested that there are three different kinds of nativism: *minimal rationalism* (children must have some innate mechanism for learning language); *antiempiricism* (no ordinary learning mechanism could possibly account for the learning of language); and *rationalism* (some specific set of language mechanisms must be part of the genetic endowment of every neurologically normal human being). Noam Chomsky's rationalist position maintains that a **universal grammar** is part of our native inheritance, while **Jerry Fodor** goes further by suggesting that it also includes mentalese (or the **language of thought**).

Natural language. Any conventional, rule-governed symbolic system, naturally evolved rather than willfully created, that facilitates communication between the human members of a community—a "native language" or "mother tongue." The symbols in such a system may be written, spoken, or signed (in languages used for communication with the deaf). Examples include English, French, Russian, Chinese, German, Spanish, Japanese, Chinese, Swahili, Maori, and American Sign Language. Natural languages (as contrasted to **artificial languages**) typically subserve broad communicative purposes and tend to display rich and varied expression rather than emphasizing efficiency and economy. Although nonhuman animals such as bees, dolphins, and chimpanzees are sometimes described as using language, the range and expressive power of any such systems of communication appear to be extremely limited in comparison with that of human languages. Cognitive (as opposed to **behaviorist**) accounts of natural language learning stress the use of cognitive resources to form hypotheses about language structures and the reference of terms; these hypotheses are corrected in the light of errors that are pointed out in the learning process. See also **Language of thought**.

Natural language processing. The analysis of sentence generation and understanding by reference to computational processes. The ultimate goal of this approach for cognitive science is to build a computer model that reflects the processes actually used by human beings—processes that are not fully understood at this time. See also **Parsing**.

Necessity. See **Modal operators**.

Neural chauvinism. The doctrine that only entities with brains and nervous systems are capable of cognition. Although this view is a consequence of the **identity theory**, it is one that cognitive science generally wishes to avoid since it would rule out the possibility that computers and other, nonhumanoid entities in the universe might be endowed with cognition.

Neural networks. See **Connectionism**.

Newell, Allen (b. 1927). University professor of computer science at Carnegie-Mellon University, he has contributed to virtually every fundamental aspect of artificial intelligence, including the nature of mentality, the character of knowledge, techniques of problem-solving, and the structure of cognitive architectures. See also **Physical symbol system hypothesis**.

Nodes. The entities contained in a **graph**, with relations between them indicated by **links**. Their use is quite general: in an **IS-A hierarchy**, nodes may represent types of animals; in a **transition network**, they may represent word categories.

Nonterminal symbol. A component of a **grammar** that is a phrase or combination of phrases rather than a single word category. Nonterminal symbols can be further decomposed into smaller syntactical units, according to the specifications provided in the grammar's "rewrite rules." Unlike **terminal symbols**, nonterminal symbols may appear on the left-hand side of a grammatical rule.

Nonterminating procedure. A procedure (**algorithm** or **program**) that never halts, for at least one input configuration. Unfortunately, there is no general method for determining whether a given procedure is of the nonterminating variety. See also **Halting problem**.

Norman, Donald A. (b. 1935). American cognitive psychologist currently at the University of California, San Diego; author of many professional articles and books on human information processing, memory and attention, human-computer interaction, and design.

Noun phrase (NP). A unit of grammatical analysis consisting either of a pronoun, or a **determiner** (optional) plus one or more adjectives (optional) plus a noun. Examples of NPs are: "it," "she"; "frog"; "a slimy frog"; "the beautiful old guitar." NPs provide one level of analysis in **phrase structure grammars**.

O

Object code. The **machine language** program produced by a **compiler** from a program written in a higher-level language such as Pascal. An object-level program carries out the instructions that were specified in the higher-level program from which it is derived, but by being translated into machine language those higher-level instructions are put into a form that a computer can respond to directly.

Object recognition. Operating on a sensory stimulus so as to determine what object produced that stimulus— for example, identifying a cup or a cat or a tree. The ease with which humans can accomplish this task masks its underlying complexity; computer systems that can recognize objects in anything other than highly controlled environments are far from being perfected.

Observational/theoretical distinction. A traditional distinction between properties (or predicates that refer to properties) that are directly accessible to sense experience and those that are not. It can be drawn in several different ways. One way is to define *observable properties* as properties whose presence or absence can be directly ascertained, under suitable conditions, by means of direct inspection; *theoretical properties* are then defined as non-observational. Alternatively, a distinction can be drawn between observable, theoretical, and *dispositional* predicates, where observable predicates describe observable properties of observable entities, theoretical predicates describe unobservable properties of unobservable entities, and dispositional predicates describe unobservable properties of observable entities. The problems of the nature of mind, of the relation of mind to body, and of other minds are difficult in part because minds are unobservable (or theoretical).

Occam's Razor. A methodological maxim asserting that entities should not be multiplied beyond necessity: "It is in vain to do by many what could be done by fewer!" Occam's Razor thus suggests that simpler theories ought to be preferred to more complex theories. But simpler theories surely ought to be preferred to more complex theories only when they are also adequate.

Ontology. Among the most central domains of philosophical inquiry, ontology (sometimes called metaphysics) aims at discovering the basic categories of existence. Examples of ontological inquiry include the nature of truth, the existence of God, the status of **propositions**, and the interpretation of **possible worlds**. Furthermore, in discussions of the nature of mind, two major ontological alternatives have been apparent. Dualists identify two primary categories of existence: the physical and the nonphysical. Because dualists also regard mind as being part of the nonphysical realm, they in effect make it off limits to scientific inquiry. In contrast, most contemporary cognitive scientists opt for a materialist ontology, holding that the mechanisms of mind are implemented by the brain (and also that perhaps someday they will be implemented in a computer). See also **Brain/mind**, **Descartes**, **Dualism**, **Physicalism**.

Opacity. See **Referential opacity**.

Original meaning. The ultimate source of semantic interpretation for a system of representation. Suppose, for example, that a conscious thought results from the brain's manipulation of symbols; the thought's content then presumably derives from the underlying meanings in the brain's symbols. Arguably, *some* symbols must have original meaning, or an infinite regress of derived meanings would result. At the same time, this gives rise to the "mystery of original meaning" (Haugeland, 1985): *How* could the brain's symbols have original semantic content? See also **Language of thought**, **Problem of primitives**, **Symbol grounding problem**.

Ostensive definition. Definition by means of samples. The meaning of the word "chair," for example, could be explained to somebody by showing a variety of sample chairs. Ostensive definition provides a means for relating words to things without reliance upon other words, which means that, strictly speaking, ostensive definitions are only "definitions" in an extended sense. The risk involved in their use is that of overgeneralization; namely, that properties of the samples (such as the color, size, and shape of an overstuffed chair) might be taken to be properties of every thing of that kind. A variety of samples can help to address this problem. See also **Definitions**.

Other minds problem. The traditional problem of showing how observable evidence can justify the claim that other people (and at least some animals) have thoughts, feelings, etc. The problem arises because of an asymmetry between our access to our own mental states and our access to the mental states of others. Whereas in the first case, we are typically "immediately aware" of what we are thinking or experiencing, our evidence for what goes on in the minds of others comes only indirectly, through verbal and nonverbal behavior. But this behavioral evidence is less than entirely conclusive, as can be seen from the fact that another person may only pretend to be having a particular experience; or (more radically) that, despite agreement in behavior, other people's inner experiences could be qualitatively very different from the ones you have; or (more radically still) that other people might lack minds altogether. With the development of increasingly sophisticated computers, the question whether machines might possess minds is also coming to the fore. See also **Inverted spectrum problem**, **Observational/theoretical distinction**, **Total Turing test**, **Turing test**.

P

Papert, Seymour (b. 1928). A mathematician by training, originally from South Africa and now professor of media technology and director of the Artificial Intelligence Laboratory at MIT. Papert, who once studied with the Swiss psychologist Jean Piaget, has conducted pioneering studies on the use of computers in education (see Papert, 1980). He developed the programming language **LOGO** to enable students to explore mathematical and geometrical concepts in an intuitive way.

Parallel processing. Carrying out independent, multiple calculations simultaneously, in contrast to **serial processing** as is done by a **Von Neumann machine**. Parallel processing may be accomplished in a computer system through multiple, independent **CPUs**; the brain also is presumed to operate in a parallel fashion through functionally independent neurological structures. Simultaneous calculations allow large amounts of information to be processed quickly, but are possible only when the information being worked on by one structure is not needed by another structure. See also **Connectionism**.

Parallel distributed processing. See **Connectionism**.

PARRY. An artificial intelligence program designed by Kenneth Colby. PARRY, which simulated a paranoid patient, was able to trick several psychiatrists into believing that they were communicating with a human being; thus PARRY was claimed by some writers to have passed the **Turing test**.

Parsing. The process of analyzing and identifying the grammatical structure of a sentence. For a detailed example see **Bottom-up/top-down parsing**.

Pattern recognition. The identification of information and order in perceptual content, for example identifying a particular stimulus pattern as the letter A. Theories as to how this is accomplished include **feature analysis** and **template matching**. **Gestalt** theories of perception emphasize the context in which the information is embedded.

Peirce, Charles S. (1839–1914). One of the most important American philosophers; scholar of metaphysics and epistemology. Originator of the theory of signs (or semiotics), Peirce was the first and greatest of the classic pragmatists (the others being William James and John Dewey) and elaborated a model of science as a process of "abduction" built on the principle of **inference to the best explanation**. His theory of signs provides a basis for contemporary theorizing about the nature of mind (see **Minds as semiotic systems**).

Penfield, Wilder Graves (1891–1976). American neurosurgeon who pioneered surgical techniques for treating epilepsy. Part of the procedure involved electrically stimulating the brains of conscious patients, whose reports on the resulting experiences provided important clues to the localization of various brain functions.

Percept. An imagelike entity traditionally thought to be produced in a perceiver by acts of perception. Percepts are generally assumed to be available to **introspection**.

Perception. The acquiring of information about the external world by means of the senses. Although some researchers (such as **J. J. Gibson**) have argued that a significant amount of information about the environment is contained immediately in perceptual stimuli, the primary research paradigm of contemporary cognitive science maintains that information must be "recovered" or extracted from sensory stimuli by means of internal processing mechanisms (for the most part unconscious).

Perceptron. An artificial intelligence approach to perceptual recognition tasks, devised in the late 1950s by Frank Rosenblatt. A perceptron contains three basic components: (1) an input unit, consisting of a two-dimensional array of photosensitive cells; (2) an associative unit, which regulates current between input and output; and (3) a response unit, which compares various voltages in the associative unit and attempts to identify the stimulus. Although intended to model perceptual learning strategies, the limitations of this technique were famously detailed in 1969 by Minsky and **Papert** in their book titled *Perceptrons*. For a time this critique was taken to establish that the **neural network** approach to recognition tasks is doomed to failure; however, later and more sophisticated systems involving multiple, connected perceptrons have proved fruitful. See also **Connectionism**, **XOR problem**.

Performance. See **Competence/performance distinction**.

Performative utterances. Sometimes in using words we perform a particular kind of act (more specifically, a **speech act**). Examples include a minister's *pronouncing* a couple husband and wife, thereby marrying them; or a judge's *announcing* that a convict will serve twenty years for a crime, thereby passing sentence. In order for these speech acts to be efficacious as performances, several conditions must be met, including that the person uttering them must be authorized to perform those acts, that the participants in those acts must be appropriate for their roles, and so on. The nature of performative utterances has been elaborated in work by **J. L. Austin** and by Paul Grice, among others.

PET (positron emission tomography) imaging. A technique used in nuclear medicine for obtaining images of the interior of a body. Positron emission tomography requires the introduction of radioactive chemicals (or isotopes) into the subject's body. These isotopes emit positively charged electrons (positrons), which tend to collide with electrons, emitting pairs of photons in opposite directions. The interactions are detectable and provide the basis for composite images of the subject's body by means of what qualifies as a kind of chemical map.

Phoneme. The basic unit of sound in a natural language. For example, the word "dog" contains three phonemes; its identity would be affected by changing the *d* sound to a *b*, or the *o* sound to an *i*, or the *g* sound to a *t*. Slight variations in the pronunciation of a particular phoneme are tolerable as long as those variations do not alter the perceived identity of the word in which the phoneme appears—a fact that poses an obvious challenge for automatic speech recognition systems. On standard computational models of speech recognition, phonemes must be identified, and then grouped into **morphemes**, which in turn are grouped into words, phrases, and sentences. Although phonemes differ from one language to another, the total number of phonemes in any given language is relatively small.

Phonology. The study of rules that analyze auditory stimuli into sequences of **phonemes**.

Phrase marker. A **tree** diagram depicting the syntactical analysis of a sentence.

Phrase structure grammar. A **grammar** that features groupings of syntactic components in a hierarchical fashion. Thus, for example, a sentence may be decomposed into a **noun phrase** and a **verb phrase**, with these elements further decomposable according to the grammar's rules. Phrase structure grammars are often taken to correspond to levels 1 and 2 on the **Chomsky hierarchy**, although some writers associate them with Level 2 only.

Physical symbol system. An information processing approach whose manipulation of physical units (symbols) is based exclusively on their formal (syntactic) properties. This conception has been developed in the work of **Allen Newell** and **Herbert Simon**. See also **Information Processing, Physical symbol system hypothesis**.

Physical symbol system hypothesis. According to **Newell** and **Simon**, the necessary and sufficient conditions for something to be capable of intelligent action (or to have mentality, to have a mind) is that it is a **physical symbol system**. They thereby endorse a conception of **mentality** according to which the capacity to manipulate symbols by reference to syntactical rules is what it takes to have a **mind**. According to this conception, physically embodied universal **Turing machines** possess the necessary and sufficient conditions to have minds.

Physicalism. The view that physical reality is the only reality, and that mental states must, therefore, ultimately be nothing over and above physical states. Various approaches to the study of mental phenomena are ultimately physicalistic: examples include **behaviorism**, **eliminative materialism**, and the **identity theory**.

Pixel (picture element). A point on a display monitor (such as a computer or television screen). The screen's image is composed of a two-dimensional array of pixels, each capable of displaying various levels of intensity. Similarly, a retinal image may be regarded as a pixel display, a fact that is extremely useful in computer-based visual processing systems; for more on this see **Gray-level array**.

PLANNER. An early artificial intelligence programming language, proposed by Carl Hewitt in 1969 as a doctoral project at MIT. PLANNER, an ancestor of the programming language **PROLOG**, was partially implemented as MICRO-PLANNER—the language used by **SHRDLU**.

Plasticity. The modifiability of neurological structures, which are described as plastic because their functions can be altered. Thus, for example, a brain injury that results in some behavioral impairment may be compensated for when undamaged areas take over the functions of the damaged portion. See also **Equipotentiality**.

Plato (427–347 B.C.). Greek philosopher, a student of Socrates and teacher of **Aristotle**. Among the most important thinkers in the history of philosophy, Plato introduced a theory of Forms, according to which everything in the ever-changing physical world is an imperfect instance of a corresponding eternal and unchanging immaterial realm. The world of Forms specifies various categories to which things in the physical world belong, and by investing the world of Forms with a hierarchical structure Plato strikingly anticipated contemporary accounts of human conceptual structures (see **Semantic memory**). Moreover, he maintained that humans are born with **a priori** knowledge already encoded within them, a view to which contemporary **nativism** is heir. Especially in his later writings, Plato adopted a synoptic view of knowledge that integrated psychology, **epistemology**, ethics, and **ontology**.

Positivism. The doctrine that all theories must be constructed from basic sensory data by means of logical principles. **Behaviorism** may be viewed as exemplifying this tradition. Positivism assumes a rigid distinction between a theory's empirical (or experienced-based) elements and its logical elements—a philosophical distinction that is no longer widely held. Moreover, the idea of basic sensory data has been challenged; see **Introspection**.

Possible worlds. Descriptions of ways the world might

be or might have been. When the described worlds are logically consistent (compatible with the laws of logic), they are *logically* possible worlds. When they are both logically consistent and physically possible (compatible with the laws of nature), they are *physically* possible worlds, and when they are logically consistent, physically possible, and historically possible (compatible with the history of the world up until time *t*), then they are *historically* possible relative to time *t*. Due to seminal work by **Saul Kripke**, the notion of possible worlds plays a key role in the interpretation of **modal operators**. The **ontology** and interpretation of possible worlds has been the subject of a substantial literature.

Possibility. See **Modal operators**.

Poverty of stimulus. The relatively small amount of linguistic information contained in sentences and surroundings that a child encounters in the process of learning its native language. From this "impoverished" information, however, the child is soon able to produce an indefinitely large number of sentences, many of which are highly novel, not only in content but also in form (this is the **creativity in language** phenomenon). **Noam Chomsky** and others have argued that the disparity between poverty of stimulus and a speaker's output ability calls for explanation in terms of innate language mechanisms. See also **Universal grammar**.

Pragmatics. The study of the relations between signs (or words), what they stand for, and sign users. See also **Semantics, Syntax**.

Prepositional Phrase (PP). A linguistic structure consisting of a preposition plus a **noun phrase**. PPs provide one unit of analysis in **phrase structure grammars**.

Primal sketch. A hypothetical stage of representation in the account of early visual processing proposed by **David Marr**. The primal sketch is produced from a series of computations performed on the **gray-level array** and consists of a description of primitive elements (**blobs, bars,** and **edges**) giving their sizes, orientations, positions, etc.

Priming. The **activation** of an area of memory by the presentation of a stimulus, thereby making that area more quickly accessible when subsequent, related stimuli are presented. This phenomenon is accounted for in **semantic network** models of memory that provide for **spreading activation**.

Primitives. Elements of a system that are not defined within that system. The meaning of these elements might be explained contextually, as in the case of **truth table** definitions, or they might be understood extra-systemically. The difficulty of understanding the meaning of primitives is called the **problem of primitives**. See also **Original meaning, Symbol grounding problem**.

Problem of primitives. Within the framework of minds as semiotic (or sign-using) systems, the problem is that of establishing the meaning of the undefined (or primitive) signs for any system. In the absence of a solution to this problem, systems of signs may be altogether devoid of meaning. Since the kinds of signs that are utilized by a semiotic system may include icons, indices, and symbols, the **symbol grounding problem** appears to be a special case of the problem of primitives. According to the solution advanced by James H. Fetzer, the meaning of a primitive for a system is determined by the totality of dispositions toward behavior for that system when conscious of that sign's presence in various contexts. The meaning of a sign is thus identified with its causal role in influencing a system's behavior—a role that cannot be conclusively determined by means of observable symbol manipulation, observable robotic behavior, or even access to internal processes by means of **CT scans, MRI,** or **PET imaging**.

Since, on this view, meanings of signs are located within a system rather than in its relations to objects and properties in the world, it is called an internalist approach, in contrast to an externalist conception (which locates meanings in the connection between signs and what they designate in the world). See also **Original meaning**.

Problem reduction. An approach to problem-solving that decomposes an initial problem into a group of smaller subproblems to which problem-solving algorithms can be applied.

Problem space. The domain in which attempts to solve a problem take place. First introduced by **Allen Newell** and **Herbert Simon** in connection with their **General Problem Solver**, the concept of a problem space includes a given problem state and a set of rules that can change one problem state into another one. Also needed for problem-solving tasks is some method for ascertaining whether a given problem state represents a solution. For an example, an equation to be solved may be regarded as the initial problem state; a set of operations on the "given" must then be carried out until a solution is eventually reached. See also **Search space**.

Procedural representation. A method for storing information (implicitly) in a computer system by providing it with a set of actions to be taken in order to arrive at new facts. This stands in contrast to **declarative representation**, which provides a set of explicit facts (declarative statements). Artificial intelligence systems commonly employ both types of representation, although the declarative/procedural distinction is not always perfectly sharp. Procedural representation is akin to *knowing how*: possessing a skill. See also **Knowing how, knowing that**.

Procedural semantics. An approach to semantic processing according to which the meaning of a linguistic unit (word, phrase, or sentence) term is a function of the actions that the system carries out when it encounters that unit. It may be argued, however, that this account leaves out one important component of meaning: the relationship between a linguistic unit and the object to which it refers. See also **Model-theoretic semantics**, **Semantic network**, **Semantics**.

Processing units in connectionist systems. A typical connectionist system contains three types of units (on analogy to neurons in the brain). These units constitute a three-layered architecture: *input* units, whose sources of stimulation are external to the system; *output* units, whose results are passed to recipients outside the system; and *hidden* units, whose inputs and outputs lie entirely within the system. Connections among units may run in one direction only or may be bidirectional; they may also be excitatory (stimulating other units to increased activity) or inhibitory (reducing the activity of other units). The "training phase" for a connectionist system typically involves making adjustments to the hidden units (for example, altering the threshold at which they fire), which in effect alters the strengths of connections between the system's inputs and outputs. Although connectionist systems can theoretically consist of just input and output units, hidden units are required for problems in which significant transformations occur between input and output. A classic example is the **XOR problem**.

Production system. A system for **knowledge representation** consisting of three components: (1) a collection of **condition-action rules** ("If . . . then—"); (2) a context or working memory that represents the system's current state; (3) an interpreter that applies appropriate production rules to the context (using **conflict-resolution** strategies if necessary to adjudicate among multiple applicable rules). Production systems provide one important theoretical approach to **cognitive architecture**. They figure

103

importantly in many **expert systems**, of which **MYCIN** is one famous example.

Productions. See **Condition-action rules**.

Program. A set of instructions in a **programming language** that controls the operation of a computer. The concept of a program is used in various ways, (1) sometimes meaning **algorithm**, and (2) at other times meaning encodings of algorithms in a form that can be executed by a physical machine. An algorithm is more abstract than a program, however, since the same algorithm might be implemented in various programs suitable for execution by various machines running a variety of programming languages. From this perspective, the sense of program defined by (2) *contrasts to* (1). See also **Artificial language**.

Programming language. A set of **formal language** constructs that permit **algorithms** to be written as **programs**—that is, in a vocabulary and structure to which a computer can respond. A distinction is sometimes drawn between high-level and low-level programming languages. High-level languages typically provide for a rich set of constructs that can reflect in a fairly direct way many of the categories and patterns of human thought. Thus, high-level languages (such as Ada, Pascal, **LISP**, **PROLOG**) are relatively easy to remember and are easy to use. High-level languages do not, however, closely reflect a computer's underlying processes and must therefore be translated by a **compiler** or **interpreter** into computer-usable form or **object code**. In contrast, low-level languages such as **assembly language** reflect a computer's operations pretty directly, but their distance from natural human thought categories and processes makes them considerably less intuitive.

PROLOG (PROgramming in LOGic). A **programming language** designed by Alain Colmerauer in the early 1970s. PROLOG is especially well suited for **natural language processing** systems and is enjoying increasing popularity in various artificial intelligence applications. Programs written in PROLOG consist of various facts and rules but do not include explicit problem-solving procedures. Instead, given a problem, the program attempts to deduce the solution from its set of facts and rules. PROLOG was chosen by the Japanese for their Fifth Generation Project, a multibillion-dollar research effort aimed at producing new computerized knowledge systems.

Proposition. (a) That which a declarative sentence asserts to be the case. The same proposition might be expressed by an English sentence, an Arabic sentence, Morse code, and sign language. Propositions are sometimes regarded as the bearers of truth value by virtue of the facts or states of affairs they describe. On such accounts, it is a proposition, rather than the various sentences expressing it, that may be described as either true or false. Alternatively, (b) an equivalence class of sentences where every sentence in such a class says the same thing (or has the same meaning).

Propositional attitudes. Relations that persons have toward propositions. If a person believes (doubts, questions, assumes, etc.) that p, then his or her attitude is one of believing (doubting, questioning, assuming, etc.) that p. There is a vast philosophical literature on propositional attitudes in the philosophy of mind. See also **Representational theory of mind**.

Propositional network. See **Semantic network**.

PROSPECTOR. An **expert system** developed at Stanford Research Institute in the late 1970s to assist geologists in mineral exploration. PROSPECTOR, which uses **Bayesian** inference, achieved some fame for identifying a previously unknown deposit of molybdenum.

Protocols. Introspective reports issued by subjects in experimental settings, typically problem-solving situations. For example, a subject confronting a problem-solving task may be asked to "think out loud" while working on the problem; alternatively, after the solution is obtained, a retrospective report may be provided. These reports, or protocols, provide data for theorizing about cognitive processes and strategies—theorizing that may be validated (or falsified) through implementation in computer systems. See also **Introspection**.

Prototype. The set of properties judged to be most commonly exhibited by members of a particular category. For example, a prototypical bird has wings, is able to fly, sings, and nests. Category members can then be specified, not by necessary and sufficient conditions for category membership but by their degree of resemblance to the category's prototype. Thus, although robins and geese are both birds, robins are more central examples. Prototypes provide an approach to **knowledge representation** akin to the idea of **family resemblance**. See also **Categorization, Concepts, Fuzzy set, Typicality effects**.

Psycholinguistics. The study of language in relation to the associated psychological processes that make language possible. Topics include **attention**, **memory**, and the question of innate capacities for language acquisition, representation, and utilization. See also **Chomsky, Fodor, Nativism**.

Putnam, Hilary (b. 1926). American philosopher who has made important contributions in the fields of logic, metaphysics, philosophy of language, and philosophy of mind. Putnam was one of the first thinkers to suggest that computation (specifically, a **Turing machine**) provides a telling comparison to human mental phenomena. He is currently Walter Beverly Pearson Professor of Modern Mathematics and Mathematical Logic at Harvard.

Pylyshyn, Zenon W. (b. 1937). Professor of psychology and computer science, and director of the Centre for Cognitive Science at the University of Western Ontario.

Pylyshyn has argued for a **representational theory of mind** and has developed a theory of cognition as computation. He also proposed the criterion of **cognitive penetrability** for determining appropriate explanatory levels in cognitive science.

Q

Qualia (singular *quale*). The alleged intrinsic qualitative characteristics of sensory experiences—for example, the throbbing sensation of a pain, the sour taste of a lemon, or the distinctive tonal quality in the sound of a violin. A challenge for cognitive science is to show how qualia could ultimately consist of physical states (of the brain, or perhaps of a computer system). See also **Absent qualia problem**, **Inverted spectrum problem**.

Quantifier. In elementary predicate **logic**, two quantifiers are introduced. One is the *existential* quantifier, usually symbolized as $(\exists x)$, which asserts the existence of at least one thing of the kind described by the corresponding sentential function (a sentence containing a variable instead of an individual name). Thus, if Rx stands for "x is red," then prefixing an existential quantifier creates an existential generalization of the form $(\exists x)Rx$, which asserts that something is red. The other quantifier is the universal *quantifier*, usually symbolized as $(\forall x)$ or (x), which asserts that everything is of the kind described by the corresponding sentential function. Thus, using the same example, prefixing a universal quantifier creates a universal generalization of the form $(\forall x)Rx$, which asserts that everything is red.

Queue. A structure in an **algorithm** or computer **program** that permits the storing of data in a systematic, serial fashion, with access to that data restricted by the following principle: first in, first out (FIFO). Contrast **Stack**.

Quine, Willard Van Orman (b. 1908). American philosopher and logician, perhaps best known for his critique of the **analytic/synthetic** distinction for emphasizing the **underdetermination of theories** by evidence and for the thesis of the **indeterminacy of translation**.

R

RAM (Random Access Memory). That portion of a computer system's memory in which both programs and data can be stored and retrieved. RAM is volatile, meaning that its contents disappear when the computer is turned off. For long-term storage, secondary memory (tape or disk) is required.

Rationalism. The view that there exists some knowledge that has not been acquired directly through sense experience, or by inferences from sense experience. Some rationalists, such as **Plato** and **Descartes**, assert the strong view that although some knowledge exists, none of it can be based upon or otherwise derived from sense experience. Other rationalists, especially **Kant**, maintain that there are other sources of knowledge as well—such as knowledge that is **synthetic** and **a posteriori**, and even **synthetic a priori knowledge**. Contrast **Empiricism**.

Reaction time (RT). The time required for an experimental subject to react in some specified way to a presented stimulus. Typically measured in milliseconds (thousandths of a second), RTs provide a rich and widely used source of data for theorizing about underlying cognitive processes.

Realism. The doctrine that the world's objects, structure, and properties exist independently of human knowledge and perception. On this view, theories and observations may reflect or describe an external reality, but they do not create that reality. Some forms of realism maintain that there is only one true description of the world, in contrast to other forms which hold that the truth or falsity of statements about the world depends upon the overall theory in which they are formulated.

Recall. A form of **memory** that involves retrieving a previously encountered item in response to a query or cue. This form of memory would be called upon for an essay examination as opposed to a multiple-choice test. Contrast **Recognition**.

Recognition. (a) A form of **memory** that involves identifying a stimulus as one that has been previously encountered. This form of memory would be called upon for a multiple-choice test as opposed to an essay examination. Contrast **Recall**. (b) Determining that a sequence of words constitutes a sentence.

Recursion. A technique in which new results are generated by a component that operates by repeatedly invoking itself (direct recursion) or by two or more components that invoke each other (indirect recursion). Clearly, this process must provide for some stopping mechanism, or an infinite process (nonterminating recursion) will result; see the final (three-word) sentence of this entry for an example. A common illustration of direct recursion is the following definition of a natural number's factorial (the product of that number times all of its predecessors down to and including 1):

factorial 1 = 1
Factorial $N = N \times$ factorial $(N - 1)$.

Applying this two-part formula to factorial 5 yields 5 × factorial 4, which equals 5 × 4 × factorial 3, etc. Finally, the calculation reaches $5 \times 4 \times 3 \times 2 \times 1 = 120$. The second line of the definition contains a recursive step, since "factorial" on the left side invokes itself on the right. Although this may appear circular it is not in fact so, since the value of N decreases by one each time the procedure is invoked: eventually the value 1 is reached, at which point line 1 of the definition takes over and brings the recursion to an end (this is called the base case). Recursive calculation of a factorial illustrates the concept of a **TOTE unit**. Recursion is an important concept in linguistics, because it suggests how a finite number of rules might generate an infinite number of possible sentences. It also lies at the heart of many structures in computer programming and is an essential idea in the **LISP** programming language. See also **Recursion**.

Recursive Transition Network (RTN). See **Transition network**.

Reductionism. Any attempt to reduce theories of one (higher) level to those of another (lower) level. Important instances include attempts to reduce the mind to the body (**physicalism**) and the theoretical to the observable. Contrast **Holism** (a).

Referential opacity. A linguistic construct is said to exhibit referential opacity when co-referential terms cannot be exchanged in contexts to which that construct applies. This point is easily made with an example: "belief" is referentially opaque, for although the terms "Abraham Lincoln" and "the sixteenth president of the United States" in fact designate the same person they cannot be assumed to do so when some individual's belief about former presidents is being characterized. Thus, if A believes that Abraham Lincoln was a Republican, it does not follow that A believes that the sixteenth president of the United States was a Republican. In fact, A may not hold the latter belief at all, say, if A does not realize that

Lincoln was the sixteenth president. Referential opacity figures importantly in explanations of behavior, because (as the Lincoln example shows) the *way in which* a person describes or represents information determines what that person can say or do. Typically, contexts governed by psychological terms are referentially opaque; examples in addition to "believes" are "knows," "wants," "hopes," and "remembers." Contrast **Referential transparency**.

Referential transparency. The intersubstitutability of co-referential terms without affecting the truth value of the expression in which the substitution occurs. Consider the sentence "Abraham Lincoln was a Republican." Not only is this sentence true; it remains true if the name "Abraham Lincoln" is replaced by the phrase "the sixteenth president of the United States." There are some contexts, however, in which a substitution such as this would alter the truth value of the original sentence; for further discussion, see **Referential opacity**.

Regular grammar. A **grammar** whose rules are restricted as follows: The right side of a rule consists of either a **terminal symbol** followed by a **nonterminal symbol** or else simply a nonterminal symbol. Regular grammars occupy Level 3 in the **Chomsky hierarchy**.

Relaxation. The process whereby a **connectionist** system settles into a state representing an optimal solution to a set of constraints that must be satisfied. See also **Constraint satisfaction**.

Representation. A symbol or process that *stands for* something else. A particular symbol may be arbitrary and need not resemble the thing it stands for (both of these points are illustrated by the English word *horse* and the German word *Pferd*, which are alternative representations of the same thing). An important topic in cognitive science concerns the way in which mental symbols or processes come to represent reality. See also **Original**

meaning, **Representational Theory of the Mind**, **Symbol grounding problem**.

Representational Theory of the Mind (RTM). Any theory that views mental processes as the manipulation of representations (meanings, contents, symbols); this may include combining them, altering them, storing or retrieving them, etc. Although representations are assumed to display **intentionality**, their manipulations may be accomplished according to features that are purely syntactic. See also **Mentality**, **Methodological solipsism**, **Minds**, **Original meaning**, **Symbol grounding problem**. Contrast **Syntactical theory of the mind**.

Rewrite rules. See **Grammar**.

ROM (Read Only Memory). The permanently fixed portion of a computer system's memory from which data or programs can be retrieved but in which nothing new can be stored. ROM is nonvolatile, meaning that the information preserved there is maintained when the system is shut down. Among other things, ROM contains start-up instructions which govern a computer's behavior when it is first turned on.

Rule-based system. See **Expert system**.

Rumelhart, David E. (b. 1942). Professor of psychology at Stanford University, author, and a leading theoretician of **connectionism** as a model of cognitive processing.

Russell, Bertrand (1872–1970). British mathematician and philosopher, perhaps the most distinguished of the twentieth century. Russell wrote prolifically on the central problems of epistemology, philosophy of science, and mathematical logic; he also produced a variety of popular works on such topics as marriage, values, the existence of God, and the history of philosophy.

Ryle, Gilbert (1900–1976). British philosopher whose 1949 work *The Concept of Mind* argued against Cartesian **dualism** (which he referred to disparagingly as "the dogma of the Ghost in the Machine") and developed a case for a behaviorist-style account of mental phenomena. According to Ryle, philosophers have erred in regarding mental terms as referring to events in a nonphysical realm; instead, mental terms typically refer to **dispositions** (or propensities to behave in particular ways). Because of Ryle's acute sensitivity to the way in which words are actually used in a variety of contexts, he is often described as an "ordinary language" philosopher. See also **Behaviorism**.

S

Sapir—Whorf hypothesis. The hypothesis that categories in a speaker's native language determine his or her cognitive categories (as in thought, perception, and memory). Often cited in this connection is the claim that Eskimos have some twenty words for snow, each indicating a different condition (powdery, wet, etc.), and, consequently, that Eskimos view the world differently than do speakers of English or similar languages. Although the substance of the Sapir—Whorf hypothesis has been much discussed and disputed, it does raise important questions about the origin of conceptual structures and the criteria for determining when two or more conceptual structures are appreciably different.

Satisficing. Finding solutions that are less than optimal but still acceptable. **Herbert Simon** (who coined the term) stressed the need for finding satisficing methods in cases where exact answers to real-world questions are either theoretically unattainable or computationally intractable. An important feature of this approach involves the recognition of acceptable solutions fairly early in a search process.

Schank, Roger C. (b. 1946). Professor of information science at Northwestern University, Schank is among the leading theoreticians of **knowledge representation** and learning theory in artificial intelligence. His contributions include **conceptual dependency** theory, studies of the nature of **scripts**, and work on computers and cognition.

Schemas. See **Scripts**.

Scripts. Sequences of events that are typical in a given, restricted context. Armed with an appropriate script, an agent can make probable inferences about situations for which no information has been explicitly provided. For example, if you are told that Jane ate a hamburger at a fast-food restaurant, you can conclude that she placed an order by going to a counter rather than sitting down and waiting for service; that she paid for her meal; and that payment was made prior to eating. In this case, a restaurant script is being activated; however, scripts are available for many other scenarios (getting a haircut, going to the movies, going to a birthday party, etc.). Various artificial intelligence systems have employed scripts as vehicles of **knowledge representation**, and some psychological studies indicate that scripts may play an important role in humans' representation of knowledge as well. Scripts represent dynamic, unfolding events, whereas **frames**, which are similar, represent static objects or states of affairs.

Search. The investigation of alternatives in a **search space**. Problem-solving may be thought of as a search for an efficient route from some given condition to a goal.

Search space. The set of alternatives that may be explored in looking for a path between an initial, given state and an end-state or goal. The set of all legal board positions in a chess game, for example, constitutes a search space. Since the total number of alternatives in a search space may be astronomical (owing to **combinatorial explosion**), computational search procedures must devise strategies—often **heuristic**—for limiting the number of states to be explored. See also **Problem space**.

Searle, John R. (b. 1932). Professor of philosophy at the University of California, Berkeley, who is well known for his studies in the philosophy of language, especially **speech act** theory, and for his **Chinese Room** argument as a counterexample to the **Turing test** as a criterion of intelligence.

Semantic memory. Memory organized by associative structures, such as those represented in a **semantic network**. Semantic memory involves the vocabulary of a language along with general facts about the world, as contrasted to **episodic memory** of personally experienced specific events. Arguments that the semantic/episodic distinction has a physical basis in the brain draw heavily from physiological measures (such as blood flow in various parts of the brain and the effects of frontal lobe lesions); however, the interpretation of this evidence is not univocal.

Semantic network. A **knowledge representation** structure consisting of **nodes** (representing words or concepts) and **links** (representing relationships among words or concepts). Together, nodes and links can represent propositions, or statements, such as "Ronald Reagan was re-elected to a second term in the White House," or "A variety of satellites are orbiting the earth." One basic semantic network structure uses **IS-A** links for displaying conceptual hierarchies; however, the network approach is highly flexible and capable of capturing a variety of conceptual interconnections (such as part-whole, subject-object, giver-recipient). Semantic networks provide an excellent vehicle for representing **inheritance of properties** and may be taken as a model of association among ideas in memory. Ross Quillian, who introduced semantic network representation in this context, also argued that the full *meaning* of a term or concept is given by the semantic network in which it is embedded. Despite their name, however, semantic networks do not provide for any connection between terms and their referents.

Semantics. The study of relations between signs and what they stand for. Among the most important semantic concepts involving signs are those of meaning and of truth. See also **Pragmatics**, **Model-theoretic semantics**, **Syntax**.

Semiotics. The study of systems of signs. The subject is very broad and may include communication, not only through ordinary language but also through whistles, drumbeats, smoke signals, facial expressions, gestures, film, dance, architecture, etc. See also **Icons**, **Indices**, **Minds as semiotic systems**.

Serial processing. Processing that proceeds sequentially (one calculation at a time), as contrasted to **parallel processing** which permits multiple operations to be carried out simultaneously. Serial processing is characteristic of **Von Neumann machines** and gives rise to the notorious **Von Neumann bottleneck**.

Set effect. Clinging to a particular problem-solving strategy due to the influence of past experience with problems that appear similar to the current one. The set effect may help or hinder, depending on whether the strategy being employed is a good strategy. Many everyday activities are viewed by cognitive scientists as problem-solving tasks, often exhibiting set effects. For example, driving a new brand of car takes little effort because the relevant operations are essentially standardized from one model to another; hence, a person's usual procedures apply from one case to another. But Americans who take up driving in England are likely to find themselves getting into a car on the passenger side and activating the windshield wipers instead of the turn signal.

Short-term memory (STM). Temporary, limited, and rapidly accessible storage. Short-term memories do not normally persevere unless they are given a high degree of **activation**, as might be attained by conscious repetition. There is some evidence that short-term memories may also be maintained through rehearsal procedures of which we are unaware. The capacity of short-term memory appears subject to the **magic number seven** phenomenon.

SHRDLU. A well-known artificial intelligence program devised in 1970 by **Terry Winograd** as a doctoral thesis project at MIT. The purpose of SHRDLU was to investigate some aspects of knowledge representation that underlie natural language communication. The program accepted commands in English for manipulating objects in a **blocks world** and requested clarification when an unfamiliar term was employed or when a command was ambiguous (for example, *which* cube was meant in the command "Pick up the cube"?). SHRDLU was also able to answer questions about what it had done—and why; its ultimate answer to the latter question was "Because you told me to." Like **ELIZA**, SHRDLU has sometimes been discussed in connection with the **Turing test**, although its restricted blocks world scope does not begin to meet the wide-open questioning that Turing's test envisaged.

Simon, Herbert Alexander (b. 1916). Nobel laureate in economics and university professor of computer science and psychology at Carnegie-Mellon University. Simon is widely noted for his contributions to a variety of fields, including artificial intelligence. He has often collaborated with **Allen Newell**, for example in designing the **General Problem Solver** and in elaborating the **physical symbol system hypothesis**.

Simple transition network. See **Transition network**.

Skinner, B. F. (1904–1990). Highly influential American behavioral psychologist who taught at Harvard, where he also directed a research laboratory for many years. Skinner was noted for his studies of animal behavior, which involved attempts to determine probabilities of response as a function of the kind of organism under study together with its history of reinforcement. He wrote numerous books, some (such as *Verbal Behavior; Science and Human Behavior*) primarily for an audience of psychologists, and others (for example, *Beyond Freedom and Dignity; About Behaviorism*) aimed at popularizing **behaviorism**. His 1948 novel *Walden Two*, which imagined a utopian community based on behavioristic principles, has been widely read by several generations; the book has also inspired several attempts to set up experimental communities incorporating Skinnerian ideas.

Slot/filler notation. A structure used in a variety of **knowledge representation** systems (including **frames**, **scripts**, and **semantic networks**), based on the idea that an object or situation can be described by reference to a set of properties and their associated values. For example, a robin normally has the following properties: it belongs to the bird category; it has body parts consisting of wings, bill, etc.; it can fly; it can sing. In a semantic network, the property of belonging to the general category could be modeled by an **IS-A link** from a **node** labeled "robin" to another node labeled "bird"; the property of having wings could be captured by a "has part" link to a node labeled "wings"; and the flying and singing abilities could be captured by "is able to" links directed from "robin" to other appropriately labeled nodes. Some of the properties in this example represent **default values** and may be overridden in a particular instance (an individual robin whose wings were broken would of course be unable to fly).

Smolensky, Paul (b. 1955). A member of the department of computer science at the University of Colorado and a former research scientist at the University of California, San Diego, Smolensky is perhaps best known for his contributions to **connectionism**, but his interests also include the methodology and foundations of cognitive science, as well as mathematical approaches to integrating connectionist and symbolic computation in the theory of higher cognition—especially language.

SOAR. An artificial intelligence system embodying a theory of **cognitive architecture** (the fundamental components required for the processing of **mental representations**). SOAR contains a short-term working memory and a long-term memory configured as a **production system** (essentially, a set of **condition-action** or if-then rules). When relevant productions are called into action, they all fire simultaneously, thus obviating the need to assign priorities to those rules in advance. When SOAR encounters a problem that is not directly solvable (for example, if multiple productions produce contradictory results), the system creates its own subtasks, solving them first as a means to solving the previous problem. Thus, in the course of carrying out its operations, the system sets up its own hierarchy of goals.

Society of mind. An approach to cognition introduced by **Marvin Minsky** and based on the idea that cognitive processing involves a large number of discrete processes or agents, often hierarchically arranged (**demons** are one example). Each process is charged with performing a particular task, and various processes may exchange the results of their computations. Although on this account the mind consists of a society of simple agents, no individual agent is itself a mind or **homunculus**; otherwise, minds would be explained in terms of minds and an infinite regress would result. Moreover, the explanation of consciousness by way of underlying agents does not imply that anyone is conscious of those agents' operation.

Soundness. The property of a formal system such that every statement that is provable by the rules of that system is true in that system. Alternatively, a system of logic is said to be sound when every formula that is provable as a theorem of that system is true (as a tautology) in that system.

Soundness of arguments. See **Deductive arguments**.

Source code. The computer program which is run through a **compiler** in order to create an **object code** to which a computer can directly respond.

Spatial neglect. A pathological condition (affecting one or more of the senses) in which an individual is unable to be aware of a particular area of space. A variety of cases have been documented, including patients who have no awareness of one side of their bodies (most commonly, the left side) and others who have no awareness of distant objects. Varieties of spatial neglect suggest that underlying, specialized mechanisms are responsible for specialized aspects of spatial **attention**.

Speech acts. Actions that are performed by the use of words. **J. L. Austin** drew an important distinction among three dimensions of speech acts: *locutionary* (the use of words on a certain occasion), *illocutionary* (the purpose for which the words were used on that occasion), and *perlocutionary* (the effect that the words used achieved on that occasion). See also **Performative utterances**.

Sperry, Roger Wolcott (b. 1913). American neuroscientist, now professor emeritus of psychobiology at California Institute of Technology. Sperry's studies of split-brain patients made a major contribution to our knowledge of **hemispheric specialization** (he shared a Nobel Prize in 1981). See also **Commisurotomy**.

Split-brain. See **Commisurotomy**.

Spreading activation. When a particular area of **long-term memory** undergoes **activation**, other connected areas tend to be activated as well. This spreading activation phenomenon, which can be modeled in **semantic networks**, captures the intuitively obvious idea that one concept often leads naturally to (is associated with) another. The level of activation of a memory area decreases with the number of related areas to which the activation spreads. See also **Fan effect**.

Stack. A structure in an **algorithm** or computer **program** that permits the storing of data in a systematic, serial fashion, with access to that data restricted by the following principle: last in, first out (LIFO). Contrast **Queue**.

State transition diagram. See **Finite-state automaton**.

Stereopsis. The fusion of two retinal images, resulting in three-dimensional perception. A good deal of computation underlies this process, since the left and right retinal images differ slightly due to **binocular disparity**. Thus, a point from the retinal image on one eye must be matched with a corresponding point on the eye's other retinal image. The trick is to figure out the correct pairs of matching points. Various **constraint satisfaction** mechanisms (neurologically "wired into" the brain) are believed to be involved and have been used in computational models of vision as well.

Stich, Stephen P. (b. 1943). Professor of philosophy at Rutgers University who has elaborated important distinctions in the theory of cognition, including those between the **Syntactical Theory of the Mind** (STM) and the **Representational Theory of the Mind** (RTM).

Strong AI. The claim that, under appropriate conditions (such as running the proper program), a computer actually would possess a mind; that is, a computer would be endowed with cognition in a nonmetaphorical sense. Contrast **Weak AI**.

STUDENT. An artificial intelligence designed in the 1970s by Daniel Bobrow as his Ph.D. thesis project at MIT. Presented with algebraic "story problems" in English, STUDENT solved them by creating (and solving) the appropriate equations. Its performance reportedly approximated that of an average high school student.

Subroutine. A special-purpose component of a computer **program**, typically invoked by the main program in order to get a specific task performed. When a subroutine is invoked, it takes over control from the main program, temporarily assuming responsibility for carrying out its own instructions. At the conclusion of its operations control is returned from the subroutine to the point in the main program from which it was called. The invocation of a subroutine is an example of **branching**.

Surface structure. A level of analysis employed in a **transformational grammar** and contrasted to **deep structure** (the distinction was introduced by **Noam Chomsky**). At the level of surface structure, a straightforward correspondence exists between a sentence and its grammatical representation. The relationship between the surface structure and deep structure of a sentence is revealed by a transformational grammar.

Syllogism. An argument consisting of two premises and a conclusion that follows from them by **deductive inference**. The premises and conclusion of a syllogism are restricted to the following four forms: (1) All A are B; (2) Some A are B; (3) No A are B; (4) Some A are not B. Thus, the following is a valid syllogism:

All humans are animals.
All animals are mortals.
Therefore, all humans are mortals.

Aristotle was the first to develop a theory of the syllogism, showing which combinations of statement forms result in valid arguments (validity is purely a function of statement form and is independent of statement content).

Symbols. One of three kinds of representative entity in a famous classification introduced by **C. S. Peirce**, symbols (such as written words) represent as a consequence of conventional agreement. The other two categories are **icons** and **indices**.

Symbol grounding problem. The problem of securing the meaning of the symbols that are used by **physical symbol systems**. If at least some of these symbols do not have extrasymbolic meaning apart from their relations to other symbols, the set of symbols may possess no meaning at all. This problem frequently lurks in the type of cognitive models proposed by **symbolic AI**, although proponents of symbolic AI are not always aware of it. **Connectionist** approaches tend to circumvent the issue insofar as they do not appeal to symbol manipulation at all. Harnad (1990) has put forth a hybrid cognitive theory that assigns a prominent role to symbols while employing the pattern-recognition capabilities of connectionist systems to establish links between symbols and features of the external world. The symbol grounding problem may be viewed as a special case of the **problem of primitives**. See also **Original meaning, Representational Theory of the Mind**.

Symbolic AI. An approach to **artificial intelligence** that stresses the importance of rules for manipulating symbols of various sorts (such as those found in **semantic networks**, **scripts**, or **frames**). The symbolic paradigm in AI reflects the attitude of those cognitive scientists who regard human intelligence as emerging from the brain's manipulation of symbols. A contrasting approach in AI research (and theories of human cognition) is **connectionism**.

Syntactical Theory of the Mind (STM). Any theory that maintains that the nature of mentality can be adequately captured by means of mental operations on symbols that ignore what those symbols mean or stand for. On this view, mental *content* is irrelevant to the nature of cognition and the mind is likened to a calculating machine, whose symbols' connection to the world is left unspecified. See also **Mentality**. Contrast **Representational Theory of the Mind (RTM)**.

Syntax. The study of the relations that signs bear to other signs—especially how signs can be combined to produce new signs. Purely syntactical systems are often studied in their own right without concern for their possible interpretation as meaningful assertions about the physical world, for example. Indeed, one domain of purely syntactical systems is pure mathematics. Among the most important concepts of syntax is that of a **well-formed formula**. See also **Grammar**, **Pragmatics**, **Semantics**.

Synthetic a priori knowledge. Knowledge that is both informative about experience (hence synthetic) yet knowable independently of experience (hence a priori). Most rationalists endorse some variety of synthetic a priori knowledge; the most important such figure is **Immanuel Kant**.

Systemic grammar. An approach that views language within the social context of interpersonal communication rather than as an abstract system of rules presumed to be internalized by an individual speaker. It emphasizes various social roles that linguistic expressions can play (for example, a declarative sentence such as "It's getting late" appears to state a fact but may function as a suggestion that it is time to leave or go to bed). Although not originally conceived as a computational theory of language, systemic grammars have influenced natural language processing systems. From that perspective, social linguistic transactions are viewed as resulting from speakers' generating sentences through the choice of various functional linguistic units that exhibit mutually interacting constraints (analogous to those in a **case grammar**). See also **Conversational implicatures**.

T

Tarski, Alfred (1901–1983). Polish-American philosopher and logician affiliated with the University of California, Berkeley, from which he retired in 1973. Among the most important contributors to formal semantics, Tarski formulated an important conception of truth known as the semantic theory of truth.

TEIRESIAS. A computer program developed as a Ph.D. project at Stanford in the 1970s by Randall Davis. Originally designed for use with **MYCIN**, TEIRESIAS assisted a human expert in expanding or correcting the knowledge base of various **expert systems**.

Template matching. An approach to **recognition** tasks that proceeds by comparing an input pattern with a set of stored specimens, aiming to discover a close fit. Except for highly standardized inputs, however (such as the account number printed on a typical bank check), this method does not work very well because a given object may be viewed from a variety of perspectives, each of which alters the input pattern. Moreover, the same category of object—such as a given alphabetic character—may admit of a tremendous variety of patterns, as is evident from the great variation in handwriting styles. A more promising approach is **feature analysis**.

Terminal symbol. A grammatical symbol that is the smallest syntactical unit (for example, noun, verb, **determiner**). Terminal symbols are not further decomposable, as is indicated by the fact that they do not appear on the left-hand side of any rewrite rule in a **grammar**. Contrast **Nonterminal symbol**.

Token identity theory. The theory that each psychological state is identical with one or another physical state. While preserving a commitment to **physicalism**, the token identity theory does not insist that the same mental state in two different individuals must have the same physical identification—only that each mental state is identical with one or another physical state. This leaves open the possibility that nonhumanlike systems, or even nonbiological systems (such as computers), though physical in nature, might nevertheless be capable of mentality (a central tenet of **functionalism**). Contrast **Type identity theory**.

Top-down parsing. See **Bottom-up/top-down parsing**.

Top-down processing. See **Bottom-up/top-down processing**.

Total Turing Test (TTT). A criterion proposed by Harnad (1991) for identifying the presence of minds in others (humans or machines), relying not only upon linguistic behavior (as did the original **Turing test**), but also upon nonverbal bodily behavior. The underlying assumption of the TTT is that the original Turing test is too weak, because a mindless computer might display language capabilities comparable to that of a human. However, if a robotic device were to behave in ways indistinguishable from a person *in all respects*—both verbal and nonverbal—then the question of whether it had a mind would be more firmly settled. In fact, Harnad suggests, the TTT is essentially what people rely on in everyday situations when attributing mentality to other people. Even stronger versions of such tests could also be constructed by testing not only outward behavior, but also internal processes, using **CT scans**, **PET imaging**, **MRI imaging**, and the like. While granting all this, it may still be argued that *no* test based entirely upon observable evidence can provide conclusive proof of the presence of mental powers, since those powers involve nonobservable cognitive capacities. Thus the **problem of other minds** can still be raised, even in the face of high-tech examinations of bodily interiors. See also **Inference to the best explanation**, **Observational/theoretical distinction**.

TOTE unit (Test-Operate-Test-Exit). Introduced by Miller, Galanter, and Pribram in their *Plans and the Structure of Behavior* (1960), the TOTE unit is a vehicle that when given a goal, carries out a set of operations to achieve that goal, then confirms that the goal has been met, and finally either terminates or establishes a new goal and repeats. The TOTE unit proceeds by establishing a hierarchy of subroutines, with control passed back to the points of departure as the subroutines conclude their work. For an example, see **Recursion**.

Tower of Hanoi. A classic problem-solving task, consisting of three vertical pegs and a set of disks with different diameters. In their initial configuration, the disks are stacked on the left-hand peg, with the largest-diameter disk on the bottom and progressively smaller diameter disks placed on top of it. The goal is to arrange the disks on the right-hand peg in the same order by moving one disk at a time, using any of the pegs as intermediate storage places. Smaller disks may be placed on top of larger ones, but not vice versa. The Tower of Hanoi problem can be decomposed into a series of subgoals; hence it can be represented naturally as a case of **problem reduction**. The repetitive nature of establishing and solving subgoals suggests the use of **recursion**.

Transducer. Any process or procedure (or any structure performing the process or procedure) of converting an input of one kind into an output of another kind. The senses (eyes, ears, etc.) are transducers, as are microphones and television cameras.

Transformational grammar (TG). A **grammar** developed by **Chomsky**, employing two levels of representation: **deep structure** and **surface structure**. The essential hypothesis is that the production of natural language sentences relies on derivations from underlying structures by processes of which a speaker is unaware. Deep structures are generated by a **phrase structure grammar**; a set of transformation rules is then applied in order to yield the surface structure corresponding to an actual sentence. It turns out that an unrestricted transformational grammar is extremely powerful—so much so that rules not required for the description of any known human language can be cast into TG format. As such, an unrestricted TG is not a viable candidate for a **universal grammar**; possibly, however, some suitably restricted TG might serve in that capacity.

Transition network (also called **simple transition network**). A simple transition network is characteristically depicted as a **graph** and may be used to generate a sentence or to recognize that a given string of words is a sentence (but not to analyze a sentence into its grammatical components). Links in a simple transition network are labeled as syntactic categories (arranged so as to constitute a grammar). Although transition networks are relatively weak, corresponding to **regular grammars**, they can be enhanced in various ways to increase their power. For example, a recursive transition network (RTN) consists of a group of subnetworks, each resembling a simple transition network, but with the proviso that links may refer to (and thereby invoke) themselves as well as other subnetworks. With **recursion**, RTNs gain the power of a **context-free grammar** and can be used for

parsing. More powerful yet is the augmented transition network (ATN), which builds upon the RTN idea; its most notable addition is the incorporation of what are essentially **condition-action rules** associated with the network's links. ATNs are able to handle some of the more complex constructions in English, and ever since their introduction by William Woods in conjunction with his **LUNAR** program, ATNs have been popular in artificial intelligence approaches to **parsing**.

Transitivity. A logical property of relations that obtains when the following is true: If x bears relation R to y, and y bears relation R to z, then x bears relation R to z. The "ancestor" relation is transitive, as is the relation "taller than." Thus, if Sandy is an ancestor of Chris, and Chris is an ancestor of Pat, it follows that Sandy is an ancestor of Pat. Similarly, if Sandy is taller than Chris, and Chris is taller than Pat, it follows that Sandy is taller than Pat.

Tree. A hierarchical structure consisting of a single **node** (called the root node) to which multiple branches or **links** attach, leading to other nodes. (If all nodes have exactly two branches, the structure is called a *binary* tree.) The branching may continue through any number of levels. A familiar example is a hierarchical corporate organization chart depicting the president at the top and various managers and other employees on lower levels, but tree representations are also extremely useful in many other domains where hierarchical organization is present. They have been used to display the grammatical structure of sentences, to lay out possible solutions to a problem by decomposing the original into layers of subproblems, and to display sets of alternatives from a given starting point (such as the theorems that can be derived from a given axiom or the possible moves in a game). A tree may be defined as a **graph**, restricted by the allowance of just one path between any two nodes.

Truth table. In elementary logic, truth tables are employed for the definition of the connectives (including "not- ——," ". . . and ——," ". . . or ——," and so forth) whereby the truth values of molecular sentences that are built out of atomic sentences as their components are completely determined by the truth values of those atomic sentences. Examples are:

p q	Not-p	p and q	p or q	if p then q
T T	F	T	T	T
T F	F	F	T	F
F T	T	F	T	T
F F	T	F	F	T

The leftmost column indicates the various combinations of truth values that can be taken on by p and by q. The remaining columns show how the truth values of compound sentences change as a function of the truth values of their constituents. Thus the negation of a sentence reverses its truth value; conjunctions of sentences are only true when both of their component sentences (conjuncts) are true; disjunctions are only false when both of their component sentences (disjuncts) are false; and conditionals are only false when their "if" sentences (antecedents) are true and their "then" sentences (consequents) are false.

Turing, Alan Mathison (1912–1954). English mathematician whose theoretical work on computation lies at the foundation of computer science (see **Turing machine** and **Church–Turing thesis** for examples). Turing also proposed what has come to be known as the **Turing test** for determining whether a machine displays intelligence. During World War II he headed a team that built several computer systems which succeeded in deciphering German military ciphers—a fact that was not revealed until many years later. The definitive biography of Turing is by Hodges (1983).

Turing machine. An abstract device consisting of an indefinitely long "tape," divided into cells, each of which may contain either a 0 or a 1. A scanner passes over the tape, reading the contents of one cell at a time and performing a set of serial operations, each of which depends jointly upon the content of a current cell and the machine's current "control state." The machine's program instructs it what to do at each point—for example, "If the symbol 0 is being scanned and the machine is in control state 6, then replace the 0 with a 1 and shift into control state 4." Any marks on the tape at the beginning of the machine's operations may be viewed as input, and any marks that remain when its program has been executed may be viewed as output. Turing machines that are designed to operate on the basis of just one set of instructions are "special purpose" machines. Universal Turing machines, in contrast, can imitate the performance of any special-purpose machine when provided with the corresponding program. In this sense, they are general-purpose machines. The striking feature of universal Turing machines is their enormous computational power: Any problem for which an algorithmic solution exists can be solved by a Turing machine. The difference between a modern digital machine and a Turing machine is a matter of design rather than of function; also, real-world computers, unlike Turing machines, have limited memories. See also **Algorithm**, **Church-Turing thesis**, **Program**.

Turing test. An operational test introduced by Alan Turing as a means for answering the question "Can a machine think?" The test initially involves an interrogator who poses various questions on any topic to a man and a woman sequestered in a different location; communication is carried out by a message system. The interrogator's goal is to ascertain which of the contestants is the man and which is the woman. At a later phase, the game is played with a computer replacing the male contestant. If the interrogator continues to believe that both contestants are human, the computer's performance clearly matches that of a human, and the computer should thereby be credited with the capacity to think. The adequacy of the Turing test for determining the presence of cognition has been challenged by **John Searle** with his famous counterexample of the **Chinese Room**. See also **Total Turing test**.

Two and one-half-dimensional sketch. The final stage in early visual processing, as theorized by **David Marr**. The $2\frac{1}{2}$-dimensional sketch, produced by various computational operations on a **primal sketch**, represents an object's depth and surface orientations from the perspective of an observer (the perspectival limitation is the reason for calling the sketch $2\frac{1}{2}$ rather than 3-dimensional, since a fully 3-dimensional model would not present the object from just one point of view).

Type identity theory. The theory that each type of mental state is identical to a particular type of physical state (in the case of humans, a brain state). Although the type identity theory is a version of **physicalism**, it is arguably undermined by its commitment to **neural chauvinism**. Suppose, for example, that the state of believing that Lincoln was the sixteenth president of the U.S. were identical to brain state B. It would then follow that anything lacking brain state B would be incapable of holding that belief. Thus computers, and even highly advanced outer space creatures with nonhuman physical makeups, would be automatically disqualified as candidates for mentality. Contrast **Functionalism**, **Token identity theory**.

Typicality. A measure of the degree to which an entity represents the category to which it belongs, as determined by subjects' ratings. For example, a robin is a highly typical bird, whereas a flamingo is much less so; and an apple is a more typical fruit than is a mango. Degrees of typicality can be used to predict **typicality effects**.

Typicality effects. Performance variations that reflect **typicality** ratings. In **recall** tasks, aimed at producing as many instances of a given concept as possible, subjects tend to produce typical instances first. And in **recognition** tasks where subjects are asked to decide whether a given item belongs in a particular category (for example, "Is a minnow a fish?"), the **reaction time** for typical instances is faster than for atypical ones. These and other typicality effects point to an apparent difficulty with the traditional view of categories, according to which category membership is a matter of satisfying a set of defining conditions. For if that view were correct, why should some identifications take longer than others with respect to the same category? An alternative to the traditional view is the suggestion that category membership can be construed in terms of sufficient proximity to a **prototype**; items closely resembling a prototype would be "central" and therefore more quickly identified.

U

Unconscious. Areas of the mind whose contents and operations are not available to **introspection**. Under special circumstances such as psychoanalysis, some of those contents may be brought to consciousness. But many of the mechanisms that are presumed to underlie cognition are not available to introspection under any circumstances, and introspection alone simply cannot reveal all the facts about mental processes. For example, a huge amount of computational processing is required in order for data presented in a retinal image to result in a perceptual experience, but people recognize objects so immediately and effortlessly that some argument is often required to convince them of the magnitude of their accomplishment.

Undecidability. The nonexistence of a finite procedure for determining whether a given statement or its negation can be proved in a particular formal system. Thus, in a system that is undecidable, no mechanical procedure (or recipe) is available to determine whether an arbitrary given formula can be proven using the axioms and the rules of inference of that system. This result was established by **Alonzo Church** in 1936. For an analog, see **Halting problem**.

Underdetermination of theories. The thesis that the content of a scientific theory is always greater than its set of empirically testable consequences, which implies that theories, however testable, are never completely verifiable. **W. V. O. Quine** has advanced a special instance of this thesis, known as the **indeterminacy of translation**.

Universal grammar. Proposed by **Noam Chomsky**, a universal grammar is a set of constraints that the grammar of any natural language must satisfy. Chomsky argued that the paucity of linguistic data received by a child engaged in learning a language requires the hypothesis of an *innate* linguistic framework; more technically, that the **poverty of stimulus**, when viewed in the context of **creativity in language**, requires the hypothesis of **nativism**. On this view, all natural languages (both actual and possible) share some central underlying features.

V

Validity of arguments. See **Deductive arguments**.

Vector. An ordered list of numbers that, in **connectionist** systems, displays patterns of activity (such as the levels of activation of various **processing units** or the set of the system's output units). Insofar as representation is accomplished by patterns of activity, a vector can indicate what is being represented by the system.

Vector completion. The ability of a **connectionist** network to function properly even when some of the normal input to that network is degraded or missing. This is accomplished by providing feedback connections from the system's output units back to its input units, thereby in effect either increasing or decreasing input levels.

Verb phrase (VP). A unit of grammatical analysis, whose simplest forms consist merely of a verb or a verb plus an object (represented as a **noun phrase**). Examples include "eat," and "played the banjo." VPs provide one level of analysis in **phrase structure grammars**.

Virtual machine. A machine (either abstract or physically embodied) that can be programmed in such a way that its behavior mimics the behavior of something else. For example, a computer running a word processing program is a "virtual word processor," although different programs can turn it into a virtual calculator or a virtual arcade game. The same virtual machine may have a variety of underlying physical implementations, as is the case when differently constructed computers nevertheless offer the same capabilities and screen displays.

Visual neglect. An instance of **spatial neglect** in which patients are unaware of part of their visual field.

Von Neumann, John (1903–1957). Hungarian-born professor of mathematics at Princeton University who conceived the basic architecture for the modern (serial) computer; one of its key elements was the stored program (a program that could be maintained in a computer's memory). Von Neumann was associated with the **ENIAC**

project and designed the specifications for later computer systems as well. He theorized extensively on the relationship between computers and human brains.

Von Neumann bottleneck. The channeling of all processing sequentially through a single **CPU** in a typical computer (**Von Neumann machine**), thereby limiting the speed with which instructions can be carried out. For many tasks this is not a problem, especially insofar as millions of instructions per second may be executed. Even so, calculations that are highly computation-intensive (for example, those involved in visual object recognition) may suffer appreciably from this limitation. An alternative approach currently gaining favor is **parallel processing**.

Von Neumann machine. The most common type of computer architecture (invented by **Von Neumann**), the basic components of which are a memory unit (which stores both programs and data) and a central processing unit (**CPU**) that maintains physical control and performs basic operations. To these components may be attached various peripheral devices such as a disk drive for long-term storage; an output display (monitor or printer); a keyboard or mouse for input. Despite its great usefulness for many processing tasks, this type of design is ultimately limited by the **Von Neumann bottleneck**; alternatives such as the **connection machine** are now under development.

W

Weak AI. The view that computers are useful and powerful tools for studying the mind, for example by formulating and testing hypotheses about language processing or memory organization. In contrast to **strong AI**, however, weak AI does not claim that computers literally are (or could be) cognitive agents.

Weizenbaum, Joseph (b. 1923). A major figure in the

early development of artificial intelligence and author of the famous **ELIZA** program. Weizenbaum, a professor emeritus of computer science at MIT, has in recent years devoted considerable energy to discussing the social implications of artificial intelligence (see Weizenbaum, 1976).

Well-formed formula (WFF). A sequence of symbols that is permitted by the formation rules in a **formal language**.

Wh-questions. Interrogatives that seek information beyond what can be provided by a simple yes or no answer. In English, wh-questions typically begin with the letters *wh* ("who," "what," "when," "why," etc.), although this does not necessarily hold for other languages. In linguistics, wh-questions have been extensively investigated in connection with augmented **transition networks** and **transformational grammars**.

Whorfian hypothesis. See **Sapir-Whorf Hypothesis**.

Wiener, Norbert (1864–1964). American mathematical prodigy (he received his Ph.D. from Harvard at eighteen) who pioneered the field of **cybernetics**. At MIT during the 1930s and 1940s, Wiener worked on missile and aircraft guidance systems, which led him to propose that there are general principles of self-regulating (cybernetic) systems independent of their physical makeup (electrical, mechanical, or biological). He also contributed to discussion of the social effects of technology in his book *The Human Use of Human Beings: Cybernetics and Society*.

Winograd, Terry (b. 1946). Professor of computer science at Stanford University, Winograd is noted for his **SHRDLU** program and for his overall contributions to the study of language as a cognitive process. More recently, in collaboration with Fernando Flores, he has provided a critique of the computational conception of the mind. Winograd has also exhibited an ongoing concern about the social uses of computers and has served as a president of Computer Professionals for Social Responsibility.

Word. An informational unit in a computer system. Composed of **bits** (which may be chunked into **bytes**), a word's size may vary, depending upon the system in which it is employed. In the original IBM PC, a word consisted of 16 bits; however, other, larger and more powerful computers may employ a word length of 32 bits or higher.

Working memory. See **Short-term memory**.

X

XCON. An **expert system** developed by Digital Equipment Corporation for use in configuring computer installations. XCON maintained a rule base of some 10,000 **condition-action rules** and was said to be capable of doing the work of hundreds of human employees. The system uses **forward chaining**.

XOR problem. The problem of implementing the "exclusive or" function ("Either p or q, but not both"), which, when applied to the truth values of two input statements, yields the value TRUE if just one of those statements is true, and FALSE otherwise. Thus the XOR function's output is the same when both input statements are TRUE and again when both input statements are FALSE. Due to the disparity between input and output, the XOR function cannot be computed by a **perceptron**—a fact that at one time was thought to spell doom for **connectionist**-style systems. However, with the addition of hidden **processing units**, the problem is rather easily solved.

References

Anderson, John R. (1983). *The Architecture of Cognition.* Cambridge, MA: Harvard University Press.

Dretske, Fred I. (1981). *Knowledge and the Flow of Information.* Cambridge, MA: MIT Press.

Dreyfus, Hubert L. (1979). *What Computers Can't Do: The Limits of Artificial Intelligence* (rev. ed.). New York: Harper.

Grice, Paul (1989). *Studies in the Way of Words.* Cambridge, MA: Harvard University Press.

Harnad, Stevan (1990). "The Symbol Grounding Problem." *Physica D,* 42: 335–346.

——— (1991). "Other Bodies, Other Minds: A Machine Incarnation of an Old Philosophical Problem." *Minds and Machines,* Vol. 1, No. 1: 43–54.

Hodges, Alan (1983). *Alan Turing: The Enigma.* New York: Simon & Schuster.

Hofstadter, Douglas R. (1979). *Gödel, Escher, Bach: An Eternal Golden Braid.* New York: Basic Books.

Johnson-Laird, Philip N. (1983). *Mental Models: Towards a Cognitive Science of Language, Inference, and Consciousness.* Cambridge, MA: Harvard University Press.

Kosslyn, Stephen Michael (1980). *Image and Mind.* Cambridge, MA: Harvard University Press.

Nagel, Ernest, and James R. Newman (1958). *Gödel's Proof*. New York: New York University Press.

Papert, Seymour (1980). *Mindstorms: Children, Computers, and Powerful Ideas*. New York: Basic Books.

Rumelhart, David E., James L. McClelland, and the PDP Research Group (1986). *Parallel Distributed Processing: Explorations in the Microstructure of Cognition* (2 vols). Cambridge, MA: MIT Press.

Tversky, Amos, and Daniel Kahneman (1983). "Extensional vs. Intuitive Reasoning: The Conjunction Fallacy in Probability Judgment." *Psychological Review*, 90: 293–315.

Weizenbaum, Joseph (1976). *Computer Power and Human Reason*. New York: W. H. Freeman.

Wittgenstein, Ludwig (1968). *Philosophical Investigations* (3rd ed.). New York: Macmillan.

Bibliography

Anderson, John R. (1990). *Cognitive Psychology and Its Implications* (3rd ed.). New York: W. H. Freeman.

Bechtel, William, and Adele Abrahamsen (1991). *Connectionism and the Mind: An Introduction to Parallel Processing in Networks*. Cambridge, MA: Basil Blackwell.

Bruner, Jerome S., Jacqueline J. Goodnow, George A. Austin (1956). *A Study of Thinking*. New York: Wiley.

Churchland, Patricia Smith (1986). *Neurophilosophy: Toward a Unified Science of the Mind/Brain*. Cambridge, MA: MIT Press.

————, and Terrence J. Sejinowski (1992). *The Computational Brain*. Cambridge, MA: MIT Press.

Churchland, Paul (1988). *Matter and Consciousness: A Contemporary Introduction to the Philosophy of Mind* (rev. ed.). Cambridge, MA: MIT Press.

————(1989). *A Neurocomputational Perspective: The Nature of Mind and the Structure of Science*. Cambridge, MA: MIT Press.

Crystal, David (1987). *The Cambridge Encyclopedia of Language*. New York: Cambridge University Press.

Cummins, Robert (1988). *Meaning and Mental Representation*. Cambridge, MA: MIT Press.

Dennett, Daniel C. (1978). *Brainstorms: Philosophical*

Essays on Mind and Psychology. Montgomery, VT: Bradford Books.

———(1987). *The Intentional Stance*. Cambridge, MA: MIT Press.

———(1991). *Consciousness Explained*. Boston: Little, Brown.

Dretske, Fred (1981). *Knowledge and the Flow of Information*. Cambridge, MA: MIT Press.

———(1988). *Explaining Behavior: Reasons in a World of Causes*. Cambridge, MA: MIT Press.

Dreyfus, Hubert L., and Stuart E. Dreyfus (1986). *Mind Over Machine: The Power of Human Intuition and Expertise in the Era of the Computer*. New York: Free Press.

Edelman, Gerald M. (1992). *Bright Air, Brilliant Fire: On the Matter of the Mind*. New York: Basic Books.

Feigenbaum, Edward A. et al. (1982, 1989). *The Handbook of Artificial Intelligence*, Vols. I–IV. Reading, MA: Addison-Wesley.

Fetzer, James H. (1990). *Artificial Intelligence: Its Scope and Limits*. Dordrecht/Boston/London: Kluwer Academic Publishers.

———(1991). *Philosophy and Cognitive Science*. New York: Paragon House.

Fodor, Jerry A. (1975). *The Language of Thought*. New York: Crowell.

———(1981). *Representations: Philosophical Essays on the Foundations of Cognitive Science*. Cambridge, MA: MIT Press.

———(1983). *The Modularity of Mind: An Essay on Faculty Psychology*. Cambridge, MA: MIT Press.

Gardner, Howard (1984, 1987). *The Mind's New Science: A History of the Cognitive Revolution*. New York: Basic Books.

Garfield, Jay, ed. (1990). *Foundations of Cognitive Science*. New York: Paragon House.

142

Graubard, Stephen R, ed. (1990). *The Artificial Intelligence Debate: False Starts, Real Foundations*. Cambridge, MA: MIT Press.

Haugeland, John (1985). *Artificial Intelligence: The Very Idea*. Cambridge, MA: MIT Press.

Hofstadter, Douglas R., and Daniel C. Dennett (1981). *The Mind's I: Fantasies and Reflections on Self and Soul*. New York: Basic Books.

Johnson-Laird, Philip N. (1988). *The Computer and the Mind: An Introduction to Cognitive Science*. Cambridge, MA: Harvard University Press.

Kosslyn, Stephen M., and Oliver Koenig (1992). *Wet Mind: The New Cognitive Neuroscience*. New York: Free Press.

Kurzweil, Raymond (1990). *The Age of Intelligent Machines*. Cambridge, MA: MIT Press.

Lyons, John. *Noam Chomsky* (1970). New York: Viking.

Minsky, Marvin (1985, 1986). *The Society of Mind*. New York: Simon & Schuster.

Posner, Michael I., ed. (1989). *Foundations of Cognitive Science*. Cambridge, MA: MIT Press.

Rich, Elaine (1983). *Artificial Intelligence*. New York: McGraw-Hill.

Shapiro, Stuart C., ed. (1987). *Encyclopedia of Artificial Intelligence*. New York: Wiley.

Stich, Stephen P. (1983). *From Folk Psychology to Cognitive Science: The Case Against Belief*. Cambridge, MA: MIT Press.

Stillings, Neil A. et al. (1987). *Cognitive Science: An Introduction*. Cambridge, MA: MIT Press.

Winograd, Terry (1983). *Language as a Cognitive Process*. Reading, MA: Addison-Wesley.

———, and Fernando Flores (1986, 1987). *Understanding Computers and Cognition*. Reading, MA: Addison-Wesley.

About the Authors

Charles E. M. Dunlop is professor of philosophy at the University of Michigan, Flint. In addition to his Ph.D. in philosophy from Duke, he has an M.S. in computer science from Wright State University. The senior editor of *Computerization and Controversy: Value Conflicts and Social Choices* (1991) and the editor of *Philosophical Essays in Dreaming* (1977), his articles and reviews have appeared in *Synthese, Philosophical Studies, Philosophia, Minds and Machines*, the *Australasian Journal of Philosophy*, and other well-known journals. His areas of special interest include cognitive science, artificial intelligence, and the social aspects of computer use. He has held recent visiting positions at the University of Cincinnati, Wright State University, and the University of Waikato (New Zealand).

James H. Fetzer is professor of philosophy at the University of Minnesota, Duluth. He is the author of *Scientific Knowledge* (1981), *AI: Its Scope and Limits* (1990), *Philosophy and Cognitive Science* (1991), and *Philosophy of Science* (1993), as well as the editor or co-editor of eleven other books, including *Aspects of Artificial Intelligence* (1988), *Philosophy, Language, and Artificial Intelligence*

(1988), *Philosophy, Mind, and Cognitive Inquiry* (1990), and *Epistemology and Cognition* (1991). He is editor of the journal *Minds and Machines*, co-editor of *Synthese*, and series editor of *STUDIES IN COGNITIVE SYSTEMS*. He has published more than seventy articles and reviews.

Europe

Through the Back Door
PHRASE BOOK

ITALIAN

Rick Steves

John Muir Publications
Santa Fe, New Mexico

ii

Thanks to the team of people at *Europe Through the Back Door* who helped make this book possible: Mary Carlson, Steve Smith, Kendra Roth, Anne Kirchner, Margaret Berger, Colleen Murphy, Mary Romano, Plum Moore, Gene Openshaw and...

Italian translation: Giulia Fiorini and Giuseppe Leporace
Phonetics: Risa Laib
Layout: Rich Sorensen
Maps: Dave Hoerlein

Edited by Risa Laib and Rich Sorensen

John Muir Publications, P.O. Box 613, Santa Fe, NM 87504

ISBN 1-56261-099-6

Distributed to the book trade by
W.W. Norton & Company, Inc.
New York, NY

While every effort has been made to keep the content of this book accurate, the author and publisher accept no responsibility whatsoever for anyone ordering the wrong meal or getting messed up in any other way because of the linguistic confidence this phrase book has given them.

JMP travel guidebooks by Rick Steves:

2 to 22 Days in Italy
Europe Through the Back Door
Europe 101: History and Art for the Traveler
   (with Gene Openshaw)
Mona Winks: Self-Guided Tours of Europe's Top Museums
   (with Gene Openshaw)
2 to 22 Days in Europe
2 to 22 Days in France (with Steve Smith)
2 to 22 Days in Great Britain
2 to 22 Days in Germany, Austria & Switzerland
2 to 22 Days in Norway, Sweden & Denmark
2 to 22 Days in Spain & Portugal
Europe Through the Back Door Phrase Books:
   French, Italian and German
Asia Through the Back Door
Kidding Around Seattle

Rick Steves' company, *Europe Through the Back Door*,
provides many services for budget European travelers,
including a free quarterly newsletter/catalog, budget travel
books and accessories, Eurailpasses (with free video and
travel advice included), a free computer BBS Travel
Information Line, a travel partners list, intimate European bus
tours, and a user-friendly Travel Resource Center in
Edmonds, WA. For more information and a free newsletter
subscription, call or write to:

Europe Through the Back Door
109 Fourth Avenue N, Box 2009
Edmonds, WA 98020 USA
Tel: 206/771-8303, Fax: 206/771-0833
BBS: 206/771-1902 (1200-2400 baud, 8/N/1)

iv

CONTENTS

Hi, I'm Rick Steves.

I'm the only mono-lingual speaker I know who's had the nerve to design a series of European phrase books. But that's one of the things that makes them better. You see, after twenty summers of travel through Europe, I've learned first-hand (1) what's essential for communication in another country, and (2) what's not. I've assembled these essential words and phrases in a logical, no-frills format, and I've worked with native Europeans and seasoned travelers to give you the simplest, clearest translations possible.

But this book is more than just a pocket translator. The words and phrases have been carefully selected to help you have a smarter, smoother trip in my favorite country without going broke. Italy used to be cheap and chaotic. These days it's neither. It's better organized than ever -- and often more expensive than France or Germany. The key to getting more out of every travel dollar is to get closer to the local people, and to rely less on entertainment, restaurants, and hotels that cater only to foreign tourists. This book will not only help you order a meal at a locals-only Venetian restaurant -- it will also help you discuss politics, social issues and other topics with the family that runs the place. Long after your memories of museums have faded, you'll still treasure the personal encounters you had with your new Italian friends.

A good phrase book should help you enjoy your Italian experience -- not just survive it -- so I've added a healthy dose of humor. But please use these phrases carefully, in a self-effacing spirit. Remember that one ugly American can undo the goodwill built by dozens of culturally-sensitive ones.

To get the most out of this book, take the time to internalize and put into practice my Italian pronunciation tips. Remember that Italians, more than their European neighbors, are forgiving of your linguistic fumbling. Don't worry too much about memorizing grammatical rules, like which gender a particular noun is -- the important thing is to rise above sex... and communicate!

You'll notice this book has a tear-out "cheat sheet." Tear this out and keep it in your pocket, so you can easily use it to memorize key words and phrases during otherwise idle moments. You'll also find my *Rolling Rosetta Stone* word guide, and special sections on Italian tongue-twisters, gestures, international words, and tips for using Italian telephones. As you prepare for your trip, you may want to read my new *2 to 22 Days in Italy* guidebook.

Italy can be the most intense, difficult and rewarding destination in Europe. Travelers either love it -- or they quickly see the big sights and flee to Switzerland. To me, someone's love of Italy is a sign that they're a good traveler -- thoughtful, confident and extroverted. If this phrase book helps make that happen, or if you have suggestions for making it better, I'd love to hear from you. Happy travels, and good luck as you hurdle the language barrier!

Rick Steves

Italy

Getting Started

User-friendly Italian

...is easy to get the hang of. Some Italian words are so familiar, you'd think they were English. If you can say *pizza, lasagna,* and *spaghetti,* you can speak Italian.

There are a few unusual twists to its pronunciation:

C usually sounds like C in cat.
    But *C* followed by *E* or *I* sounds like CH in chance.
CH sounds like C in cat.
E often sounds like AY in play.
G usually sounds like G in get.
    But *G* followed by *E* or *I* sounds like G in gentle.
GH sounds like G in *spaghetti.*
GLI sounds like LI in million. The G is silent.
GN sounds like GN in *lasagna.*
H is never pronounced.
I sounds like EE in seed.
R is rolled as in *brrravo!*
SC usually sounds like SK in skip.
    But *SC* followed by *E* or *I* sounds like SH in shape.

Have you ever noticed that all Italian words end in a vowel? It's *a* if the word is feminine and *o* if it's masculine. So a *bambina* gets pink and a *bambino* gets blue.

Word endings can differ depending on the gender of the person you're speaking of. A man is *generoso* (generous), a woman is *generosa.* A man will say,

"Sono sposato" (I am married). A woman will say,
"Sono sposata." In this book, we invariably use
masculine endings for simplicity. If you are speaking
of a woman, simply change the ending of a noun or
adjective from *o* to *a*. He is a *santo* (saint), she is a
santa. If a noun or adjective ends in *e*, such as
cantante (singer) or *gentile* (kind), the same word
applies to either sex.

Adjective endings agree with the noun, which may
be masculine or feminine. It's *cara amica* (a dear
female friend) and *caro amico* (a dear male friend).
Sometimes the adjective comes after the noun, as in
vino rosso (red wine).

Plurals are formed by changing the final letter: *a* to
e and *o* to *i*. So it's *una pizza* and *due pizze*, and one
cup of *cappuccino* and two cups of *cappuccini*.

Italians usually pronounce every letter in a word, so
due (two) is DOO-ay. Sometimes two vowels share one
syllable. *Piacere* (please) sounds like peeah-CHAY-ray.
The "peeah" is one syllable. When one vowel in a pair
should be stressed, it will appear in capital letters:
italiano is ee-tah-leeAH-noh.

The key to Italian inflection is to remember this
simple rule: most Italian words have their accent on
the second-to-last syllable. To override this rule,
Italians sometimes insert an accent: *città* (city) is
pronounced cheet-TAH.

Italians are animated. You may think two Italians
are arguing when in reality they're agreeing enthusias-
tically. When they do argue, it's fast and furious! Body
language is a very important part of communicating in

Italy -- especially hand gestures (see the Gestures section for details). Watch and imitate. Be confident, and have fun communicating in Italian. The Italians really do want to understand you, and are forgiving of a yankee-fied version of their language.

Here's a quick guide to the phonetics we've used in this book:

ah	like A in father.
ar	like AR in park.
ay	like AY in play.
eh	like E in let.
ee	like EE in seed.
ehr	sounds like "air."
g	like G in go.
o	like O in cost.
oh	like O in note.
oo	like OO in too.
or	like OR in core.
ow	like OW in cow.
s	like S in sun.
dz	like DS in kids.
ts	like TS in hits. It's a small explosive sound. Think of *pizza* (PEET-tsah).

Italian Basics

Meeting and greeting Italians:

Good day.	**Buon giorno.**	bwohn JOR-noh
Good morning.	**Buon giorno.**	bwohn JOR-noh
Good evening.	**Buona sera.**	BWOH-nah SAY-rah
Hello / Goodbye. (informal)	**Ciao.**	chow
Welcome!	**Benvenuto!**	bayn-vay-NOO-toh
Mr.	**Signor**	SEEN-yor
Mrs.	**Signora**	seen-YOH-rah
Miss	**Signorina**	seen-yoh-REE-nah
How are you?	**Come sta?**	KOH-may stah
Very well, thanks.	**Molto bene, grazie.**	MOL-toh BEH-nay GRAH-tseeay
And you?	**E lei?**	ay LEHee
My name is...	**Mi chiamo...**	mee keeAH-moh
What's your name?	**Come si chiama?**	KOH-may see keeAH-mah
Pleased to meet you.	**Piacere.**	peeah-CHAY-ray
Where are you from?	**Di dove è?**	dee DOH-vay eh
I am... / Are you...?	**Sono... / È...?**	SOH-noh / eh
...on vacation	**...in vacanza**	een vah-KAHN-tsah
...on business	**...qui per lavoro**	kwee pehr lah-VOH-roh
See you later!	**Arrivederci!**	ar-ree-vay-DEHR-chee
Good luck!	**Buona fortuna!**	BWOH-nah for-TOO-nah
Have a good trip!	**Buon viaggio!**	bwohn veeAH-joh

The Top 50 survival phrases

Yes, you can survive in Italy using only these fifty
phrases (okay, so maybe there are 53). Most are
repeated on your tear-out cheat sheet later in this
book.

The essentials:

Hello. / Goodbye.	**Ciao.**	chow
Do you speak English?	**Parla inglese?**	PAR-lah een-GLAY-zay
Yes.	**Si.**	see
No.	**No.**	noh
I don't understand.	**Non capisco.**	nohn kah-PEE-skoh
I'm sorry.	**Mi dispiace.**	mee dee-speeAH-chay
Please.	**Per favore. /**	pehr fah-VOH-ray /
	Per piacere.	pehr peeah-CHAY-ray
Thanks.	**Grazie.**	GRAH-tseeay
A thousand thanks.	**Grazie mille.**	GRAH-tseeay MEEL-lay

Where?

Where is...?	**Dov'è...?**	doh-VEH
...a hotel	**...un hotel**	oon oh-TEHL
...a youth hostel	**...un ostello**	oon oh-STEHL-loh
	della gioventù	DAY-lah joh-vehn-TOO
...a restaurant	**...un ristorante**	oon ree-stoh-RAHN-tay
...a grocery store	**...un negozio**	oon nay-GOH-tsoh
	di alimentari	dee ah-lee-mayn-TAH-ree

...the train station	...la stazione	lah stah-tseeOH-nay
...tourist information	...informazioni per turisti	een-for-mah-tseeOH-nee pehr too-REE-stee
...the toilet	...il gabinetto	eel gah-bee-NAYT-toh
men	uomini, signori	WAW-mee-nee, seen-YOH-ree
women	donne, signore	DON-nay, seen-YOH-ray

How much?

How much does it cost?	Quanto costa?	KWAHN-toh KOS-tah
Wil you write it down?	Lo può scrivere?	loh pwoh SKREE-vay-ray
Cheap.	Economico.	ay-koh-NOH-mee-koh
Cheaper.	Più economico.	peeOO ay-koh-NOH-mee-koh
Included?	È incluso?	eh een-KLOO-zoh
I would like...	Vorrei....	vor-REHee
We would like...	Vorremo...	vor-RAY-moh
Just a little. / More.	Un pochino. / Di più.	oon poh-KEE-noh / dee peeOO (say "P.U.")
A ticket.	Un biglietto.	oon beel-YAYT-toh
A room.	Una camera.	OO-nah KAH-may-rah
The bill.	Il conto.	eel KOHN-toh

Number crunching:

one	**uno**	OO-noh
two	**due**	DOO-ay
three	**tre**	tray
four	**quattro**	KWAHT-troh
five	**cinque**	CHEENG-kway
six	**sei**	SEHee
seven	**sette**	SEHT-tay
eight	**otto**	OT-toh
nine	**nove**	NOV-ay
ten	**dieci**	deeEH-chee
hundred	**cento**	CHEHN-toh
thousand	**mille**	MEEL-lay

You'll find more numbers in the Numbers section on page 18.

Moving on:

I go to...	**Vado a...**	VAH-doh ah
We go tp...	**Andiamo a...**	ahn-deeAH-moh ah
today	**oggi**	OJ-jee
tomorrow	**domani**	doh-MAN-nee
departure	**partenza**	par-TEHN-tsah
At what time?	**A che ora?**	ah kay OH-rah

What's up?

Excuse me. (to get attention)	**Mi scusi.**	mee SKOO-zee
Just a moment.	**Un momento.**	oon moh-MAYN-toh

It's a problem.	**È un problema.**	eh oon proh-BLAY-mah
It's good.	**Va bene.**	vah BEH-nay
Fantastic.	**Fantastico.**	fahn-TAH-stee-koh
You are very kind.	**Lei è molto gentile.**	LEHee eh MOL-toh jayn-TEE-lay

Be creative! You can combine these phrases to say: "Two, please," or "No, thank you," or "I'd like a cheap hotel," or "Cheaper, please?" Please is a magic word in any language. If you want something and you don't know the word for it, just point and say *"Per favore"* (Please). If you know the word for what you want, such as the bill, simply say, *"Il conto, per favore"* (The bill, please).

Struggling with Italian:

Do you speak English?	**Parla inglese?**	PAR-lah een-GLAY-zay
Even a teeny weeny bit?	**Nemmeno un pochino?**	nehm-MAY-noh oon poh-KEE-noh
Please speak English.	**Parli inglese, per favore.**	PAR-lee een-GLAY-zay pehr fah-VOH-ray
You speak English well.	**Lei parla l'inglese bene.**	LEHee PAR-lah leen-GLAY-zay BEH-nay
I don't speak Italian.	**Non parlo l'italiano.**	nohn PAR-loh lee-tah-leeAH-noh
I speak a little Italian.	**Parlo un po' d'italiano.**	PAR-loh oon poh dee-tah-leeAH-noh

I speak ten words in Italian.	**Parlo dieci parole d'italiano.**	PAR-loh deeEH-chee pah-ROH-lay dee-tah-leeAH-noh
I study Italian.	**Studio l'italiano.**	STOO-deeoh lee-tah-leeAH-noh
Excuse...	**Scusi...**	SKOO-zee
Correct...	**Corregga...**	kor-RAY-jah
...my pronunciation.	**...la mia pronuncia.**	lah MEE-ah proh-NOON-chah
What is this in Italian?	**Come si dice questo in italiano?**	KOH-may see DEE-chay KWAY-stoh een ee-tah-leeAH-noh
Repeat.	**Ripeta.**	ree-PAY-tah
Speak slowly.	**Parli lentamente.**	PAR-lee layn-tah-MAYN-tay
Excuse me? (didn't hear)	**Come?**	KOH-may
Do you understand?	**Capisce?**	kah-PEE-shay
I understand.	**Capisco.**	kah-PEE-skoh
I don't understand.	**Non capisco.**	nohn kah-PEE-skoh
Wil you write it down?	**Lo può scrivere?**	loh pwoh SKREE-vay-ray
Does anybody here speak English?	**C'è qualcuno che parla inglese?**	cheh kwahl-KOO-noh kay PAR-lah een-GLAY-zay

Common questions:

How much?	**Quanto?**	KWAHN-toh
How many?	**Quanti?**	KWAHN-tee
How long? (time)	**Quanto tempo?**	KWAHN-toh TEHM-poh
How far?	**Quanto dista?**	KWAHN-toh DEE-stah
How?	**Come?**	KOH-may
Is it possible?	**È possibile?**	eh pohs-SEE-bee-lay
What?	**Che cosa?**	kay KOH-zah
What is that?	**Che cos'è quello?**	kay koh-ZEH KWAY-loh
What is better?	**Che cos'è meglio?**	kay koh-ZEH MEHL-yoh
When?	**Quando?**	KWAHN-doh
What time is it?	**Che ora è?**	kay OH-rah eh
At what time?	**A che ora?**	ah kay OH-rah
When does this...?	**A che ora...?**	ah kay OH-rah
...open	**...aprite**	ah-PREE-tay
...close	**...chiudete**	keeoo-DAY-tay
Do you have...?	**Ha...?**	ah
Where is...?	**Dov'è...?**	doh-VEH
Where are...?	**Dove sono...?**	DOH-vay SOH-noh
Who?	**Chi?**	kee
Why?	**Perchè?**	pehr-KEH
Why not?	**Perchè no?**	pehr-KEH noh

You can easily turn a word or sentence into a question, by asking it in a questioning tone. *"Va bene"* (It's good) becomes *"Va bene?"* (Is it good?). *"Gabinetto?"* (Toilet?) is a simple way to ask, "Where is the toilet?"

Yin and yang:

cheap / expensive	**economico / caro**	ay-koh-NOH-mee-koh / KAH-roh
big / small	**grande / piccolo**	GRAHN-day / PEEK-koh-loh
hot / cold	**caldo / freddo**	KAHL-doh / FRAYD-doh
open / closed	**aperto / chiuso**	ah-PEHR-toh / keeOO-zoh
entrance / exit	**entrata / uscita**	ayn-TRAH-tah/oo-SHEE tah
arrive / depart	**arrivare / partire**	ar-ree-VAH-ray / par-TEE-ray
soon / later	**presto / tardi**	PREHS-toh / TAR-dee
fast / slow	**veloce / lento**	vay-LOH-chay / LEHN-toh
here / there	**qui / lì**	kwee / lee
near / far	**vicino / lontano**	vee-CHEE-noh / lohn-TAH-noh
good / bad	**buono / cattivo**	booOH-noh / kaht-TEE-voh
best / worst	**il migliore / il peggiore**	eel meel-YOH-ray / eel pay-JOH-ray
a little / lots	**poco / tanto**	POH-koh / TAHN-toh
more / less	**più / meno**	peeOO / MAY-noh
easy / difficult	**facile / difficile**	FAH-chee-lay / deef-FEE-chee-lay

beautiful / ugly	**bello / brutto**	BEHL-loh / BROOT-toh
intelligent / stupid	**intelligente / stupido**	een-tehl-lee-JAYN-tay / STOO-pee-doh
vacant / occupied	**libero / occupato**	LEE-bay-roh / oh-koo-PAH-toh
with / without	**con / senza**	kohn / SEHN-tsah

Little words that are big in Italy:

I	**io**	EEoh
you (formal)	**Lei**	LEHee
you (informal)	**tu**	too
he	**lui**	LOOee
she	**lei**	LEHee
we	**noi**	NOHee
and	**e**	ay
at	**a**	ah
but	**ma**	mah
by (via)	**in**	een
for	**per**	pehr
from	**da**	dah
not	**non**	nohn
now	**adesso**	ah-DEHS-soh
only	**solo**	SOH-loh
or	**o**	oh
this	**questo**	KWAY-stoh
that	**quello**	KWAY-loh
to	**a**	ah
very	**molto**	MOHL-toh

Handy Italian expressions:

Pronto.	PRON-toh	Hello (answering phone) / Ready (other situations).
Prego.	PRAY-goh	Can I help you? / Please / Thanks / You're welcome / All right.
Tutto va bene.	TOOT-toh vah BEH-nay	Everything's fine.
Ecco.	AY-koh	Here it is.
È tutto.	eh TOOT-toh	That's all.
la dolce vita	lah DOHL-chay VEE-tah	the sweet life
il dolce far niente	eel DOHL-chay far neeEHN-tay	the sweetness of doing nothing

Italian names for places:

Italy	**Italia**	ee-TAHL-yah
Venice	**Venezia**	vay-NEH-tseeah
Florence	**Firenze**	fee-REHN-tsah
Rome	**Roma**	ROH-mah
Naples	**Napoli**	NAH-poh-lee
Italian Riviera	**Riviera Ligure**	ree-veeEH-rah lee-GOO-ray
Vatican City	**Città del Vaticano**	cheet-TAH dayl vah-tee-KAH-noh
Munich	**Monaco**	MOH-nah-koh
Germany	**Germania**	jehr-MAHN-yah
Paris	**Parigi**	pah-REE-jah
France	**Francia**	FRAHN-chah
England	**Inghilterra**	een-geel-TEHR-rah
Netherlands	**Paesi Bassi**	pah-AY-zee BAHS-see
Austria	**Austria**	OW-streeah
Switzerland	**Svizzera**	SVEET-tsay-rah
Spain	**Spagna**	SPAHN-yah
Greece	**Grecia**	GRAY-chah
Europe	**Europa**	ay-oo-ROH-pah
United States	**Stati Uniti**	STAH-tee oo-NEE-tee
world	**mondo**	MOHN-doh

Numbers

Numbers you can count on:

0	**zero**	TSAY-roh
1	**uno**	OO-noh
2	**due**	DOO-ay
3	**tre**	tray
4	**quattro**	KWAHT-troh
5	**cinque**	CHEENG-kway
6	**sei**	SEHee
7	**sette**	SEHT-tay
8	**otto**	OT-toh
9	**nove**	NOV-ay
10	**dieci**	deeEH-chee
11	**undici**	OON-dee-chee
12	**dodici**	DOH-dee-chee
13	**tredici**	TRAY-dee-chee
14	**quattordici**	kwaht-TOR-dee-chee
15	**quindici**	KWEEN-dee-chee
16	**sedici**	SAY-dee-chee
17	**diciassette**	dee-chahs-SEHT-tay
18	**diciotto**	dee-CHOHT-toh
19	**diciannove**	dee-chahn-NOV-ay
20	**venti**	VAYN-tee
21	**ventuno**	vayn-TOO-noh
22	**ventidue**	vayn-tee-DOO-ay
23	**ventitrè**	vayn-tee-TRAY
30	**trenta**	TRAYN-tah
31	**trentuno**	trayn-TOO-noh
40	**quaranta**	kwah-RAHN-tah
41	**quarantuno**	kwah-rahn-TOO-noh
50	**cinquanta**	cheeng-KWAHN-tah

60	**sessanta**	say-SAHN-tah
70	**settanta**	say-TAHN-tah
80	**ottanta**	oh-TAHN-tah
90	**novanta**	noh-VAHN-tah
100	**cento**	CHEHN-toh
101	**centouno**	chehn-toh-OO-noh
102	**centodue**	chehn-toh-DOO-ay
200	**duecento**	doo-ay-CHEHN-toh
1000	**mille**	MEEL-lay
1994	**mille**	MEEL-lay
	novecento	noh-vay-CHEHN-toh
	novantaquattro	noh-vahn-tah-KWAT-troh
2000	**duemila**	doo-ay-MEE-lah
10,000	**diecimila**	deeEH-chee-MEE-lah
1,000,000	**un milione**	oon mee-leeOH-nay
first	**primo**	PREE-moh
second	**secondo**	say-KOHN-doh
third	**terzo**	TEHR-tsoh
half	**mezzo**	MEHD-dzoh
fifty percent	**cinquanta**	cheeng-KWAHN-tah
	per cento	pehr CHEHN-toh
number one	**numero uno**	NOO-may-roh OO-noh

Money

Key money words:

bank	**banca**	BAHN-kah
money	**denaro**	day-NAH-roh
change money (v)	**cambiare dei soldi**	kahm-beeAH-ray DEHee SOHL-dee
exchange (n)	**cambio**	KAHM-beeoh
traveler's check	**traveler's check**	"traveler's check"
credit card	**carta di credito**	KAR-tah dee KRAY-dee-toh
cash advance	**prelievo**	pray-leeAY-voh
cash machine	**cassa automatica**	KAHS-sah ow-toh-MAH-tee-kah
cashier	**cassiere**	kahs-seeEH-ray
receipt	**ricevuta**	ree-chay-VOO-tah

Changing money:

Can you change dollars?	**Può cambiare dollari?**	pwoh kahm-beeAH-ray DOL-lah-ree
What is your exchange rate for dollars...?	**Qual'è il cambio del dollaro?**	kwah-LEH eel KAHM-beeoh dayl DOL-lah-ree
...in traveler's checks	**...per traveler's checks**	pehr "traveler's checks"
Are there extra fees?	**Ci sono altre spese?**	chee SOH-noh AHL-tray SPAY-zay

What is the service charge?	**Quant'è la tariffa bancaria?**	kwahn-TEH lah tah-REEF-fah bahn-KAH-reeah
What is the commission?	**Quant'è la commissione?**	kwahn-TEH lah kohm-mees-seeOH-nay
I would like...	**Vorrei....**	vor-REHee
...small bills.	**...banconote di piccolo taglio.**	bahn-koh-NOH-tay dee PEEK-koh-loh TAHL-yoh
...large bills.	**...banconote di grosso taglio.**	bahn-koh-NOH-tay dee GROHS-soh TAHL-yoh
...coins.	**...moneta.**	moh-NAY-tah
I think you've made a mistake.	**Penso che ci sia un errore.**	PEHN-soh kay chee SEE-ah oon ehr-ROH-ray
I'm rich / poor / broke.	**Sono ricco / povero / al verde.**	SOH-noh REEK-koh / POH-vay-roh / ahl VEHR-day
L. 17,000	**diciassette-mila lire**	dee-chahs-seht-tay-MEE-lah LEE-ray
L. 500	**cinquecento lire**	cheeng-kway-CHEHN-toh LEE-ray

The *lire* is nearly microscopic -- it takes around 1300 to make a dollar. Italian prices sound huge. You'll often hear the words *mille* (thousand) and *mila* (thousands). To minimize confusion, you can figure out roughly how many dollars you're talking about by covering up the last three numbers, and subtracting about 25%. *Ventimila* = L. 20,000 = around $15. Change money carefully in Italy, where bank fees can be steep.

Public Transportation

Tickets:

ticket	**biglietto**	beel-YAYT-toh
ticket office	**biglietteria**	beel-yayt-tay-REE-ah
schedule	**orario**	oh-RAH-reeoh
one way	**andata**	ahn-DAH-tah
roundtrip	**ritorno**	ree-TOR-noh
overnight	**notte**	NOT-tay
direct	**diretto**	dee-REHT-toh
connection	**coincidenza**	koh-een-chee-DEHN-tsah
first class	**prima classe**	PREE-mah KLAHS-say
second class	**seconda classe**	say-KOHN-dah KLAHS-say
reservation	**prenotazione**	pray-noh-tah-tseeOH-nay
seat	**posto**	POH-stoh
window seat	**posto vicino al finestrino**	POH-stoh vee-CHEE-noh ahl fee-nay-STREE-noh
aisle seat	**posto vicino al corridoio**	POH-stoh vee-CHEE-noh ahl kor-ree-DOH-yoh
non-smoking	**non fumare**	nohn foo-MAH-ray
refund	**rimborso**	reem-BOR-soh

At the station:

arrival	**arrivo**	ar-REE-voh
departure	**partenza**	par-TEHN-tsah
delay	**ritardo**	ree-TAR-doh

waiting room	**sala di attesa, sala d'aspetto**	SAH-lah dee aht-TAY-zah, SAH-lah dah-SPAYT-toh
check room	**sala di controllo, consegna**	SAH-lah dee kohn-TROHL-loh, kohn-SAYN-yah
lockers	**armadietti**	ar-mah-deeAYT-tee
baggage	**bagaglio**	bah-GAHL-yoh
lost and found office	**ufficio oggetti smarriti**	oo-FEE-choh oh-JEHT-tee smah-REE-tee
tourist information	**informazioni per turisti**	een-for-mah-tseeOH-nee pehr too-REE-stee

Trains:

Italian State Railways	**Ferrovie dello Stato (FS)**	fehr-ROH-veeay DAY-loh STAH-toh
train station	**stazione**	stah-tseeOH-nay
train information	**informazioni sui treni**	een-for-mah-tseeOH-nee SOOee TRAY-nee
train	**treno**	TRAY-noh
high speed train	**inter-city (IC)**	"inter-city"
to the trains	**ai treni**	AHee TRAY-nee
track or platform	**binario**	bee-NAH-reeoh
train car	**vagone**	vah-GOH-nay
dining car	**carrozza ristorante**	kar-ROT-tsah ree-stoh-RAHN-tay
sleeper car	**carrozza letto**	kar-ROT-tsah LEHT-toh
sleeper berth	**cuccetta**	koo-CHAYT-tah
...upper	**...di sopra**	dee SOH-prah
...middle	**...in mezzo**	een MEHD-dzoh

| ...lower | **...di sotto** | dee SOHT-toh |
| conductor | **conduttore** | kohn-doot-TOH-ray |

Buses

bus station	**stazione**	stah-tseeOH-nay
	degli autobus	DAYL-yee OW-toh-boos
long distance bus	**pullman**	POOL-mahn
city bus	**autobus**	OW-toh-boos
bus stop	**fermata**	fehr-MAH-tah

Boats

boat	**barca**	BAR-kah
cabin	**cabina**	kah-BEE-nah
gondola ferry (Venice)	**traghetto**	trah-GEHT-toh
motorized ferry (Venice)	**vaporetto**	vah-poh-REHT-toh

Subway

subway	**metropolitana**	may-troh-poh-lee-TAH-nah
subway entrance	**stazione della**	stah-tseeOH-nay DAY-lah
	metropolitana	may-troh-poh-lee-TAH-nah

Handy transportation phrases:

English	Italian	Pronunciation
How much is the fare to...?	**Quant'è la tariffa per...?**	kwahn-TEH lah tah-REEF-fah pehr
I'd like...	**Vorrei...**	vor-REHee
...to go to ___.	**...andare a ___.**	ahn-DAH-ray ah
...a ticket to ___.	**...un biglietto per ___.**	oon beel-YAYT-toh pehr
Is a reservation required?	**È obbligatoria la prenotazione?**	eh oh-blee-gah-TOH-reeah lah pray-noh-tah-tseeOH-nay
I'd like to leave...	**Vorrei partire...**	voh-REHee par-TEE-ray
I'd like to arrive...	**Vorrei arrivare...**	voh-REH-ee ar-ree-VAH-ray
...by ___. (fill in time)	**...per le ___.**	pehr lay
...in the morning.	**...la mattina.**	lah maht-TEE-nah
...in the afternoon.	**...il pomeriggio.**	eel poh-may-REE-joh
...in the evening.	**...la sera.**	lah SAY-rah
Is there...?	**C'è...?**	cheh
...an earlier departure	**...una partenza più presto**	OO-nah par-TEHN-tsah peeOO PREHS-toh
...a later departure	**...una partenza più tardi**	OO-nah par-TEHN-tsah peeOO TAR-dee
...a supplement	**...un supplemento**	oon soop-play-MAYN-toh
...a cheaper ticket	**...un biglietto più economico**	oon beel-YAYT-toh peeOO ay-koh-NOH-mee-koh
When is the next departure?	**A che ora è la prossima partenza?**	ah kay OH-rah eh lah PROS-see-mah par-TEHN-tsah
Will you write it down?	**Lo può scrivere?**	loh pwoh SKREE-vay-ray

Where does it leave from?	**Da dove parte?**	dah DOH-vay PAR-tay
On what track?	**Su quale binario?**	soo KWAH-lay bee-NAH-reeoh
When will it arrive?	**Quando arriva?**	KWAHN-doh ar-REE-vah
Is it direct?	**È diretto?**	eh dee-REHT-toh
Must I transfer?	**Devo cambiare?**	DAY-voh kahm-beeAH-ray
When? / Where?	**Dove? / Quando?**	DOH-vay / KWAHN-doh
Which train to...?	**Quale treno per....?**	KWAH-lay TRAY-noh pehr
Which train car to...?	**Quale vagone per....?**	KWAH-lay vah-GOH-nay pehr
Which bus to...?	**Quale autobus per....?**	KWAH-lay OW-toh-boos pehr
Does it stop at...?	**Si ferma a...?**	see FEHR-mah ah
Is this (seat) free?	**È libero?**	eh LEE-bay-roh
That's my seat.	**Quello è il mio posto.**	KWAY-loh eh eel MEE-oh POH-stoh
Save my place.	**Mi tenga il posto.**	mee TAYN-gah eel POH-stoh
Where are you going?	**Dove va?**	DOH-vay vah
I'm going to...	**Vado a...**	VAH-doh ah
Can you tell me when to get off?	**Mi può dire quando devo scendere?**	mee pwoh DEE-ray KWAHN-doh DAY-voh SHEHN-day-ray

Italian stations have wonderful (and fun) new schedule computers. Once you've mastered these (start by punching the "English" button), you'll save lots of time figuring out the right train connections.

Italian trains come in four types: *accelerato* or *locale* which are very slow milk-run trains; the not-as-slow *diretto* trains; and the *espresso* trains which stop only at big stations. The *rapido* or *IC* (inter-city) trains are the fastest. All fast trains require a supplement, which is a confusion that railpass travelers avoid.

Reading train and bus schedules:

a	to
arrivo (a)	arrival
da	from
domenica	Sunday
eccetto	except
feriali	weekdays including Saturday
fermi in tutte le stazione	stops at all the stations
festivi	Sundays and holidays
fino	until
giorni	days
non fermi a...	doesn't stop in...
ogni	every
partenza (p)	departure
per	for
sabato	Saturday
solo	only
tutti i giorni	daily
vacanza	holiday

Italian schedules use the 24-hour clock. It's like American time until noon. After that, subtract twelve and add p.m. So 13:00 is 1 p.m., 20:00 is 8 p.m., and 24:00 is midnight. Train travelers take note: if your train is scheduled to depart at 00:01, it'll leave one minute after midnight. Days of the week are often referred to by number, with *lunedì* (Monday) being #1 and *domenica* (Sunday) being #7.

Taking taxis:

taxi	**tassì**	tahs-SEE
Where is a taxi stand?	**Dov'è una fermata dei tassì?**	doh-VEH OO-nah fehr-MAH-tah DEHee tahs-SEE
Are you free?	**È libero?**	eh LEE-bay-roh
Occupied.	**Occupato.**	oh-koo-PAH-toh
How much will it cost to go to...?	**Quanto per andare a...?**	KWAHN-toh pehr ahn-DAH-ray ah
Too much.	**Troppo.**	TROP-poh
How many people can you take?	**Quante persone può portare?**	KWAHN-tay pehr-SOH-nay pwoh por-TAH-ray
Is there an extra fee?	**Ci sono altre tariffe?**	chee SOH-noh AHL-tray tah-REEF-fay
The meter, please.	**Il tassimetro, per favore.**	eel tahs-SEE-meht-roh pehr fah-VOH-ray
The most direct route.	**Il percorso più breve.**	eel pehr-KOR-soh peeOO BRAY-vay
Slow down.	**Rallenti.**	rahl-LEHN-tee
If you don't slow down, I'll throw up.	**Se non rallenta, vomito.**	say nohn rahl-LEHN-tah, VOH-mee-toh
Stop here.	**Si fermi qui.**	see FEHR-mee kwee
Can you wait?	**Può aspettare?**	pwoh ah-spayt-TAH-ray

I'll never forget this ride.	**Non dimenticherò mai questo viaggio.**	nohn dee-mayn-tee-kay-ROH MAHee KWAY-stoh veeAH-joh
Where did you learn to drive?	**Ma dove ha imparato a guidare?**	mah DOH-vay ah eem-pah-RAH-toh ah gwee-DAH-ray
I'll only pay what's on the meter.	**Pago solo la cifra sul tassimetro.**	PAH-goh SOH-loh lah CHEE-frah sool tahs-SEE-meht-roh
My change, please.	**Il resto, per favore.**	eel REHS-toh pehr fah-VOH-ray
Keep the change.	**Tenga il resto.**	TAYN-gah eel REHS-toh

Italian cab fares are reasonable and most drivers are honest. Three or more tourists are usually better off hailing a cab than messing with city buses in Italy. If cabs won't stop for you, your luck may improve at a nearby *fermata dei tassì* (taxi stand).

Driving

Wheeling and dealing:

I'd like to rent...	**Vorrei affittare...**	vor-REHee ahf-feet-TAH-ray
...a car.	**...una macchina.**	OO-nah MAHK-kee-nah
...a motorcycle.	**...una motocicletta.**	OO-nah moh-toh-chee-KLAYT-tah
...a motor scooter.	**...un motorino.**	oon moh-toh-REE-noh
...a bicycle.	**...una bicicletta.**	OO-nah bee-chee-KLAYT-tah
...Venice.	**...Venezia.**	vay-NEH-tseeah
How much...?	**Quanto...?**	KWAHN-toh
...per hour	**...all'ora**	ahl-LOH-rah
...per day	**...al giorno**	ahl JOR-noh
...per week	**...alla settimana**	AHL-lah sayt-tee-MAH-nah

Gassing up:

gas station	**stazione di servizio**	stah-tseeOH-nay dee sehr-VEE-tseeoh
self-service	**self-service**	"self service"
Where is the nearest gas station?	**Dov'è il benzinaio più vicino?**	doh-VEH eel bayn-dzee-NAH-yoh peeOO vee-CHEE-noh
Fill the tank.	**Il pieno.**	eel peeEH-noh
I need...	**Ho bisogno di...**	oh bee-ZOHN-yoh dee
...gas.	**...benzina.**	bayn-DZEE-nah

...unleaded.	...senza piombo.	SEHN-tsah peeOHM-boh
...regular.	...normale.	nor-MAHL-lay
...super.	...super.	SOO-pehr
...diesel.	...gasolio.	gah-ZOH-leeoh
...oil.	...olio.	OH-leeoh
Check the...	Controlli...	kohn-TROHL-lee
...oil.	...l'olio.	LOH-leeoh
...tires.	...le gomme.	lay GOHM-may
...water.	...l'acqua.	LAHK-kwah
...radiator.	...il radiatore.	eel rah-deeah-TOH-ray
...battery.	...la batteria.	lah baht-tay-REE-ah
...fuses.	...i fusibili.	ee foo-ZEE-bee-lee
...fanbelt.	...la cinghia del ventilatore.	lah CHEENG-geeah dayl vehn-tee-lah-TOH-ray
...brakes.	...i freni.	ee FRAY-nee

Filling up the tank in Italy is just like at home, except the pump says lire and liters rather than dollars and gallons. The freeway rest stops and city *automat* gas pumps are the only places that sell gas during the afternoon siesta hours. Gas is always more expensive on the super highways. Italy's famous coupons for cheaper gas (available only to tourists at the border crossings) are not worth the complexity they add to your travels.

Car trouble:

accident	**incidente**	een-chee-DEHN-tay
breakdown	**guasto**	gooAH-stoh
funny noise	**rumore strano**	roo-MOH-ray STRAH-noh
electrical problem	**problema elettrico**	proh-BLAY-mah ay-LEHT-tree-koh
It won't start.	**Non parte.**	nohn PAR-tay
This doesn't work.	**Non funziona.**	nohn foon-tseeOH-nah
It's overheating.	**Si sta surriscaldando.**	see stah soor-ree-skahl-DAHN-doh
I need...	**Ho bisogno di...**	oh bee-ZOHN-yoh dee
...a tow truck.	**...un carro attrezzi.**	oon KAR-roh aht-TRAYT-tsee
...a mechanic.	**...un meccanico.**	oon may-KAH-nee-koh
...a stiff drink.	**...whiskey.**	"whiskey"
Can you fix it?	**Lo può aggiustare?**	loh pwoh ah-joo-STAH-ray
Just do the essentials.	**Faccia solamente le cose essenziali.**	FAH-chah soh-lah-MAYN-tay lay KOH-zay ays-sayn-tseeAH-lee
When will it be ready?	**Quando è pronta?**	KWAHN-doh eh PRON-tah
How much will it cost to make it run?	**Quanto costa ripararla?**	KWAHN-toh KOS-tah ree-pah-RAR-lah
I'm going to faint.	**Mi sa che adesso svengo.**	mee sah kay ah-DEHS-soh ZVEHN-goh

Parking:

parking garage	**garage**	gah-RAHJ
Where can I park?	**Dove posso parcheggiare?**	DOH-vay POS-soh par-kay-JAH-ray
Is parking nearby?	**È vicino il parcheggio?**	eh vee-CHEE-noh eel par-KAY-joh
Can I park here?	**Posso parcheggiare qui?**	POS-soh par-kay-JAH-ray kwee
How long can I park here?	**Per quanto tempo posso parcheggiare qui?**	pehr KWAHN-toh TEHM-poh POS-soh par-kay-JAH-ray kwee
Must I pay to park here?	**È a pagamento questo parcheggio?**	eh ah pah-gah-MAYN-toh KWAY-stoh par-KAY-joh
Is this a safe place to park?	**È sicuro parcheggiare qui?**	eh see-KOO-roh par-kay-JAH-ray kwee

Parking in Italian cities is expensive and hazardous.
Plan to pay to use a parking garage in big cities.
Leave nothing in your car at night. Always ask at your
hotel about safe parking. Take parking restrictions
seriously to avoid getting fines and having your car
towed away (an interesting but costly experience).

Bike bits:

bicycle	**bicicletta**	bee-chee-KLAYT-tah
tire	**gomma**	GOHM-mah
inner tube	**camera d'aria**	KAH-may-rah DAH-reeah
wheel	**ruota**	rooOH-tah
spoke	**raggio**	RAH-joh
chain	**catena**	kah-TAY-nah
freewheel	**ruota di scorta**	rooOH-tah dee SKOR-tah
shifter	**cambio**	KAHM-beeoh
brakes	**freno**	FRAY-noh
I brake for bakeries.	**Mi fermo ad ogni pasticceria.**	mee FEHR-moh ahd OHN-yee pah-stee-chay-REE-ah

Finding Your Way

Key navigation words:

straight ahead	**sempre diritto**	SEHM-pray dee-REET-toh
left / right	**sinistra / destra**	see-NEE-strah / DEHS-trah
first / next	**prima / prossima**	PREE-mah / PROS-see-mah
intersection	**intersezione**	een-tehr-say-tseeOH-nay
stoplight	**semaforo**	say-mah-FOH-roh
square	**piazza**	peeAHT-tsah
street	**strada, via**	STRAH-dah, VEE-ah
bridge	**ponte**	POHN-tay
tunnel	**tunnel**	TOON-nel
overpass	**ponte**	POHN-tay
underpass	**sottopassaggio**	soht-toh-pahs-SAH-joh
highway	**autostrada**	ow-toh-STRAH-dah
freeway	**superstrada**	soo-pehr-STRAH-dah
map	**cartina**	kar-TEE-nah

In Italy, the shortest distance between any two points is the *autostrada*, though the tolls are not cheap (about a dollar for each ten minutes). There are not as many signs as we are used to, so stay alert or you may miss your exit! Italy's *autostrada* rest stops are among the best in Europe.

Getting directions:

I am going to...	**Vado a...**	VAH-doh ah
How do I get to...?	**Come si va a...?**	KOH-may see vah ah
How many minutes...?	**Quanti minuti...?**	KWAHN-tee mee-NOO-tee
...on foot	**...a piedi**	ah peeAY-dee
...by car	**...in macchina**	een MAHK-kee-nah
How many kilometers to...?	**Quanti chilometri per...?**	KWAHN-tee kee-LOH-may-tree pehr
What is the... route to ___?	**Qual'è la strada... per andare a ___?**	kwah-LEH lah STRAH-dah... pehr ahn-DAH-ray ah
...best	**...migliore**	meel-YOH-ray
...fastest	**...più veloce**	peeOO vay-LOH-chay
...most interesting	**...più interessante**	peeOO een-tay-rays-SAHN-tay
Show me on this map.	**Me lo mostri sulla cartina.**	may loh MOH-stree SOOL-lah kar-TEE-nah
I'm lost.	**Sono perso.**	SOH-noh PEHR-soh
Where am I?	**Dove sono?**	DOH-vay SOH-noh
Who am I?	**Chi sono io?**	kee SOH-noh EEoh
Where is...?	**Dov'è...?**	doh-VEH
Where is the nearest...?	**Dov'è il più vicino...?**	doh-VEH eel peeOO vee-CHEE-noh
Where is this address?	**Dov'è questo indirizzo?**	doh-VEH KWAY-stoh een-dee-REET-tsoh

Reading road signs:

alt / stop	stop
carabinieri	police
centro città	to the center of town
circonvallazione	ring road
dare la precedenza	yield
deviazione	detour
entrata	entrance
lavori in corso	road work ahead
rallentare	slow down
senso unico	one-way street
tutte le (altre) destinazioni	to all (other) destinations
uscita	exit
zona pedonale	pedestrian zone

As in any country, the flashing lights of a patrol car are a sure sign that someone's in trouble. If it's you, practice this handy phrase: *"Mi dispiace, sono un turista."* (Sorry, I'm a tourist.)

Other signs you may bump into:

acqua non potabile	undrinkable water
affittasi, in affitto	for rent or for hire
aperto	open
aperto da... a...	open from... to...
attenzione	caution

bagno	toilet
chiuso	closed
chiuso per ferie	closed for vacation
chiuso per restauro	closed for restoration
divieto di fumo	no smoking
donne	women
entrata libera	free admission
entrata vietata	no entry
gabinetto	toilet
non toccare	do not touch
occupato	occupied
parcheggio vietato	no parking
pericolo	danger
sciopero	on strike
signore	women
signori	men
toletta	toilet
uomini	men
uscita d'emergenza	emergency exit
vendesi, in vendita	for sale
vietato	forbidden
vietato l'accesso	keep out
WC	toilet

Telephones

Key telephone words:

Post & Telegraph Office	**Poste e Telegrafi**	POH-stay ee tay-LAY-grah-fee
telephone	**telefono**	tay-LAY-foh-noh
operator	**centralinista**	chayn-trah-lee-NEE-stah
international assistance	**assistenza per chiamate internazionali**	ahs-see-STEHN-tsah pehr keeah-MAH-tay een-tehr-nah-tseeoh-NAH-lee
country code	**prefisso per il paese**	pray-FEES-soh pehr eel pah-AY-zay
area code	**prefisso**	pray-FEES-soh
phone card	**carta telefonica**	KAR-tah tay-LAY-foh-nee-kah
telephone token (200 lire)	**gettone**	jayt-TOH-nay
telephone book	**elenco telefonico**	ay-LEHN-koh tay-lay-FOH-nee-koh
yellow pages	**pagine gialle**	PAH-jee-nay JAHL-lay
metered phone	**telefono a scatti**	tay-LAY-foh-noh ah SKAHT-tee
out of service	**guasto**	gooAH-stoh

Handy phone phrases:

Where is the nearest phone?	**Dov'è il telefono più vicino?**	doh-VEH eel tay-LAY-foh-noh peeOO vee-CHEE-noh
It doesn't work.	**Non funziona.**	nohn foon-tseeOH-nah
Where is the Post Office?	**Dov'è la Poste?**	doh-VEH lah POH-stay
I'd like to telephone the USA.	**Vorrei fare una telefonata negli Stati Uniti.**	vor-REHee FAH-ray OO-nah tay-lay-foh-NAH-tah NAYL-yee STAH-tee oo-NEE-tee
How much per minute?	**Quanto costa al minuto?**	KWAHN-toh KOS-tah ahl mee-NOO-toh
I'd like to make a... call.	**Vorrei fare una telefonata...**	vor-REHee FAH-ray OO-nah tay-lay-foh-NAH-tah
...local	**...urbana.**	oor-BAH-nah
...collect	**...a carico dell'utente.**	ah KAH-ree-koh day-loo-TEHN-tay
...credit card	**...con la carta di credito.**	kohn lah KAR-tah dee KRAY-dee-toh
...person to person	**...con preavviso.**	kohn pray-ahv-VEE-zoh
...long distance (within Italy)	**...interurbana.**	een-tay-roor-BAH-nah
...international	**...internationale.**	een-tehr-nah-tseeoh-NAH-lay
May I use your phone?	**Posso usare il telefono?**	POS-soh oo-ZAH-ray eel tay-LAY-foh-noh
Can you dial for me?	**Può fare il numero per me?**	pwoh FAH-ray eel NOO-may-roh pehr may

Can you talk for me?	**Può parlare per me?**	pwoh par-LAH-ray pehr may
It's busy.	**È occupato.**	eh oh-koo-PAH-toh
Will you try again?	**Desidera riprovare?**	day-SEE-day-rah ree-proh-VAH-ray
Hello. (on the phone)	**Pronto.**	PRON-toh
My name is...	**Mi chiamo...**	mee keeAH-moh
My number is...	**Il mio numero è...**	eel MEE-oh NOO-may-roh eh
Speak slowly and clearly.	**Parli lentamente e chiaramente.**	PAR-lee layn-tah-MAYN-tay ay keeah-rah-MAYN-tay
Wait a moment.	**Un momento.**	oon moh-MAYN-toh
Don't hang up.	**Non agganci.**	nohn ah-GAHN-chee

Telephoning in Italy can be expensive, and a real headache. When dealing on the phone with someone who only speaks Italian, you might try asking someone to talk for you on your end.

The traditional public phones use coins or *gettoni* (L. 200 tokens). Whenever possible, use the much handier magnetic *carta telefonica* (Italian phone card), sold at post offices, train stations and *tabaccheria* (tobacco shops).

You can call locally or internationally from public phone booths and post offices. Unless you're using toll-free "USA Direct"-style services, long distance calls from your hotel, as in any country, are a terrible rip-off. For more details, see "Let's Talk Telephones" later in this book.

Finding a Room

If you keep it very simple and use these phrases, you will be able to reserve a hotel room over the phone. A good time to reserve a room is the morning of the day you plan to arrive. Related words and phrases can be found in the Telephone and Time sections.

Key room-finding words:

hotel	**hotel, albergo**	OH-tehl, ahl-BEHR-goh
small hotel	**pensione, locanda**	payn-seeOH-nay, loh-KAHN-dah
room in a private home	**camera in affitto**	KAH-may-rah een ahf-FEET-toh
youth hostel	**ostello della gioventù**	oh-STEHL-loh DAY-lah joh-vehn-TOO
room	**camera**	KAH-may-rah
people	**persone**	pehr-SOH-nay
night	**notte**	NOT-tay
arrive	**arrivare**	ar-ree-VAH-ray
today	**oggi**	OJ-jee
tomorrow	**domani**	doh-MAH-nee
vacancy	**camere libere**	KAH-may-rah LEE-bay-ray
no vacancy	**completo**	kohm-PLAY-toh

Handy hotel-hunting phrases:

I'd like to reserve a room...	**Vorrei prenotare una camera...**	vor-REHee pray-noh-TAH-ray OO-nah KAH-may-rah
Do you have a room...?	**Avete una camera...?**	ah-VAY-tay OO-nah KAH-may-rah
...for one person / two people	**...per una persona / due persone**	pehr OO-nah pehr-SOH-nah / DOO-ay pehr-SOH-nay
...for tonight	**...per stanotte**	pehr stah-NOT-tay
...for two nights	**...per due notti**	pehr DOO-ay NOT-tee
...for this Monday night	**...per questo lunedì notte**	pehr KWAY-stoh loo-nay-DEE NOT-tay
...for Monday, August 28	**...per lunedì ventotto agosto**	pehr loo-nay-DEE vayn-TOT-toh ah-GOH-stoh
with / without / and	**con / senza / e**	kohn / SEHN-tsah / ay
...a toilet	**...gabinetto**	gah-bee-NAYT-toh
...a shower	**...doccia**	DOH-chah
...a private bathroom	**...bagno privato**	BAHN-yoh pree-VAH-toh
...a double bed	**...letto matrimoniale**	LEHT-toh mah-tree-moh-neeAH-lay
...twin beds	**...letti singoli**	LEHT-tee SEENG-goh-lee
...a view	**...vista**	VEE-stah
...only a sink	**...solo un lavandino**	SOH-loh oon lah-vahn-DEE-noh
How much does it cost?	**Quanto costa?**	KWAHN-toh KOS-tah

You may hear: *"Mi dispiace"* (I'm sorry). *"Siamo al*

completo" (We're full). Or, *"Deve arrivare prima delle sedici"* (You must arrive before 16:00).

Working out the details:

My name is...	**Mi chiamo...**	mee keeAH-moh
I'm coming now.	**Arrivo subito.**	ar-REE-voh SOO-bee-toh
I arrive in one hour.	**Arrivo tra un'ora.**	ar-REE-voh trah oon-OH-rah
I arrive before 16:00.	**Arrivo prima delle sedici.**	ar-REE-voh PREE-mah DAY-lay SAY-dee-chee
We arrive Monday, depart Wednesday.	**Arriviamo lunedì, ripartiamo mercoledì.**	ar-ree-veeAH-moh loo-nay-DEE, ree-par-teeAH-moh mehr-koh-lay-DEE
I have a reservation.	**Ho una prenotazione.**	oh OO-nah pray-noh-tah-tseeOH-nay
Confirm my reservation.	**Confermi la mia prenotazione.**	kohn-FEHR-mee lah MEE-ah pray-noh-tah-tseeOH-nay
I'll sleep anywhere. I'm desperate.	**Posso dormire ovunque. Sono disperato.**	POS-soh dor-MEE-ray oh-VOON-kway. SOH-noh dee-spay-RAH-toh
I have a sleeping bag.	**Ho un sacco a pelo.**	oh oon SAHK-koh ah PAY-loh
How much is your cheapest room?	**Quant'è la camera più economica?**	kwahn-TEH lah KAH-may-rah peeOO ay-koh-NOH-mee-kah
Is it cheaper if I stay three nights?	**È più economico se mi fermo tre notti?**	eh peeOO ay-koh-NOH-mee-koh say mee FEHR-moh tray NOT-tee

I will stay three nights.	**Mi fermo tre notti.**	mee FEHR-moh tray NOT-tee
Breakfast included?	**La colazione è inclusa?**	lah koh-lah-tseeOH-nay eh een-KLOO-zah
Is breakfast required?	**È obbligatoria la colazione?**	eh oh-blee-gah-TOH-reeah lah koh-lah-tseeOH-nay
How much without breakfast?	**Quant'è senza la colazione?**	kwahn-TEH SEHN-tsah lah koh-lah-tseeOH-nay
Complete price?	**Prezzo completo?**	PREHT-tsoh kohm-PLAY-toh
Service included?	**Servizio incluso?**	sehr-VEE-tseeoh een-KLOO-zoh
Can I see the room?	**Posso vedere la camera?**	POS-soh vay-DAY-ray lah KAH-may-rah
Show me another room.	**Mi mostri un'altra camera.**	mee MOH-stree oo-NAHL-trah KAH-may-rah
Do you have something...?	**Avete qualcosa...?**	ah-VAY-tay kwahl-KOH-zah
...larger / smaller	**...di più grande / di più piccolo**	dee peeOO GRAHN-day / dee peeOO PEEK-koh-loh
...better / cheaper	**...di meglio / più economico**	dee MEHL-yoh / peeOO ay-koh-NOH-mee-koh
...in the back	**...nella parte di dietro**	NAY-lah PAR-tay dee deeEH-troh
...quieter	**...di più tranquillo**	dee peeOO trahn-KWEEL-loh
No, thank you.	**No, grazie.**	noh GRAH-tseeay
This is good.	**Questa va bene.**	KWAY-stah vah BEH-nay
I'll take it.	**La prendo.**	lah PREHN-doh

My key, please.	**La mia chiave, per favore.**	lah MEE-ah keeAH-vay pehr fah-VOH-ray
Sleep well.	**Sogni d'oro.**	SOHN-yee DOH-roh
Good night.	**Buona notte.**	BWOH-nah NOT-tay

Italian hotels almost always have larger rooms to fit three to six people. Your price per person plummets as you pack more into a room. Breakfasts are very basic (coffee, rolls and marmalade), expensive ($6 to $8), and often optional.

Hotel help and hassles:

I'd like...	**Vorrei...**	vor-REHee
...clean sheets.	**...delle lenzuola pulite.**	DAY-lay lehn-tsooOH-lah poo-LEE-tay
...a pillow.	**...un cuscino.**	oon koo-SHEE-noh
...a blanket.	**...una coperta.**	OO-nah koh-PEHR-tah
...a towel.	**...un asciugamano.**	oon ah-shoo-gah-MAH-noh
...toilet paper.	**...della carta igenica.**	DAY-lah KAR-tah ee-JAY-nee-kah
...a crib.	**...una culla.**	OO-nah KOOL-lah
...a small extra bed.	**...un extra letto singolo.**	oon EHK-strah LEHT-toh SEENG-goh-loh
...silence.	**...silenzio.**	see-LEHN-tseeoh
Is there an elevator?	**Un ascensore?**	oon ah-shayn-SOH-ray
Come with me.	**Venga con me.**	VAYN-gah kohn may

I have a problem in my room.	Ho un problema con la mia camera.	oh oon proh-BLAY-mah kohn lah MEE-ah KAH-may-rah
bad odor	cattivo odore	kaht-TEE-voh oh-DOH-ray
bugs	insetti	een-SEHT-tee
mice	topi	TOP-ee
prostitutes	prostitute	proh-stee-TOO-tay
The bed is too soft / hard.	Il letto è troppo morbido / duro.	eel LEHT-toh eh TROP-poh MOR-bee-doh / DOO-roh
I'm covered with bug bites.	Sono pieno di punture di insetti.	SOH-noh peeEH-noh dee poon-TOO-ray dee een-SEHT-tee
There is no hot water.	Non c'è acqua calda.	nohn cheh AHK-kwah KAHL-dah
When is the water hot?	A che ora è calda l'acqua?	ah kay OH-rah eh KAHL-dah LAHK-kwah
Where can I... my laundry?	Dove posso... bucato?	DOH-vay POS-soh... boo-KAH-toh
...wash	...fare del	pehr FAH-ray dayl
...hang	...stendere il	STEHN-day-ray eel
I'd like to stay another night.	Vorrei fermarmi un'altra notte.	vor-REHee fehr-MAR-mee oo-NAHL-trah NOT-tay
Where shall I park?	Dove posso parcheggiare?	DOH-vay POS-soh par-kay-JAH-ray
What time do you lock up?	A che ora chiude?	ah kay OH-rah keeOO-day
What time is breakfast?	A che ora è la colazione?	ah kay OH-rah eh lah koh-lah-tseeOH-nay

| Wake me at 7:00. | **Mi svegli alle sette.** | mee ZVAYL-yee AHL-lay SEHT-tay |

Checking out:

I'll leave... / We'll leave...	**Parto... / Partiamo...**	PAR-toh / par-teeAH-moh
...today / tomorrow.	**...oggi / domani.**	OJ-jee / doh-MAH-nee
When is check-out time?	**A che ora devo lasciare la camera?**	ah kay OH-rah DAY-voh lah-SHAH-ray lah KAH-may-rah
Can I pay now?	**Posso pagare subito?**	POS-soh pah-GAH-ray SOO-bee-toh
The bill, please.	**Il conto, per favore.**	eel KOHN-toh pehr fah-VOH-ray
Credit card okay?	**Una carta di credito è OK?**	OO-nah KAR-tah dee KRAY-dee-toh eh oh-KAY
I slept like a rock.	**Ho dormito come un sasso.**	oh dor-MEE-toh KOH-may oon SAHS-soh
Everything was great.	**Tutto magnifico.**	TOOT-toh mahn-YEE-fee-koh
Can I leave my bag here...?	**Posso lasciare il mio bagaglio qui...?**	POS-soh lah-SHAH-ray eel MEE-oh bah-GAHL-yoh kwee
Can we leave our bags here...?	**Possiamo lasciare il nostro bagaglio qui...?**	pos-seeAH-moh lah-SHAH-ray eel NOH-stroh bah-GAHL-yoh kwee
...until ___	**...fino a ___**	FEE-noh ah

Camping:

Where is the nearest campground?	**Dov'è il campeggio più vicino?**	doh-VEH eel kahm-PAY-joh peeOO vee-CHEE-noh
Can I... / Can we...?	**Posso... / Possiamo...?**	POS-soh / pos-seeAH-moh
...camp here for one night	**...campeggiare qui per la notte**	kahm-pay-JAH-ray kwee pehr lah NOT-tay
Do showers cost extra?	**Costano extra le doccie?**	koh-STAH-noh EHK-strah lay DOH-chay
shower token	**gettone**	jayt-TOH-nay

In some Italian campgrounds and youth hostels, you must buy a *gettone* (token) to activate a coin-operated hot shower. It has a timer inside, like a parking meter. To avoid a sudden cold rinse, buy at least two *gettoni* before getting undressed.

Eating

Finding a restaurant:

Where's a good... restaurant?	**Dov'è un buon ristorante...?**	doh-VEH oon bwohn ree-stoh-RAHN-tay
...cheap	**...economico**	ay-koh-NOH-mee-koh
...local-style	**...con cucina casereccia**	kohn koo-CHEE-nah kah-zay-RAY-chah
...untouristy	**...non per turisti**	nohn pehr too-REE-stee
...Chinese	**...cinese**	chee-NAY-zay
...fast food (Italian-style)	**...tavola calda**	TAH-voh-lah KAHL-dah

Ordering meals:

What would you like?	**Cosa desidera?**	KOH-zah day-SEE-day-rah
I'd like...	**Vorrei...**	vor-REHee
...a table for two.	**...un tavolo per due.**	oon TAH-voh-loh pehr DOO-ay
...nonsmoking.	**...non fumare.**	nohn foo-mah-ree
...just a drink.	**...soltanto qualcosa da bere.**	sohl-TAHN-toh kwahl-KOH-zah dah BAY-ray
...a snack.	**...un spuntino.**	oon spoon-TEE-noh
...only a pasta dish.	**...solo un primo piatto.**	SOH-loh oon PREE-moh peeAHT-toh
...to see the menu.	**...vedere il menù.**	vay-DAY-ray eel may-NOO

...to order.	...ordinare.	or-dee-NAH-ray
...to eat.	...mangiare.	mahn-JAH-ray
...to pay.	...pagare.	pah-GAH-ray
...to throw up.	...vomitare.	voh-mee-TAH-ray
What do you recommend?	Che cosa raccomanda?	kay KOH-zah rahk-koh-MAHN-dah
What's your favorite?	Qual'è il tuo preferito?	kwah-LEH eel TOO-oh pray-fay-REE-toh
Is it ...?	È...?	eh
...good	...buono	booOH-noh
...expensive	...caro	KAH-roh
...light	...leggero	leh-JAY-roh
...filling	...che riempie	kay ree-EHM-peeay
What is...?	Che cosa c'è...?	kay KOH-zah cheh
...that	...quello	KWAY-loh
...local	...di locale	dee loh-KAH-lay
...fast	...di veloce	dee vay-LOH-chay
...cheap and filling	...di economico che riempie	dee ay-koh-NOH-mee-koh kay ree-EHM-peeay
Do you have...?	Avete...?	ah-VAY-tay
...an English menu	...un menù in inglese	oon may-NOO een een-GLAY-zay
...children's portions	...le porzioni per bambini	lay por-tseeOH-nee pehr bahm-BEE-nee

Dietary restrictions:

I'm allergic to...	**Sono allergico al...**	SOH-noh ahl-LEHR-jee-koh ahl
I cannot eat...	**Non posso mangiare...**	nohn POS-soh mahn-JAH-ray
...dairy products.	**...prodotti casearei.**	proh-DOT-tee kah-zay-ah-RAYee
...fat.	**...grassi.**	GRAHS-see
...meat.	**...carne.**	CAR-nay
...salt.	**...sale.**	SAH-lay
...sugar.	**...zucchero.**	TSOOK-kay-roh
I am diabetic.	**Ho il diabete.**	oh eel deeah-BAY-tay
No alcohol.	**Niente alcool.**	neeEHN-tay AHL-kohl
I am a...	**Sono un...**	SOH-noh oon
...vegetarian.	**...vegetariano.**	vay-jay-tah-reeAH-noh
...strict vegetarian.	**...strettamente vegetariano.**	strayt-tah-MAYN-tay vay-jay-tah-reeAH-noh
...carnivore.	**...carnivoro.**	kar-NEE-voh-roh

Pay attention to the money-saving words in this section. Without them, Italy is a very expensive place to eat. Most menus explain the *servizio* charge which will be added to your bill along with the *coperto* (cover charge).

Budget eaters do best in places with no or minimal service and cover charges, and by sticking to the *primo piatto* (first course dishes). A hearty *minestrone* and/or *pasta* fills the average American. Pricier restaurants are wise to this, and some don't allow you to eat without ordering the expensive *secondo* course.

Key menu words:

breakfast	**colazione**	koh-lah-tseeOH-nay
lunch	**pranzo**	PRAHN-tsoh
dinner	**cena**	CHAY-nah
menu of the day	**menù del giorno**	may-NOO dayl JOR-noh
chef's speciality	**capricciosa**	kah-pree-CHOH-sah
specialty of the house	**specialità della casa**	spay-chah-lee-TAH DAY-lah KAH-zah
tourist menu	**menu turistico**	may-NOO too-REE-stee-koh
appetizers	**antipasti**	ahn-tee-PAH-stee
salad	**insalata**	een-sah-LAH-tah
bread	**pane**	PAH-nay
soup	**minestra**	mee-NEHS-trah
first course (pasta, soup)	**primo piatto**	PREE-moh peeAHT-toh
main course (meat, fish)	**secondo piatto**	say-KOHN-doh peeAHT-toh
meat	**carni**	KAR-nee
poultry	**pollame**	pohl-LAH-may
seafood	**frutti di mare**	FROOT-tee dee MAH-ray
side dishes	**contorni**	kohn-TOR-nee
vegetables	**legumi**	lay-GOO-mee
dessert	**dolce**	DOHL-chay

beverages	**bevande,**	bay-VAHN-day,
	bibite	BEE-bee-tay
beer	**birra**	BEER-rah
wine	**vino**	VEE-noh
cover charge	**coperto**	koh-PEHR-toh
service included	**servizio incluso**	sehr-VEE-tseeoh
		een-KLOO-zoh
service	**servizio**	sehr-VEE-tseeoh
not included	**non incluso**	nohn een-KLOO-zoh
with / and /	**con / e /**	kohn / ay /
or / without	**o / senza**	oh / SEHN-tsah

Restaurant requests and regrets:

A little.	**Un po.'**	oon poh
More.	**Un altro po.'**	oon AHL-troh poh
Another.	**Un altro.**	oon AHL-troh
I did not order this.	**Io questo non**	EEoh KWAY-stoh nohn
	l'ho ordinato.	loh or-dee-NAH-toh
Is it included with	**È incluso nel**	eh een-KLOO-zoh nayl
the meal?	**pasto questo?**	PAH-stoh KWAY-stoh
I'm in a hurry.	**Sono di fretta.**	SOH-noh dee FRAYT-tah
I have an	**Ho un appunta-**	oh oon ah-poon-tah-
appointment at...	**mento alle...**	MAYN-toh AHL-lay
When will the	**Tra quanto è**	trah KWAHN-toh eh
food be ready?	**pronto il cibo?**	PRON-toh eel CHEE-boh
I've changed	**Ho cambiato**	oh kahm-beeAH-toh
my mind.	**idea.**	ee-DAY-ah

Can I get it "to go"?	**Posso averlo da portar via?**	POS-soh ah-VEHR-loh dah POR-tar VEE-ah
This is...	**Questo è...**	KWAY-stoh eh
...dirty.	**...sporco.**	SPOR-koh
...too greasy.	**...troppo grasso.**	TROP-poh GRAHS-soh
...too salty.	**...troppo salato.**	TROP-poh sah-LAH-toh
...undercooked.	**...troppo crudo.**	TROP-poh KROO-doh
...overcooked.	**...troppo cotto.**	TROP-poh KOT-toh
...inedible.	**...immangiabile.**	eem-mahn-JAH-bee-lay
...cold.	**...freddo.**	FRAYD-doh
Can you heat this up?	**Me lo può riscaldare?**	may loh pwoh ree-skahl-DAH-ray
Yuk!	**Che schifo!**	kay SKEE-foh
Do any of your customers return?	**Ritornano i vostri clienti?**	ree-TOR-nah-noh ee VOH-stree klee-EHN-tee
Enough.	**Basta.**	BAH-stah
Finished.	**Finito.**	fee-NEE-toh
Delicious!	**Delizioso!**	day-lee-tseeOH-zoh
Divinely good!	**Una vera bontà!**	OO-nah VAY-rah bohn-TAH
My compliments to the chef!	**Complimenti al cuoco!**	kohm-plee-MAYN-tee ahl kooOH-koh

Paying for your meal:

Waiter.	**Cameriere.**	kah-may-reeEH-ray
Waitress.	**Cameriera.**	kah-may-reeEH-rah
The bill, please.	**Il conto, per favore.**	eel KOHN-toh pehr fah-VOH-ray
Together.	**Conto unico.**	KOHN-toh OO-nee-koh
Separate checks.	**Conto separato.**	KOHN-toh say-pah-RAH-toh
Credit card okay?	**Una carta di credito è OK?**	OO-nah KAR-tah dee KRAY-dee-toh eh oh-KAY
Is there a cover charge?	**Si paga per il coperto?**	see PAH-gah pehr eel koh-PEHR-toh
Is service included?	**È incluso il servizio?**	eh een-KLOO-zoh eel sehr-VEE-tseeoh
This is not correct.	**Questo non è giusto.**	KWAY-stoh nohn eh JOO-stoh
Can you explain this?	**Può spiegare questo?**	pwoh speeay-GAH-ray KWAY-stoh
What if I wash the dishes?	**E se lavassi i piatti?**	ay say lah-VAHS-see ee peeAHT-tee
Keep the change.	**Tenga il resto.**	TAYN-gah eel REHS-toh
This is for you.	**Questo è per lei.**	KWAY-stoh eh pehr LEHee

In Italian bars and freeway rest stops, you need to pay first at the cash register (*cassa*), then take your receipt to the counter to get your food. In restaurants, your waiter or waitress will not give you the bill unless you ask -- to do otherwise is considered rude. When you're ready for *il conto* (the bill), ask for it.

What's on the table:

table	**tavolo**	TAH-voh-loh
plate	**piatto**	peeAHT-toh
napkin	**tovagliolo**	toh-vahl-YOH-loh
knife	**coltello**	kohl-TEHL-loh
fork	**forchetta**	for-KAYT-tah
spoon	**cucchiaio**	kook-keeAH-yoh
glass	**bicchiere**	beek-keeEH-ray
carafe	**caraffa**	kah-RAHF-fah
water	**acqua**	AHK-kwah

Edible extras:

bread	**pane**	PAH-nay
breadsticks	**grissini**	grees-SEE-nee
butter	**burro**	BOOR-roh
margarine	**margarina**	mar-gah-REE-nah
salt	**sale**	SAH-lay
pepper	**pepe**	PAY-pay
sugar	**zucchero**	TSOOK-kay-roh
honey	**miele**	meeEH-lay
mustard	**senape**	SAY-nah-pay
mayonnaise	**maionese**	mah-yoh-NAY-zay
olives	**olive**	oh-LEE-vay
pickles	**cetriolini**	chay-treeoh-LEE-nee
garlic	**aglio**	AHL-yoh
oil	**olio**	OH-leeoh
vinegar	**aceto**	ah-CHAY-toh

What's (probably not) for breakfast:

Italian breakfasts, like Italian bath towels, are ridiculously small: coffee and a roll with butter and marmalade. The coffee is strong and plentiful, and often mixed about half and half with hot milk. Local markets thrive in the morning, and a picnic breakfast followed by a *cappuccino* in a bar is a good option.

breakfast	**colazione**	koh-lah-tseeOH-nay
eggs	**uova**	ooOH-vah
fried eggs	**uova fritte**	ooOH-vah FREET-tay
scrambled eggs	**uova strapazzate**	ooOH-vah strah-paht-TSAH-tay
boiled egg	**uovo alla coque**	ooOH-voh AHL-lah kok
soft / hard	**molle / sodo**	MOL-lay / SOH-doh
omelette	**omelette, frittata**	oh-may-LEHT-tay, freet-TAH-tah
ham	**prosciutto cotto**	proh-SHOOT-toh KOT-toh
cheese	**formaggio**	for-MAH-joh
roll	**brioche**	bree-OSH
toast	**toast**	tost
butter	**burro**	BOOR-roh
jelly	**gelatina**	jay-lah-TEE-nah
pastry	**pasticcini**	pah-stee-CHEE-nee
croissant	**cornetto**	kor-NAYT-toh
yogurt	**yogurt**	YOH-goort
cereal (any kind)	**corn flex**	korn flehx

milk	**latte**	LAHT-tay
hot cocoa	**cioccolata**	choh-koh-LAH-tah
	calda	KAHL-dah
fruit juice	**succo di frutta**	SOOK-koh dee FROOT-tah
fresh orange juice	**spremuta**	spray-MOO-tah
	di arancia	dee ah-RAHN-chah
tea / lemon	**tè / limone**	teh / lee-MOH-nay
coffee (see Drinking)	**caffè**	kahf-FEH
Is breakfast included	**La colazione**	lah koh-lah-tseeOH-nay
in the room cost?	**è inclusa?**	eh een-KLOO-zah

Appetizers:

antipasto misto	mixed appetizers
prosciutto e melone	cured ham with melon
salame	cured pork sausage
olive	olives
crostini	toast with liver paté or cheese
bruschetta	toast with tomatoes and garlic

Soups and salads:

soup	**minestra**	mee-NEHS-trah
clear soup	**brodo leggero**	BROD-oh leh-JAY-roh
broth	**brodo**	BROD-oh
...chicken	**...di pollo**	dee POHL-loh
...beef	**...di carne**	dee KAR-nay
...with noodles	**...con pastina**	kohn pah-STEE-nah
...with rice	**...con riso**	kohn REE-zoh
vegetable soup	**minestrone**	mee-nay-STROH-nay
green salad	**insalata verde**	een-sah-LAH-tah VEHR-day
chef's salad	**insalata dello chef**	een-sah-LAH-tah DAY-loh shehf
mixed salad	**insalata mista**	een-sah-LAH-tah MEE-stah
seafood salad	**insalata di mare**	een-sah-LAH-tah dee MAH-ray
lettuce	**lattuga**	laht-TOO-gah
tomatoes	**pomodori**	poh-moh-DOR-ee
cucumber	**cetrioli**	chay-treeOH-lee
oil / vinegar	**olio / aceto**	OH-leeoh / ah-CHAY-toh
What is in this salad?	**Che cosa c'è in questa insalata?**	kay KOH-zah cheh een KWAY-stah een-sah-LAH-tah

In Italian restaurants, salad dressing is normally just the oil and vinegar at the table. Salad bars at fast food places and *autostrada* rest stops can be a good budget bet.

Pizza:

For fresh, fast, and frugal pizza, look for *Pizza Rustica* shops. They offer the cheapest hot meal in any Italian town, selling pizza by the slice (*pezzo*) or the weight (*etto* = 100 grams, around a quarter pound). *Due etti* (200 grams) makes a good light lunch. You'll find several varieties of pizza, including the fun-to-munch *pizza bianco* (greasy, herby pizza crust alone). You can eat your pizza on the spot, or order it *da portar via* (for the road). For handier but lousy pizza, nearly any bar has precooked microwavable pizza snacks. Important pizza words include:

Calzone	folded pizza with various fillings
Capricciosa	chef's specialty
Margherita	cheese and tomato sauce
Napoletana	cheese, anchovies and tomato sauce
Quattro Stagioni	4 toppings on separate quarters of a pizza
prosciutto	cured ham
funghi	mushrooms
carciofini	artichokes
(senza) acciughe	(without) anchovies
per una persona	for one person
per due persone	for two people

Pasta:

Italy is the land of *pasta*. You can taste over 500 types! While there are a few differences in ingredients, the big deal is basically the shape. Watch for *rigatone* (little tubes), *canneloni* (big tubes), *fettucine* (flat noodles), *farfalline* (butterfly-shaped pasta), *gnocchi* (shell-shaped noodles made from potatoes), *penne* (angle-cut tubes), *rotelline* (wheel-shaped pasta), *tagliatelle* (flat noodles), and *tortellini* (pasta "donuts" filled with meat or cheese), and, surprise, *spaghetti.* Pasta can be stuffed *ravoli*-style with various meats, herbs, and spices. Pasta sauces and styles include:

carbonara	bacon, egg and pepper
genovese	pesto
in brodo	in broth
marinara	tomato and garlic
matriciana	spicy with tomato
milanese	fried in breadcrumbs
panna	cream
pescatora	seafood
pesto	olive oil, garlic, pine nuts and basil
pomodoro	tomato only
quattro formaggi	four cheeses
ragù	meaty tomato sauce
sugo	sauce, usually tomato
vongole	with clams and spices

More Italian specialities:

polenta	moist cornbread (Venice)
focaccia	flat bread with herbs
tramezzini	crustless filled sandwiches
caprese	salad of fresh mozzarella, tomatoes and basil
ribollita	cabbage and bean soup (Tuscany)
pancetta	thick bacon
saltimbocca	veal wrapped in ham (Rome)
risotto	saffron rice dish with meat, seafood or vegetables (Northern Italy)

Seafood:

seafood	**frutti di mare**	FROOT-tee dee MAH-ray
assorted seafood	**misto di frutti di mare**	MEE-stoh dee FROOT-tee dee MAH-ray
fish	**pesce**	PAY-shay
cod	**merluzzo**	mehr-LOOT-tsoh
salmon	**salmone**	sahl-MOH-nay
trout	**trota**	TROT-ah
tuna	**tonno**	TOHN-noh
herring	**aringa**	ah-REENG-gah
sardines	**sarde**	SAR-day
anchovies	**acciughe**	ah-CHOO-gay
clams	**vongole**	VOHN-goh-lay
mussels	**cozze**	KOT-tsay

oysters	**ostriche**	OS-tree-kay
shrimp	**gamberetti**	gahm-bay-RAYT-tee
prawns	**scampi**	SKAHM-pee
crab	**granchione**	grahn-keeOH-nay
lobster	**aragosta**	ah-rah-GOH-stah
squid	**calamari**	kah-lah-MAH-ree
Where did this live?	**Da dove viene questo?**	dah DOH-vay veeEH-nay KWAY-stoh

Poultry and meat:

poultry	**pollame**	pohl-LAH-may
chicken	**pollo**	POHL-loh
turkey	**tacchino**	tahk-KEE-noh
duck	**anatra**	AH-nah-trah
meat	**carne**	KAR-nay
beef	**manzo**	MAHN-dzoh
roast beef	**roast beef**	"roast beef"
beef steak	**bistecca di manzo**	bee-STAYK-kah dee MAHN-dzoh
meat stew	**stufato di carne**	stoo-FAH-toh dee KAR-nay
veal	**vitello**	vee-TEHL-loh
thin-sliced veal	**scaloppine**	skah-lohp-PEE-nay
cutlet	**cotoletta**	koh-toh-LAYT-tah
pork	**maiale**	mah-YAH-lay
cured ham	**prosciutto**	proh-SHOOT-toh
lamb	**agnello**	ahn-YEHL-loh
bunny	**coniglio**	koh-NEEL-yoh

brains	**cervello**	chehr-VEHL-loh
sweetbreads	**animelle**	ah-nee-MEHL-lay
	di vitello	dee vee-TEHL-loh
tongue	**lingua**	LEENG-gwah
liver	**fegato**	FAY-gah-toh
tripe	**trippa**	TREEP-pah
mixed boiled meats	**bollito misto**	bohl-LEE-toh MEE-stoh
How long has this been dead?	**Da quanto tempo è morto questo?**	dah KWAHN-toh TEHM-poh eh MOR-toh KWAY-stoh

How it's prepared:

hot	**caldo**	KAHL-doh
cold	**freddo**	FRAYD-doh
raw	**crudo**	KROO-doh
cooked	**cotto**	KOT-toh
baked	**al forno**	ahl FOR-noh
boiled	**bollito**	bohl-LEET-toh
fillet	**filetto**	fee-LAYT-toh
fresh	**fresco**	FRAY-skoh
fried	**fritto**	FREET-toh
grilled	**alla griglia**	AHL-lah GREEL-yah
microwave	**forno a micro onde**	FOR-noh ah MEE-kroh OHN-day
mild	**saporito**	sah-poh-REE-toh
poached	**affogato**	ahf-foh-GAH-toh
roasted	**arrostito**	ar-roh-STEE-toh
sautéed	**saltato in padella**	sahl-TAH-toh een pah-DEHL-lah
smoked	**affumicato**	ahf-foo-mee-KAH-toh
spicy hot	**piccante**	peek-KAHN-tay

steamed	**al vapore**	ahl vah-POH-ray
stuffed	**ripieno**	ree-peeEH-noh

Avoiding mis-steaks:

raw	**crudo**	KROO-doh
rare	**al sangue**	ahl SAHN-gway
medium	**cotto**	KOT-toh
well done	**ben cotto**	bayn KOT-toh
almost burnt	**quasi bruciato**	KWAH-zee broo-CHAH-toh

Veggies and rice:

vegetables	**legumi, verdure**	lay-GOO-mee, vehr-DOO-ray
mixed vegetables	**misto di verdure**	MEE-stoh dee vehr-DOO-ray
artichoke	**carciofo**	kar-CHOH-foh
asparagus	**asparagi**	ah-spah-RAH-jee
beans	**fagioli**	fah-JOH-lee
beets	**barbabietole**	bar-bah-beeay-TOH-lay
broccoli	**broccoli**	BROK-koh-lee
cabbage	**verza**	VEHR-tsah
carrots	**carote**	kah-ROT-ay
cauliflower	**cavolfiore**	kah-vohl-feeOH-ray
corn	**granturco**	grahn-TOOR-koh
eggplant	**melanzana**	may-lahn-TSAH-nah
green beans	**fagiolini**	fah-joh-LEE-nee
green peppers	**peperoni**	pay-pay-ROH-nee
mushrooms	**funghi**	FOONG-gee
onions	**cipolle**	chee-POHL-lay
peas	**piselli**	pee-ZEHL-lee
spinach	**spinaci**	spee-NAH-chee

zucchini	**zucchine**	tsoo-KEE-nay
potatoes	**patate**	pah-TAH-tay
French fries	**patate fritte**	pah-TAH-tay FREET-tay
rice	**riso**	REE-zoh

Say cheese:

cheese	**formaggio**	for-MAH-joh
mozzarella	**mozzarella**	moht-tsah-REHL-lah
small mozzarella balls	**latticini**	laht-tee-CHEE-nee
goat	**di capra**	dee KAH-prah
bleu cheese	**gorgonzola**	gor-gohn-DZOH-lah
mild cheese	**formaggio leggero**	for-MAH-joh leh-JAY-roh
cream cheese	**formaggio philadelphia**	for-MAH-joh fee-lah-DEHL-feeah
Swiss cheese	**groviera, emmenthal**	groh-veeEH-rah, ehm-mehn-TAHL
a soft white cheese	**Bel Paese**	bel pah-AY-zay
a tasty spreadable cheese	**stracchino**	strahk-KEE-noh
A little taste?	**Un assaggio?**	oon ahs-SAH-joh

Italian fruit:

fruit	**frutta**	FROOT-tah
apple	**mela**	MAY-lah
apricot	**albicocca**	ahl-bee-KOHK-kah
banana	**banana**	bah-NAH-nah
berries	**frutti di bosco**	FROOT-tee dee BOS-koh
cherry	**ciliegia**	chee-leeAY-jah
coconut	**noce di cocco**	NOH-chay dee KOHK-koh

date	**dattere**	DAHT-tay-ray
fig	**ficho**	FEE-koh
grapefruit	**pompelmo**	pohm-PAYL-moh
grapes	**uva**	OO-vah
lemon	**limone**	lee-MOH-nay
melon	**melone**	may-LOH-nay
orange	**arancia**	ah-RAHN-chah
peach	**pesca**	PEHS-kah
pear	**pera**	PAY-rah
pineapple	**ananas**	AH-nah-nahs
plum	**susina**	soo-ZEE-nah
prune	**prugna**	PROON-yah
raspberry	**lampone**	lahm-POH-nay
strawberry	**fragola**	FRAH-goh-lah
tangerine	**mandarino**	mahn-dah-REE-noh
watermelon	**cocomero**	koh-koh-MAY-roh

Nuts to you:

almond	**mandorle**	mahn-DOR-lay
chestnut	**castagne**	kah-STAHN-yay
hazelnut	**nocciola**	noh-CHOH-lah
peanut	**noccioline**	noh-choh-LEE-nay
walnut	**noce**	NOH-chay

Italian desserts and goodies:

dessert	**dolce**	DOHL-chay
cake	**torta**	TOR-tah
ice cream	**gelato**	jay-LAH-toh
sherbet	**sorbetto**	sor-BAYT-toh
fruit cup	**coppa di frutta**	KOP-pah dee FROOT-tah
tart	**tartina**	tar-TEE-nah

pie	**torte**	TOR-tay
whipped cream	**panna**	PAHN-nah
mousse	**mousse**	moos
pudding	**budino**	boo-DEE-noh
pastry	**pasticcini**	pah-stee-CHEE-nee
strudel	**strudel**	STROO-dehl
cookies	**biscotti**	bee-SKOT-tee
candy	**caramelle**	kah-rah-MEHL-lay
low calorie	**poche calorie**	POH-kay kah-loh-REE-ay
homemade	**fatto in casa**	FAHT-toh een KAH-zah
Sinfully good.	**Un peccato**	oon payk-KAH-toh
(a sin of the throat)	**di gola.**	dee GOH-lah
So good I even licked	**Così buono che**	koh-ZEE booOH-noh kay
my moustache.	**mi sono leccato**	mee SOH-noh lay-KAH-toh
	anche i baffi.	AHN-kay ee BAHF-fee

More Italian treats:

cassata	Sicilian dessert of ice cream, sponge cake, ricotta cheese, fruit and pistachio
granita	snow-cone
panforte	dense fruit and nut cake (Siena speciality)
Tiramisu	espresso-soaked cake with fruit, chocolate and cream
Zabaglione	delicious egg and liquor cream
Zuppa Inglese	rum-soaked cake with whipped cream

Italian gelati talk:

cup / cone	**coppa / cono**	KOP-pah / KOH-noh
one scoop	**una pallina**	OO-nah pahl-LEE-nah
two scoops	**due palline**	DOO-ay pahl-LEE-nay
with whipped cream	**con panna**	kohn PAHN-nah
A little taste?	**Un assaggio?**	oon ahs-SAH-joh

Gelati gusti:

flavors	**gusti**	GOO-stee
apricot	**albicocca**	ahl-bee-KOHK-kah
berries	**frutti di bosco**	FROOT-tee dee BOS-koh
blueberry	**mirtillo**	meer-TEEL-loh
cantaloupe	**melone**	may-LOH-nay
chocolate	**cioccolato**	choh-koh-LAH-toh
chocolate chips in vanilla	**stracciatella**	strah-chah-TEHL-lah
chocolate hazelnut	**baci**	BAH-chee
coffee	**caffè**	kahf-FEH
hazelnut	**nocciola**	noh-CHOH-lah
lemon	**limone**	lee-MOH-nay
mint	**menta**	MAYN-tah
orange	**arancia**	ah-RAHN-chah
peach	**pesca**	PEHS-kah
pear	**pera**	PAY-rah
pineapple	**ananas**	AH-nah-nahs
raspberry	**lampone**	lahm-POH-nay
rice	**riso**	REE-zoh
strawberry	**fragola**	FRAH-goh-lah
super chocolate	**tartufo**	tar-TOO-foh
vanilla	**crema**	KRAY-mah

Drinking

Water, milk and juice:

mineral water	**acqua minerale**	AHK-kwah mee-nay-RAH-lay
(not) carbonated	**(non) gassata**	(nohn) gahs-SAH-tah
tap water	**acqua del rubinetto**	AHK-kwah dayl roo-bee-NAYT-toh
milk...	**latte...**	LAHT-tay
...whole	**...intero**	een-TAY-roh
...skim	**...magro**	MAH-groh
...fresh	**...fresco**	FRAY-skoh
milk shake	**frappè**	frahp-PEH
hot chocolate	**cioccolata calda**	choh-koh-LAH-tah KAHL-dah
orange soda	**aranciata**	ah-rahn-CHAH-tah
lemon soda	**limonata**	lee-moh-NAH-tah
fruit juice	**succo di frutta**	SOOK-koh dee FROOT-tah
orange juice	**succo di arancia**	SOOK-koh dee ah-RAHN-chah
apple juice	**succo di mela**	SOOK-koh dee MAY-lah
with ice / without ice	**con ghiaccio / senza ghiaccio**	kohn geeAH-choh / SEHN-tsah geeAH-choh
glass / cup	**bicchiere / tazza**	beek-keeEH-ray / TAHT-tsah
small bottle	**bottiglia piccola**	boht-TEEL-yah PEEK-koh-lah

large bottle	**bottiglia grande**	boht-TEEL-yah GRAHN-day
Is this water safe to drink?	**È potabile quest'acqua?**	eh poh-TAH-bee-lay kway-STAHK-kwah

I drink the tap water in Italy (Venice's is piped in from a mountain spring, and Florence's is very chlorinated), but it is good style and never expensive to order a liter of bottled water with your meal.

Coffee and tea:

coffee...	**caffè...**	kahf-FEH
...with water	**...lungo**	LOON-goh
...American-style	**...Americano**	ah-may-ree-KAH-noh
...with milk	**...latte**	LAHT-tay
...iced	**...freddo**	FRAYD-doh
...instant	**...solubile**	soo-LOO-bee-lay
coffee with foam	**cappuccino**	kahp-poo-CHEE-noh
decaffeinated	**decaffeinato, Hag**	day-kah-fay-NAH-toh, hahg
black	**nero**	NAY-roh
milk	**latte**	LAHT-tay
sugar	**zucchero**	TSOOK-kay-roh
hot water	**acqua calda**	AHK-kwah KAHL-dah
tea / lemon	**tè / limone**	teh / lee-MOH-nay
tea bag	**bustina di tè**	boo-STEE-nah dee teh
herbal tea (decaf)	**tè decaffeinato**	teh day-kah-fay-NAH-toh
iced tea	**tè freddo**	teh FRAYD-doh

small / big	**piccola /**	PEEK-koh-lah /
	grande	GRAHN-day
Another cup.	**Un'altra tazza.**	oo-NAHL-trah TAHT-tsah

Caffè is espresso served in a teeny tiny cup. Foamy *cappuccino* was named after the monks with their brown robes and frothy cowls. A *coretto* is coffee and firewater. When ordering coffee at a bar, you'll notice that the price board clearly lists two price levels: the cheaper level for the *bar* and the more expensive for the *tavolo* (table) or *terrazza* (out on the terrace or sidewalk). You pay at the *cassa*, then take your receipt to the guy who makes the coffee. Refills are never free.

Wine:

Italy leads the world in wine production and you'll find it on nearly every table. To save money, order *una caraffa di vino della casa* (a carafe of the house wine). The best Italian wines are from Piedmont, such as the heavy, full-bodied, expensive *barbera* and *barolo*, and the more affordable *Asti spumante*. Tuscany is famous for its *chianti* -- a black rooster on the label indicates it's from the authentic Chianti region. *Orvieto Classico* is a very popular white wine from Umbria. If you like a sweet after-dinner wine, don't miss the *Sciachetrà* from the *Cinque Terre*. Many small-town Italians in the hotel business have a cellar or cantina which they are proud to show off. They'll often jump at any excuse to descend and drink.

wine / wines	**vino / vini**	VEE-noh / VEE-nee
house wine	**vino della casa**	VEE-noh DAYL-lah KAH-zah
local	**locale**	loh-KAH-lay
red	**rosso**	ROHS-soh
white	**bianco**	beeAHN-koh
rose	**rosato**	roh-ZAH-toh
sparkling	**frizzante**	freet-TSAHN-tay
sweet	**dolce, abbocato**	DOHL-chay, ahb-boh-KAH-toh
medium	**medio**	MAY-deeoh
dry	**secco**	SAYK-koh
very dry	**molto secco**	MOHL-toh SAYK-koh
a glass...	**un bicchiere...**	oon beek-keeEH-ray
a carafe...	**una caraffa...**	OO-nah kah-RAHF-fah
...of red wine	**...di rosso**	dee ROHS-soh
...of white wine	**...di bianco**	dee beeAHN-koh
a half bottle	**una mezza bottiglia**	OO-nah MEHD-dzah boht-TEEL-yah
a bottle	**una bottiglia**	OO-nah boht-TEEL-yah
The wine list.	**La lista dei vini.**	lah LEE-stah DEHee VEE-nee

Beer:

beer	**birra**	BEER-rah
from the tap	**alla spina**	AHL-lah SPEE-nah
light / dark	**chiara / scura**	keeAH-rah / SKOO-rah
local / imported	**locale / importata**	loh-KAH-lay / eem-por-TAH-tah
small / large	**piccola / grande**	PEEK-koh-lah / GRAHN-day
alcohol-free	**analcolica**	ahn-ahl-KOH-lee-kah
cold	**fredda**	FRAYD-dah

Bar talk:

What would you like?	**Che cosa prendi?**	kay KOH-zah PREHN-dee
local specialty	**specialità locale**	spay-chah-lee-TAH loh-KAH-lay
straight	**liscio**	LEE-shoh
with / without...	**con / senza...**	kohn / SEHN-tsah
...alcohol	**...alcool**	AHL-kohl
...ice	**...ghiaccio**	geeAH-choh
One more.	**Un altro.**	oon AHL-troh
Cheers!	**Cin Cin!**	cheen cheen
To your health!	**Alla tua salute!**	AHL-lah TOO-ah sah-LOO-tay
Long life!	**Lunga vita!**	LOONG-gah VEE-tah
Long live Italy!	**Viva l'Italia!**	VEE-vah lee-TAHL-yah

I'm feeling...	**Mi sento...**	mee SEHN-toh
...a little drunk.	**...un po' ubriaco.**	oon poh oo-breeAH-koh
...blitzed. (colloq.)	**...ubriaco fradicio.**	oo-breeAH-koh FRAH-dee-choh

An Italian speciality is *Cinzano*, a red, white, and rose vermouth. After dinner, try a *digestivo*, a liqueur thought to aid in digestion. For a flammable drink, get *grappa*, firewater distilled from grape skins and stems.

For a memorable and affordable adventure in eating, have a 'pub crawl' dinner. While *cicchetti* (bar munchies) aren't as common as they used to be, many bars are still popular for their wide selection of often ugly, always tasty hors d'oeuvres on toothpicks. Some bars called *ciccheteria* specialize in this, and are worth seeking out. Otherwise, most bartenders will make you a simple, hearty *panino* (sandwich).

Groceries and Picnics

Building your own meal:

market (open air)	**mercato**	mehr-KAH-toh
grocery store	**alimentari**	ah-lee-mayn-TAH-ree
supermarket	**supermercato**	soo-pehr-mehr-KAH-toh
Is it self service?	**È self-service?**	eh "self-service"
picnic	**picnic**	PEEK-neek
sandwich or roll	**panino**	pah-NEE-noh
bread	**pane**	PAH-nay
sausage	**salsiccia**	sahl-SEE-chah
cured ham	**prosciutto**	proh-SHOOT-toh
cheese	**formaggio**	for-MAH-joh
a piece	**un pezzo**	oon PEHT-tsoh
a slice	**una fettina**	OO-nah fayt-TEE-nah
sliced	**tagliato a fettine**	tahl-YAH-toh ah fayt-TEE-nay
fifty grams	**cinquanta grammi**	cheeng-KWAHN-tah GRAHM-mee
one hundred grams	**etto**	EHT-toh
more / less	**più / meno**	peeOO / MAY-noh
yogurt	**yogurt**	YOH-goort
plastic spoon	**cucchiaio di plastica**	kook-keeAH-yoh dee PLAH-stee-kah
paper plate	**piatto di carta**	peeAHT-toh dee KAR-tah

Can you make me a sandwich?	**Mi può fare un panino?**	mee pwoh FAH-ray oon pah-NEE-noh
To take out.	**Da portar via.**	dah POR-tar VEE-ah
Is there a park nearby?	**C'è un parco qui vicino?**	cheh oon PAR-koh kwee vee-CHEE-noh
May we picnic here?	**Si possono fare picnic qui?**	see POS-soh-noh FAH-ray PEEK-neek kwee
Enjoy your meal!	**Buon appetito!**	bwohn ahp-pay-TEE-toh

You can easily make your own sandwiches by getting the ingredients at a store or a public market. Order meat and cheese by the gram. One hundred grams is about a quarter pound, enough for two sandwiches. Italians call 100 grams an *etto*. So if you say *cinque etti*, you'll get 500 grams, or half a kilo (about a pound).

Sightseeing

Handy sightseeing questions:

Where is... / Where are...?	Dov'è... / Dove sono...?	doh-VEH / DOH-vay SOH-noh
...the best view	...la vista più bella	lah VEE-stah peeOO BEHL-lah
...the main square	...la piazza centrale	lah peeAHT-tsah chehn-TRAH-lay
...the old town center	...il centro storico	eel CHEHN-troh STOH-ree-koh
...the museum	...il museo	eel moo-ZAY-oh
...the castle	...il castello	eel kah-STEHL-loh
...the palace	...il palazzo	eel pah-LAHT-tsoh
...the ruins	...le rovine	lay roh-VEE-nay
...a festival	...un festival	oon FEHS-tee-vahl
...tourist information	...informazioni per turisti	een-for-mah-tseeOH-nee pehr too-REE-stee
Do you have... in English?	Avete... in inglese?	ah-VAY-tay... een een-GLAY-zay
...information	...informazioni	een-for-mah-tseeOH-nee
...a guidebook	...una guida	OO-nah GWEE-dah
...a tour	...una gita	OO-nah JEE-tah
When is the next tour...?	Quando è la prossima gita...?	KWAHN-doh eh lah PROS-see-mah JEE-tah
...in English	...in inglese	een een-GLAY-zay
Is it free?	È gratis?	eh GRAH-tees

How much does it cost?	**Quanto costa?**	KWAHN-toh KOS-tah
Is there a discount for...?	**Fate sconti per...?**	FAH-tay SKOHN-tee pehr
...students	**...studenti**	stoo-DEHN-tee
...seniors	**...pensionati**	payn-seeoh-NAH-tee
...youth	**...giovani**	joh-VAH-nee
Is the ticket valid all day?	**Il biglietto è valido per tutto il giorno?**	eel beel-YAYT-toh eh VAH-lee-doh pehr TOOT-toh eel JOR-noh
What time does this open / close?	**A che ora apre / chiude?**	ah kay OH-rah AH-pray / keeOO-day
What time is the last entry?	**Quand'è l'ultima entrata?**	kwahn-DEH LOOL-tee-mah ayn-TRAH-tah
PLEASE let me in.	**PER FAVORE, mi faccia entrare.**	pehr fah-VOH-ray mee FAH-chah ayn-TRAH-ray
I've traveled all the way from...	**Sono venuto qui da...**	SOH-noh vay-NOO-toh kwee dah
I must leave tomorrow.	**Devo partire domani.**	DAY-voh par-TEE-ray doh-MAH-nee

In the museum:

Where can I find this? (point to photo)	**Dove posso trovare questo?**	DOH-vay POS-soh troh-VAH-ray KWAY-stoh
I'd like to see...	**Mi piacerebbe vedere...**	mee peeah-chay-RAY-bay vay-DAY-ray
Are photos / videos allowed?	**Si possono fare foto / filmini?**	see POS-soh-noh FAH-ray FOH-toh / feel-MEE-nee

No flash / tripod.	**Vietato usare flash / cavalletti.**	veeay-TAH-toh oo-ZAH-ray flahsh / kah-vahl-LAYT-tee
I like it.	**Mi piace.**	mee peeAH-chay
It's so...	**È così...**	eh koh-ZEE
...beautiful.	**...bello.**	BEHL-loh
...ugly.	**...brutto.**	BROOT-toh
...strange.	**...strano.**	STRAH-noh
...boring.	**...noioso.**	noh-YOH-zoh
...interesting.	**...interessante.**	een-tay-rays-SAHN-tay
Wow!	**Che diamine!**	kay deeAH-mee-nay
My feet hurt!	**Mi fanno male i piedi!**	mee FAHN-noh MAH-lay ee peeAY-dee
I'm exhausted!	**Sono stanco morto!**	SOH-noh STAHN-koh MOR-toh

Many museums close in the afternoon from 13:00 until 15:00 or 16:00, and are closed all day on a weekday, usually Monday. Museums often stop selling tickets 45 minutes before closing. Historic churches usually open much earlier than museums.

Art and architecture:

art	**arte**	AR-tay
artist	**artista**	ar-TEE-stah
painting	**quadro**	KWAH-droh
self-portrait	**autoritratto**	ow-toh-ree-TRAHT-toh
sculptor	**scultore**	skool-TOH-ray
sculpture	**scultura**	skool-TOO-rah

architect	**architetto**	ar-kee-TEHT-toh
architecture	**architettura**	ar-kee-teht-TOO-rah
original	**originale**	oh-ree-jee-NAH-lay
restored	**restaurato**	ray-stow-RAH-toh
B.C. / A.D.	**A.C. / D.C.**	ah chee / dee chee
century	**secolo**	SAY-koh-loh
style	**stile**	STEE-lay
Abstract	**Astratto**	ah-STRAHT-toh
Ancient	**Antico**	ahn-TEE-koh
Art Nouveau	**Arte Nouveau**	AR-tay NOO-voh
Baroque	**Barocco**	bah-ROK-koh
Classical	**Classico**	KLAHS-see-koh
Gothic	**Gotico**	GOT-ee-koh
Impressionist	**Impressionista**	eem-pray-seeoh-NEE-stah
Medieval	**Medievale**	may-deeay-VAH-lay
Modern	**Moderno**	moh-DEHR-noh
Renaissance	**Rinascimento**	ree-nah-shee-MAYN-toh
Romanesque	**Romanesco**	roh-mah-NAY-skoh
Romantic	**Romantico**	roh-MAHN-tee-koh

As you sightsee, you'll find that the Italians refer to their three greatest centuries of art in an unusual way. The 1300s are called *tre cento* (300s); the 1400s, early Renaissance, are called *quattro cento* (400s); and the 1500s, High Renaissance, are *cinque cento* (500s).

Castles and palaces:

castle	**castello**	kah-STEHL-loh
palace	**palazzo**	pah-LAHT-tsoh
ballroom	**sala da ballo**	SAH-lah dah BAHL-loh
kitchen	**cucina**	koo-CHEE-nah
cellar	**cantina**	kahn-TEE-nah
dungeon	**prigione sotterranea**	pree-JOH-nay soht-tehr-RAH-nay-ah
fortified wall	**muri fortificati**	MOO-ree for-tee-fee-KAH-tee
tower	**torre**	TOR-ray
fountain	**fontana**	fohn-TAH-nah
garden	**giardino**	jar-DEE-noh
king	**re**	ray
queen	**regina**	ray-JEE-nah
knights	**cavalieri**	kah-vah-leeEH-ree

Religious words:

cathedral	**duomo**	doo-OH-moh
church	**chiesa**	keeAY-zah
monastery	**monastero**	moh-nah-STAY-roh
synagogue	**sinagoga**	see-nah-GOG-ah
chapel	**cappella**	kahp-PEHL-lah
altar	**altare**	ahl-TAH-ray
cross	**croce**	KROH-chay
crypt	**cripta**	KREEP-tah

dome	**cupola**	KOO-poh-lah
organ	**organo**	OR-gah-noh
relics	**reliquie**	ray-LEE-kweeay
saint	**santo**	SAHN-toh
God	**Dio**	DEE-oh
Jewish	**ebreo**	ay-BRAY-oh
Christian	**cristiano**	kree-steeAH-noh
Protestant	**protestante**	proh-tay-STAHN-tay
Catholic	**cattolico**	kaht-TOH-lee-koh
When is the service?	**A che ora è la messa?**	ah kay OH-rah eh lah MAY-sah
Are there church concerts?	**Ci sono concerti in chiesa?**	chee SOH-noh kohn-CHEHR-tee een keeAY-zah

Shopping

Names of Italian shops:

antiques	**negozio di antiquariato**	nay-GOH-tseeoh dee ahn-tee-kwah-reeAH-toh
art gallery	**galleria d'arte**	gahl-lay-REE-ah DAR-tay
bakery	**fornaio, panificio**	for-NAH-yoh, pah-nee-FEE-choh
barber shop	**barbiere**	bar-beeEH-ray
beauty parlor	**parrucchiere**	par-rook-keeEH-ray
book shop	**libreria**	lee-bray-REE-ah
camera shop	**negozio di macchine fotografiche**	nay-GOH-tseeoh dee MAHK-kee-nay foh-toh-GRAH-fee-kay
department store	**grande magazzino**	GRAHN-day mah-gahd-DZEE-noh
flea market	**mercato dell'usato**	mehr-KAH-toh day-loo-ZAH-toh
flower market	**mercato dei fiori**	mehr-KAH-toh DEHee fee-OH-ree
grocery store	**negozio di alimentari**	nay-GOH-tseeoh dee ah-lee-mayn-TAH-ree
jewelry shop	**gioielliere**	joh-yayl-leeEH-ray
laundromat	**lavanderia**	lah-vahn-day-REE-ah
newsstand	**giornalaio**	jor-nah-LAH-yoh
open air market	**mercato**	mehr-KAH-toh
pharmacy	**farmacia**	far-mah-CHEE-ah

shopping mall	**centro commerciale**	CHEHN-troh koh-mehr-CHAH-lay
souvenir shop	**negozio di souvenir**	nay-GOH-tseeoh dee SOO-vay-neer
supermarket	**supermercato**	soo-pehr-mehr-KAH-toh
toy store	**negozio di giocattoli**	nay-GOH-tseeoh dee joh-KAHT-toh-lee
travel agency	**agenzia di viaggio**	ah-jehn-TSEE-ah dee veeAH-joh
used bookstore	**negozio di libri usati**	nay-GOH-tsoh dee LEE-bree oo-ZAH-tee
wine shop	**negozio di vini**	nay-GOH-tsoh dee VEE-nee

Most businesses are closed daily from 13:00 until 15:00 or 16:00. Many stores in the larger cities close for all or part of August -- not a good time to plan a shopping spree.

Shop till you drop:

sale	**saldo**	SAHL-doh
How much does it cost?	**Quanto costa?**	KWAHN-toh KOS-tah
I'd like...	**Vorrei...**	vor-REHee
Do you have...?	**Avete...?**	ah-VAY-tay
...something cheaper	**...qualcosa di meno caro**	kwahl-KOH-zah dee MAY-noh KAH-roh
Can I see more?	**Posso vederne ancora?**	POS-soh vay-DEHR-nay ahn-KOH-rah

This one.	Questo qui.	KWAY-stoh kwee
Can I try it on?	Lo posso provare?	loh POS-soh proh-VAH-ray
Do you have a mirror?	Ha uno specchio?	ah OO-noh SPAY-choh
It's too...	È troppo...	eh TROP-poh
...big.	...grande.	GRAHN-day
...small.	...piccolo.	PEEK-koh-loh
...expensive.	...caro.	KAH-roh
Did you make this?	L'avete fatto voi questo?	lah-VAY-tay FAHT-toh VOHee KWAY-stoh
What is it made out of?	Di che cosa è fatto?	dee kay KOH-zah eh FAHT-toh
Is it machine washable?	Se può lavare in lavatrice?	say pooOH lah-VAH-ray een lah-vah-TREE-chay
Will it shrink?	Si ritira?	see ree-TEE-rah
Can you ship this?	Può spedirmelo?	pwoh spay-deer-MAY-loh
Credit card okay?	Una carta di credito è OK?	OO-nah KAR-tah dee KRAY-dee-toh eh oh-KAY
Tax-free?	Esente da tasse?	ay-ZEHN-tay dah TAHS-say
I'll think about it.	Ci penserò.	chee pehn-say-ROH
What time do you close?	A che ora chiudete?	ah kay OH-rah keeoo-DAY-tay
What time do you open tomorrow?	A che ora aprite domani?	ah kay OH-rah ah-PREE-tay doh-MAH-nee
Is that your final price?	È questo il prezzo finale?	eh KWAY-stoh eel PREHT-tsoh fee-NAH-lay
My last offer.	La mia ultima offerta.	lah MEE-ah OOL-tee-mah ohf-FEHR-tah

I'm nearly broke.	**Sono quasi al verde.**	SOH-noh KWAH-zee ahl VEHR-day
Thanks, I'm just browsing.	**Grazie, sto solo guardando.**	GRAH-tseeay stoh SOH-loh gwar-DAHN-doh
My male friend...	**Il mio amico...**	eel MEE-oh ah-MEE-koh
My female friend...	**La mia amica...**	lah MEE-ah ah-MEE-kah
My husband...	**Mio marito...**	MEE-oh mah-REE-toh
My wife...	**Mia moglie...**	MEE-ah MOHL-yay
...has the money.	**...ha i soldi.**	ah ee SOHL-dee

You can look up colors and fabrics in the *Rolling Rosetta Stone* Word Guide, later in this book.

Mail

Licking the postal code:

Post & Telegraph Office	**Poste e Telegrafi**	POH-stah ay tay-LAY-grah-fee
post office	**ufficio postale**	oof-FEE-choh poh-STAH-lay
stamp	**timbro, francobollo**	TEEM-broh, frahn-koh-BOHL-loh
post card	**cartolina**	kar-toh-LEE-nah
letter	**lettera**	LEHT-tay-rah
aerogram	**aerogramma**	ah-ay-roh-GRAHM-mah
envelope	**busta**	BOO-stah
package	**pacco**	PAHK-koh
box	**scatola**	SKAH-toh-lah
string / tape	**filo / cassetta**	FEE-loh / kahs-SEHT-tah
mailbox	**cassetta postale**	kahs-SAYT-tah poh-STAH-lay
air mail	**per via aerea**	pehr VEE-ah ah-AY-ray-ah
express	**espresso**	ay-SPREHS-soh
slow and cheap	**lento e economico**	LEHN-toh ay ay-koh-NOH-mee-koh
book rate	**prezzo di listino**	PREHT-tsoh dee lee-STEE-noh
registered	**raccomandata**	rahk-koh-mahn-DAH-tah
insured	**assicurato**	ahs-see-koo-RAH-toh
fragile	**fragile**	frah-JEE-lay

contents	**contenuto**	kohn-tay-NOO-toh
customs	**dogana**	doh-GAH-nah
to / from	**da / a**	dah / ah
address	**indirizzo**	een-dee-REET-tsoh
zip code	**codice**	koh-DEE-chay
	postale	poh-STAH-lay
general delivery	**fermo posta**	FEHR-moh POH-stah

Mail bonding:

Where is the Post Office?	**Dov'è la Posta?**	doh-VEH lah POH-stah
Which window for...?	**Qual'è lo sportello per...?**	kwah-LEH loh spor-TEHL-loh pehr
To the United States.	**Per Stati Uniti.**	pehr STAH-tee oo-NEE-tee
How much does it cost?	**Quanto costa?**	KWAHN-toh KOS-tah
How many... will it take?	**Quanti... ci vogliono?**	KWAHN-tee... chee VOHL-yoh-noh
...days	**...giorni**	JOR-nee
...weeks	**...settimane**	sayt-tee-MAH-nay
...months	**...mesi**	MAY-zee

In Italy, you can often get stamps at the corner *tabaccheria* (tobacco shop). As long as you know which stamps you need, this is a great convenience.

Time

It's about time:

What time is it?	**Che ore sono?**	kay OH-ray SOH-noh
It's...	**È...**	eh
...8:00.	**...le otto.**	lay OT-toh
...13:30.	**...le tredici e mezza.**	lay TRAY-dee-chee ay MEHD-dzah
...16:00.	**...le sedici.**	lay SAY-dee-chee
...a quarter past three.	**...le tre e un quarto.**	lay tray ay oon KWAR-toh
...a quarter to eleven.	**...le undici meno un quarto.**	lay OON-dee-chee MAY-noh oon KWAR-toh
...about 4:00 in the afternoon.	**...circa le quattro del pomeriggio.**	CHEER-kah lay KWAHT-troh dayl poh-may-REE-joh
...noon.	**...mezzogiorno.**	mehd-dzoh-JOR-noh
...midnight.	**...mezzanotte.**	mehd-dzah-NOT-tay
...too early.	**...troppo presto.**	TROP-poh PREHS-toh
...too late.	**...troppo tardi.**	TROP-poh TAR-dee

Timely words:

minute	**minuto**	mee-NOO-toh
hour	**ora**	OH-rah
in one hour	**tra un'ora**	trah oon-OH-rah
immediately	**immediatamente**	eem-may-deeah-tah-MAYN-tay

anytime	**a qualsiasi ora**	ah kwahl-seeAH-zee OH-rah
every hour	**ogni ora**	OHN-yee OH-rah
every day	**ogni giorno**	OHN-yee JOR-noh
May 15	**il quindici di maggio**	eel KWEEN-dee-chee dee MAH-joh
morning	**mattina**	maht-TEE-nah
afternoon	**pomeriggio**	poh-may-REE-joh
evening	**sera**	SAY-rah
night	**notte**	NOT-tay
day	**giorno**	JOR-noh
today	**oggi**	OJ-jee
yesterday	**ieri**	YEH-ree
tomorrow	**domani**	doh-MAH-nee
tomorrow morning	**domani mattina**	doh-MAH-nee maht-TEE-nah
day after tomorrow	**dopodomani**	doh-poh-doh-MAH-nee
week	**settimana**	sayt-tee-MAH-nah
month	**mese**	MAY-zay
year	**anno**	AHN-noh
last	**passato**	pahs-SAH-toh
this	**questo**	KWAY-stoh
next	**prossimo**	PROS-see-moh
Monday	**lunedì**	loo-nay-DEE
Tuesday	**martedì**	mar-tay-DEE
Wednesday	**mercoledì**	mehr-koh-lay-DEE
Thursday	**giovedì**	joh-vay-DEE
Friday	**venerdì**	vay-nehr-DEE
Saturday	**sabato**	SAH-bah-toh
Sunday	**domenica**	doh-MAY-nee-kah

January	**gennaio**	jayn-NAHee-oh
February	**febbraio**	fay-BRAHee-oh
March	**marzo**	MAR-tsoh
April	**aprile**	ah-PREE-lay
May	**maggio**	MAH-joh
June	**giugno**	JOON-yoh
July	**luglio**	LOOL-yoh
August	**agosto**	ah-GOH-stoh
September	**settembre**	sayt-TEHM-bray
October	**ottobre**	oht-TOH-bray
November	**novembre**	noh-VEHM-bray
December	**dicembre**	dee-CHEHM-bray
spring	**primavera**	pree-mah-VAY-rah
summer	**estate**	ay-STAH-tay
fall	**autunno**	ow-TOON-noh
winter	**inverno**	een-VEHR-noh
Ice Age	**Era Glaciale**	AY-rah glah-seeAH-lay

Italian holidays:

holiday	**festa**	FEHS-tah
national holiday	**festa nazionale**	FEHS-tah nah-tseeoh-NAH-lay
religious holiday	**festa religiosa**	FEHS-tah ray-lee-JOH-zah
Ascension of Mary (Aug. 15)	**Ferragosto**	fehr-rah-GOH-stoh
Happy birthday!	**Buon compleanno!**	bwohn kohm-play-AHN-noh
Merry Christmas!	**Buon Natale!**	bwohn nah-TAH-lay
Happy New Year!	**Felice anno nuovo!**	fay-LEE-chay AHN-noh nooOH-voh

Red Tape and Profanity

Filling out forms:

Signore / Signora / Signorina	Mr. / Mrs. / Miss
nome	first name
cognome	name
indirizzo	address
domicilio	address
strada	street
città	city
stato	state
paese	country
nazionalità	nationality
origine / destinazione	origin / destination
età	age
data di nascita	date of birth
luogo di nascita	place of birth
sesso	sex
sposato / sposata	married man / married woman
scapolo / nubile	single man / single woman
professione	profession
adulto	adult
bambino / ragazzo / ragazza	child / boy / girl
bambini	children
famiglia	family
firma	signature

Handy / dangerous customs phrases:

customs	**dogana**	doh-GAH-nah
passport	**passaporto**	pahs-sah-POR-toh
Stamp it, please.	**Me lo può timbrare, per favore.**	may loh pooOH teem-BRAH-ray pehr fah-VOH-ray
I am on vacation.	**Sono in vacanza.**	SOH-noh een vah-KAHN-tsah
I have nothing to declare.	**Non ho niente da dichiarare.**	nohn oh neeEHN-tay dah dee-keeah-RAH-ray
I have no idea how that got there.	**Non ho idea di come quello sia finito quì.**	nohn oh ee-DAY-ah dee KOH-may KWAY-loh SEE-ah fee-NEE-toh kwee
Was your father in the Gestapo?	**Ma tuo padre era nella Gestapo?**	mah TOO-oh PAH-dray AY-rah NAY-lah gay-STAH-poh
Nice doggie.	**Bel cucciolo.**	bel KOO-choh-loh

Italian profanity:

Insulting an Italian customs official is a serious offense. While you languish in prison, you'll hear some rough language.

Go to hell.	**Vai al diavolo.**	VAHee ahl deeAH-voh-loh
Damn it.	**Dannazione.**	dahn-nah-tseeOH-nay
Screw it.	**Vai a fa'n culo.**	VAHee ah fahn KOO-loh
Stick it between your teeth.	**Ficcatelo tra i denti.**	feek-kah-TAY-loh trah ee DEHN-tee
bastard	**bastardo**	bah-STAR-doh
bitch	**cagna**	KAHN-yah
breasts (colloq.)	**seno**	SAY-noh
penis (colloq.)	**cazzo**	KAHT-tsoh
butthole	**stronzo**	STRON-tsoh
shit	**merda**	MEHR-dah
drunk	**ubriaco**	oo-breeAH-koh
idiot	**idiota**	ee-deeOH-tah
jerk	**imbecille**	eem-bay-CHEEL-lay
stupid	**stupido**	STOO-pee-doh
Did someone...?	**Ma qualcuno ha fatto...?**	mah kwahl-KOO-noh ah FAHT-toh
...burp	**...un rutto**	oon ROOT-toh
...fart	**...una scoreggia**	OO-nah skoh-RAY-jah

Health

Handy health words:

pain	**dolore**	doh-LOH-ray
dentist	**dentista**	dehn-TEE-stah
doctor	**dottore**	doht-TOH-ray
nurse	**infermiera**	een-fehr-meeEH-rah
health insurance	**assicurazione medica**	ahs-see-koo-rah-tseeOH-nay MEH-dee-kah
hospital	**ospedale**	oh-spay-DAH-lay
medicine	**medicina**	may-dee-CHEE-nah
pharmacy	**farmacia**	far-mah-CHEE-ah
prescription	**prescrizione**	pray-skree-tseeOH-nay
pill	**pillola**	PEEL-loh-lah
aspirin	**aspirina**	ah-spee-REE-nah
antibiotic	**antibiotici**	ahn-tee-beeOH-tee-chee
pain killer	**medicina per il dolore**	may-dee-CHEE-nah pehr eel doh-LOH-ray
bandage	**cerotti**	chay-ROT-tee

Finding a cure:

I feel sick.	**Mi sento male.**	mee SEHN-toh MAH-lay
I need a doctor who speaks English.	**Ho bisogno di un dottore che parli inglese.**	oh bee-ZOHN-yoh dee oon doht-TOH-ray kay PAR-lee een-GLAY-zay
It hurts here.	**Fa male qui.**	fah MAH-lay kwee

I'm allergic to...	**Sono allergico...**	SOH-noh ahl-LEHR-jee-koh
...penicillin.	**...alla penicillina.**	AHL-lah pay-nee-cheel-LEE-nah
I am diabetic.	**Ho il diabete.**	oh eel deeah-BAY-tay
This is serious.	**È grave.**	eh GRAH-vay
I have...	**Ho...**	oh
...a burn.	**...un bruciato.**	oon broo-CHAH-toh
...chest pains.	**...dolore al petto.**	doh-LOH-ray ahl PEHT-toh
...a cold.	**...un raffreddore.**	oon rahf-frayd-DOH-ray
...constipation.	**...stitichezza.**	stee-tee-KAYT-tsah
...a cough.	**...la tosse.**	lah TOS-say
...diarrhea.	**...diarrea.**	dee-ar-RAY-ah
...a fever.	**...la febbre.**	lah FEHB-bray
...the flu.	**...l'influenza.**	leen-floo-EHN-tsah
...a headache.	**...il mal di testa.**	eel mahl dee TEHS-tah
...indigestion.	**...una indigestione.**	OO-nah een-dee-jay-steeOH-nay
...an infection.	**...una infezione.**	OO-nah een-fay-tseeOH-nay
...nausea.	**...nausea.**	NOW-zee-ah
...a rash.	**...una in-fiammazione.**	OO-nah een-feeah-mah-tseeOH-nay
...a sore throat.	**...la gola infiammata.**	lah GOH-lah een-feeah-MAH-tah
...a stomach ache.	**...il mal di stomaco.**	eel mahl dee STOM-ah-koh
...swelling.	**...un gonfiore.**	oon gohn-feeOH-ray

...a toothache.	**...mal di denti.**	mahl dee DEHN-tee
...a venereal disease.	**...una malattia venerea.**	OO-nah mah-laht-TEE-ah vay-nay-RAY-ah
...worms.	**...vermi.**	VEHR-mee
I have body odor.	**Ho odore personale.**	oh oh-DOH-ray pehr-soh-NAH-lay
Is it serious?	**È grave?**	eh GRAH-vay

Contact lenses:

hard lenses	**lenti dure**	LEHN-tee DOO-ray
soft lenses	**lenti morbide**	LEHN-tee MOR-bee-day
cleaning solution	**soluzione al sapone**	soh-loo-tseeOH-nay ahl sah-POH-nay
soaking solution	**solvente**	sohl-VEHN-tay
I've... a contact lens.	**Ho... una lente a contatto.**	oh... OO-nah LEHN-tay ah kohn-TAHT-toh
...lost	**...perso**	PEHR-soh
...swallowed	**...inghiottito**	een-goht-TEE-toh

Help!

Help in general:

Help!	**Aiuto!**	ah-YOO-toh
Help me!	**Aiutatemi!**	ah-yoo-TAH-tay-mee
Call a doctor!	**Chiamate un dottore!**	keeah-MAH-tay oon doht-TOH-ray
ambulance	**ambulanza**	ahm-boo-LAHN-tsah
accident	**incidente**	een-chee-DEHN-tay
injured	**ferito**	fay-REE-toh
emergency	**emergenza**	ay-mehr-JEHN-tsah
police	**polizia**	poh-lee-TSEE-ah
thief	**ladro**	LAH-droh
pick-pocket	**saccheggiatore**	sah-kay-jah-TOH-ray
I've been ripped off.	**Sono stato imbrogliato.**	SOH-noh STAH-toh eem-brohl-YAH-toh
I've lost...	**Ho perso...**	oh PEHR-soh
...my passport.	**...il mio passaporto.**	eel MEE-oh pahs-sah-POR-toh
...my ticket.	**...il mio biglietto.**	eel MEE-oh beel-YAYT-toh
...my baggage.	**...il mio bagaglio.**	eel MEE-oh bah-GAHL-yoh
...my purse.	**...la mia borsa.**	la MEE-ah BOR-sah
...my wallet.	**...il mio portafoglio.**	eel MEE-oh por-tah-FOHL-yoh

...my faith in humankind.	...la fiducia nel prossimo.	lah fee-DOO-chah nayl PROS-see-moh
I'm lost.	Sono perso.	SOH-noh PEHR-soh

Help for women:

Leave me alone.	Lasciami in pace.	LAH-shah-mee een PAH-chay
I wish to be alone.	Voglio stare sola.	VOHL-yoh STAH-ray SOH-lah
I'm not interested.	Non sono interessata.	nohn SOH-noh een-tay-rays-SAH-tah
I'm married.	Sono sposata.	SOH-noh spoh-ZAH-tah
I'm a lesbian.	Sono lesbica.	SOH-noh LEHZ-bee-kah
I have a contagious disease.	Ho una malattia contagiosa.	oh OO-nah mah-laht-TEE-ah kohn-tah-JOH-zah
Stop following me.	Smettila di seguirmi.	ZMAYT-tee-lah dee SAY-gweer-mee
Don't touch me.	Non mi tocchi.	nohn mee TOHK-kee
Enough!	Basta!	BAH-stah
Get lost!	Sparisci!	spah-REE-shee
Drop dead!	Crepa!	KRAY-pah
I'll call the police.	Chiamo la polizia.	keeAH-moh lah poh-lee-TSEE-ah
Police!	Polizia!	poh-lee-TSEE-ah

Conversations

Getting to know you:

My name is...	**Mi chiamo...**	mee keeAH-moh
What's your name?	**Come si chiama?**	KOH-may see keeAH-mah
How are you?	**Come sta?**	KOH-may stah
I am fine.	**Io sto bene.**	EEoh stoh BEH-nay
I am... / You are...	**Io sono... / È...**	EEoh SOH-noh / eh
...happy.	**...felice.**	fay-LEE-chay
...sad.	**...triste.**	TREE-stay
...tired.	**...stanco.**	STAHN-koh
...lucky.	**...fortunato.**	for-too-NAH-toh
I am... / You are...	**Ho... / Ha...**	oh / ah
...hungry.	**...fame.**	FAH-may
...thirsty.	**...sete.**	SAY-tay
...cold.	**...freddo.**	FRAYD-doh
I don't smoke.	**Non fumo.**	nohn FOO-moh
Where are you from?	**Di dove è?**	dee DOH-vay eh
What... are you from?	**Da che... viene?**	dah kay... veeEH-nay
...city	**...città**	cheet-TAH
...country	**...paese**	pah-AY-zay
...planet	**...pianeta**	peeah-NAY-tah
I am...	**Io sono...**	EEoh SOH-noh
...an American.	**...un Americano. (m)**	oon ah-may-ree-KAH-noh
	...una Americana. (f)	OO-nah ah-may-ree-KAH-nah

This is my...	È mio (m) / mia (f)...	eh MEE-oh / MEE-ah
...male friend / female friend.	...amico / amica.	ah-MEE-koh / ah-MEE-kah
...boy friend / girl friend.	...ragazzo / ragazza.	rah-GAHT-tsoh / rah-GAHT-tsah
...husband / wife.	...marito / moglie.	mah-REE-toh / MOHL-yay
...son / daughter.	...figlio / figlia.	FEEL-yoh / FEEL-yah
...brother / sister.	...fratello / sorella.	frah-TEHL-loh / soh-REHL-lah
...father / mother.	...padre / madre.	PAH-dray / MAH-dray

Family, school and work:

Are you married? (asked of a woman)	È sposata?	eh spoh-ZAH-tah
Are you married? (asked of a man)	È sposato?	eh spoh-ZAH-toh
Do you have children?	Ha bambini?	ah bahm-BEE-nee
Do you have photos?	Ha foto?	ah FOH-toh
How old is your child?	Quanti anni ha il suo bambino?	KWAHN-tee AHN-nee ah eel SOO-oh bahm-BEE-noh
Beautiful child / Beautiful children!	Bel bambino / Bei bambini!	behl bahm-BEE-noh / BEHee bahm-BEE-nee
Beautiful boy / Beautiful girl!	Bel ragazzo / Bella ragazza!	behl rah-GAHT-tsoh / BEHL-lah rah-GAHT-tsah
What are you studying?	Che cosa sta studiando?	kay KOH-zah stah stoo-deeAHN-doh
How old are you?	Quanti anni ha?	KWAHN-tee AHN-nee ah

I'm... years old.	**Ho... anni.**	oh... AHN-nee
Do you have brothers and sisters?	**Ha fratelli e sorelle?**	ah frah-TEHL-lee ay soh-REHL-lay
What is your occupation?	**Che lavoro fa?**	kay lah-VOH-roh fah
I'm a...	**Sono...**	SOH-noh
...student.	**...studente.**	stoo-DEHN-tay
...teacher.	**...insegnante.**	een-sayn-YAHN-tay
...worker.	**...manovale.**	mah-noh-VAH-lay
...brain surgeon.	**...chirurgo del cervello.**	kee-ROOR-goh dayl chehr-VEHL-loh
...professional traveler.	**...turista di professione.**	too-REE-stah dee proh-fays-seeOH-nay
Do you like your work?	**Le piace il suo lavoro?**	lay peeAH-chay eel SOO-oh lah-VOH-roh

Travel talk:

Are you on vacation?	**È in vacanza?**	eh een vah-KAHN-tsah
A business trip?	**Un viaggio di affari?**	oon veeAH-joh dee ahf-FAH-ree
How long have you been traveling?	**Da quanto tempo è in viaggio?**	dah KWAHN-toh TEHM-poh eh een veeAH-joh
day / week	**giorno / settimana**	JOR-noh / sayt-tee-MAH-nah
month / year	**mese / anno**	MAY-zay / AHN-noh
When are you going home?	**Quando ritorna a casa?**	KWAHN-doh ree-TOR-nah ah KAH-zah

This is my first time in...	**Questa è la mia prima volta in...**	KWAY-stah eh lah MEE-ah PREE-mah VOHL-tah een
I've visited... and then...	**Ho visitato... e poi...**	oh vee-zee-TAH-toh... ay POHee
Tomorrow / today I go to...	**Domani / oggi vado a...**	doh-MAH-nee / OJ-jee VAH-doh ah
I'm homesick.	**Ho nostalgia.**	oh noh-STAHL-jah
I'm very happy here.	**Sono molto felice qui.**	SOH-noh MOHL-toh fay-LEE-chay kwee
The Italians are very friendly.	**Gli italiani sono molto amichevoli.**	LEEyee ee-tah-leeAH-nee SOH-noh MOHL-toh ah-mee-kay-VOH-lee
Italy is a wonderful country.	**L'Italia è un paese meraviglioso.**	lee-TAHL-yah eh oon pah-AY-zay may-rah-veel-YOH-zoh
Travel is good for your health.	**Viaggiare fa bene alla salute.**	veeah-JAH-ray fah BEH-nay AHL-lah sah-LOO-tay

Weather:

What's the weather tomorrow?	**Come sarà il tempo domani?**	KOH-may sah-RAH eel TEHM-poh doh-MAH-nee
sunny / rainy	**bello / piovoso**	BEHL-loh / peeoh-VOH-zoh
hot / cold	**caldo / freddo**	KAHL-doh / FRAYD-doh

Favorite things:

What... do you like?	**Qual'è il suo... preferito?**	kwah-LEH eel SOO-oh... pray-fay-REE-toh
...art	**...genere d'arte**	JAY-nay-ray DAR-tay
...books	**...genere di libri**	JAY-nay-ray dee LEE-bree
...hobby	**...passatempo**	pahs-sah-TEHM-poh
...ice cream	**...gelato**	jay-LAH-toh
...movie	**...film**	feelm
...male movie star	**...attore**	aht-TOH-ray
...music	**...genere di musica**	JAY-nay-ray dee MOO-zee-kah
...male singer	**...cantante**	kahn-TAHN-tay
...sport	**...sport**	sport
...vice	**...vizio**	VEE-tseeoh
What... do you like?	**Qual'è la sua... preferita?**	kwah-LEH lah SOO-ah... pray-fay-REE-tah
...female movie star	**...attrice**	aht-TREE-chay
...female singer	**...cantante**	kahn-TAHN-tay

Responses for all occasions:

I like that.	**Mi piace.**	mee peeAH-chay
I like you.	**Mi piaci.**	mee peeAH-chee
Excellent!	**Ottimo.**	OT-tee-moh
Perfect.	**Perfetto.**	pehr-FEHT-toh
Funny.	**Divertente.**	dee-vehr-TEHN-tay

Very interesting.	**Molto interessante.**	MOHL-toh een-tay-rays-SAHN-tay
Really?	**Davvero?**	dahv-VAY-roh
Congratulations!	**Congratulazioni!**	kohn-grah-too-lah-tseeOH-nee
You're welcome.	**Prego.**	PRAY-goh
Bless you! (after sneeze)	**Salute!**	sah-LOO-tay
What a pity.	**Che peccato.**	kay payk-KAH-toh
No problem.	**Non c'è problema.**	nohn cheh proh-BLAY-mah
OK.	**Va bene.**	vah BEH-nay
That's life.	**Quella è vita.**	KWAYL-lah eh VEE-tah
This is the good life!	**Questa è vita!**	KWAY-stah eh VEE-tah
I feel like a pope! (happy)	**Sto come un papa!**	stoh KOH-may oon PAH-pah
Have a good trip!	**Buon viaggio!**	bwohn veeAH-joh
Good luck!	**Buona fortuna!**	BWOH-nah for-TOO-nah
Let's go!	**Andiamo!**	ahn-deeAH-moh

Thanks a million:

A thousand thanks.	**Grazie mille.**	GRAH-tseeay MEEL-lay
You are...	**Lei è...**	LEHee eh
...kind.	**...gentile.**	jayn-TEE-lay
...wonderful.	**...meraviglioso.**	may-rah-veel-YOH-zoh
...helpful.	**...di aiuto.**	dee ah-YOO-toh
...generous.	**...generoso.**	jay-nay-ROH-zoh
...hairy.	**...peloso.**	pay-LOH-zoh

This is...	È...	eh
This was...	È stato...	eh STAH-toh
...great fun.	...un vero divertimento.	oon VAY-roh dee-vehr-tee-MAYN-toh
You've gone to much trouble.	Ti sei veramente disturbato.	tee SEHee vay-rah-MAYN-tay dee-stoor-BAH-toh
You are a saint.	Lei è un santo.	LEHee eh oon SAHN-toh
I will remember you...	Mi ricorderò di Lei...	mee ree-kor-day-ROH dee LEHee
...always.	...sempre.	SEHM-pray
...till Tuesday.	...fino a martedì.	FEE-noh ah mar-tay-DEE

Conversing with Italian animals:

rooster / cock-a-doodle-doo	gallo / chicchirichì	GAHL-loh / keek-kee-ree-KEE
bird / tweet tweet	uccello / cip cip	oo-CHEHL-loh / cheep cheep
cat / meow	gatto / miao	GAHT-toh / MEE-ow
dog / bark bark	cane / bau bau	KAH-nay / bow bow
duck / quack quack	oca / quac quac	OH-kah / kwahk kwahk
cow / moo	mucca / muu	MOOK-kah / moo
pig / oink oink	maiale / oinc oinc (or just snort)	mah-YAH-lay / oynk oynk

Politics and Philosophy

The Italians enjoy deep conversations. With this list, you can build sentences that will sound either deep or ridiculous, depending on your mood (and theirs):

Who:

politicians	**politici**	poh-LEE-tee-chee
big business	**grande attività**	GRAHN-day aht-tee-vee-TAH
mafia	**mafia**	MAH-feeah
military	**militare**	mee-lee-TAH-ray
the system	**il sistema**	eel see-STEHM-ah
the rich	**i ricchi**	ee REEK-kee
the poor	**i poveri**	ee POH-vay-ree
men / women	**uomini / donne**	WAW-mee-nee / DON-nay
children	**bambini**	bahm-BEE-nee
the Italians	**gli italiani**	LEEyee ee-tah-leeAH-nee
the Americans	**gli americani**	LEEyee ah-may-ree-KAH-nee
the French	**i francesi**	ee frahn-CHAY-zee
the Germans	**i tedeschi**	ee tay-DEHS-kee
I / you	**io / Lei**	EEoh / LEHee
everyone	**tutti**	TOOT-tee

What:

want	**volere**	voh-LAY-ray
need	**aver bisogno**	AH-vehr bee-ZOHN-yoh
take	**prendere**	PREHN-day-ray
give	**dare**	DAH-ray

prosper	**prosperare**	proh-spay-RAH-ray
suffer	**soffrire**	sohf-FREE-ray
love	**amare**	ah-MAH-ray
hate	**odiare**	oh-deeAH-ray
work	**lavorare**	lah-voh-RAH-ray
play	**giocare**	joh-KAH-ray
vote	**votare**	voh-TAH-ray

Why:

love	**amore**	ah-MOH-ray
sex	**sesso**	SEHS-soh
money	**denaro**	day-NAH-roh
power	**potere**	poh-TAY-ray
family	**famiglia**	fah-MEEL-yah
work	**lavoro**	lah-VOH-roh
food	**cibo**	CHEE-boh
health	**salute**	sah-LOO-tay
hope	**speranza**	spay-RAHN-tsah
religion	**religione**	ray-lee-JOH-nay
happiness	**felicità**	fay-lee-chee-TAH
recreational drugs	**droghe leggere**	DROH-gay leh-JAY-ray
democracy	**democrazia**	day-moh-krah-TSEE-ah
taxes	**tasse**	TAHS-say
lies	**bugie**	boo-JEE-ay
corruption	**corruzione**	kor-roo-tseeOH-nay
pollution	**inquinamento**	een-kwee-nah-MAYN-toh
war / peace	**guerra / pace**	GWEHR-rah / PAH-chay

You be the judge:

(not) important	**(non) importante**	(nohn) eem-por-TAHN-tay
(not) powerful	**(non) potente**	(nohn) poh-TEHN-tay
(not) honest	**(non) onesto**	(nohn) oh-NEHS-toh
(not) innocent	**(non) innocente**	(nohn) een-noh-CHEHN-tay
(not) greedy	**(non) avido**	(nohn) ah-VEE-doh
liberal	**liberale**	lee-bay-RAH-lay
conservative	**conservatore**	kohn-sehr-vah-TOH-ray
radical	**radicale**	rah-dee-KAH-lay
too much	**troppo**	TROP-poh
enough	**abbastanza**	ah-bah-STAHN-tsah
never enough	**mai abbastanza**	MAHee ah-bah-STAHN-tsah
worse	**peggio**	PEH-joh
same	**stesso**	STAYS-soh
better	**meglio**	MEHL-yoh
good	**buono**	booOH-noh
bad	**cattivo**	kaht-TEE-voh
here	**qui**	kwee
everywhere	**ovunque**	oh-VOON-kway

Assorted beginnings and endings:

I like...	**Mi piace...**	mee peeAH-chay
I don't like...	**Non mi piace...**	nohn mee peeAH-chay
Do you like...?	**Le piace...?**	lay peeAH-chay
I am... / Are you...?	**Sono... / È...?**	SOH-noh / eh
I believe... /	**Io credo... /**	EEoh KRAY-doh /
I don't believe...	**Non credo...**	nohn KRAY-doh
Do you believe...?	**Lei crede...?**	LEHee KRAY-day
...in God	**...in Dio**	een DEEoh

...in reincarnation	**...nella rein-carnazione**	NAY-lah ray-een-kar-nah-tseeOH-nay
...in extraterrestrial life	**...negli extra-terrestri**	NAYL-yee ehk-strah-tehr-REHS-tree
...in Clinton	**...in Clinton**	een "Clinton"
Yes. / No.	**Sì. / No.**	see / noh
Maybe. / I don't know.	**Forse. / Non lo so.**	FOR-say / nohn loh soh
What's most important in life?	**Qual'è la cosa più importante nella vita?**	kwah-LEH lah KOH-zah peeOO eem-por-TAHN-tay NAY-lah VEE-tah
The problem is...	**Il problema è...**	eel proh-BLAY-mah eh
The answer is...	**La risposta è...**	lah ree-SPOH-stah eh
We have solved the world's problems.	**Abbiamo risolto i problemi del mondo.**	ah-beeAH-moh ree-ZOHL-toh ee proh-BLAY-mee dayl MOHN-doh

Entertainment

What's happening:

movie	**cinema**	CHEE-nay-mah
...original version	**...versione originale**	vehr-seeOH-nay oh-ree-jee-NAH-lay
...in English	**...in inglese**	een een-GLAY-zay
...with subtitles	**...con sottotitoli**	kohn soht-toh-TEE-toh-lee
...dubbed	**...doppiato**	dohp-peeAH-toh
music	**musica**	MOO-zee-kah
...classical	**...classica**	KLAHS-see-kah
...folk	**...folk**	fohlk
...live	**...dal vivo**	dahl VEE-voh
old rock	**rock vecchio stile**	rok VEHK-keeoh STEE-lay
jazz	**jazz**	jahts
blues	**blues**	"blues"
singer	**cantante**	kahn-TAHN-tay
concert	**concerto**	kohn-CHEHR-toh
show	**spettacolo**	spayt-TAH-koh-loh
dancing	**ballare**	bahl-LAH-ray
folk dancing	**danze popolari**	DAHN-tsay poh-poh-LAH-ree
disco	**discoteca**	dee-skoh-TAY-kah
cover charge	**tariffa d'entrata**	tah-REEF-fah dayn-TRAH-tah

For cheap entertainment, join the locals and take *una passeggiata* (a stroll) through town.

A night on the town:

Can you recommend...?	**Può raccomandare...?**	pwoh rahk-koh-mahn-DAH-ray
What's happening tonight?	**Che cosa succede stasera?**	kay KOH-zah soo-CHAY-day stah-SAY-rah
Where can I buy a ticket?	**Dove si comprano i biglietti?**	DOH-vay see kohm-PRAH-noh ee beel-YAYT-tee
When does it start?	**A che ora comincia?**	ah kay OH-rah koh-MEEN-chah
When does it end?	**A che ora finisce?**	ah kay OH-rah fee-NEE-shay
Where's the best place to dance nearby?	**Qual'è il posto migliore per ballare qui vicino?**	kwah-LEH eel POH-stoh meel-YOH-ray pehr bahl-LAH-ray kwee vee-CHEE-noh
Do you want to dance?	**Vuoi ballare?**	VWOHee bahl-LAH-ray
Again?	**Ancora?**	ahn-KOH-rah
Let's have a wild and crazy night!	**Diamoci una notte da sballo!**	deeah-MOH-chee OO-nah NOT-tay dah ZBAHL-loh

An Italian Romance

Ah, amore:

What's the matter?	**Qual'è il problema?**	kwah-LEH eel proh-BLAY-mah
Nothing.	**Niente.**	neeEHN-tay
I / me / you	**Io / mi / ti**	EEoh / mee / tee
flirt (v)	**flirtare**	fleer-TAH-ray
kiss (v)	**baciare**	bah-CHAH-ray
hug (v)	**abbracciare**	ah-brah-CHAH-ray
love (n)	**amore**	ah-MOH-ray
make love	**fare l'amore**	FAH-ray lah-MOH-ray
condom	**preservativo**	pray-zehr-vah-TEE-voh
contraceptive	**contraccetivo**	kohn-trah-chay-TEE-voh
safe sex	**sesso prudente**	SEHS-soh proo-DEHN-tay
sexy	**sensuale**	sayn-sooAH-lay
cozy	**accogliente**	ahk-kohl-YEHN-tay
romantic	**romantico**	roh-MAHN-tee-koh
honey bunch	**dolce come il miele**	DOHL-chay KOH-may eel meeEH-lay
cupcake	**pasticcino**	pah-stee-CHEE-noh
sugar pie	**zuccherino**	tsook-kay-REE-noh
pussy cat	**gattino**	gaht-TEE-noh

I am...	**Sono...**	SOH-noh
...gay.	**...gay.**	gay
...straight.	**...normale.**	nor-MAH-lay
...undecided.	**...indeciso.**	een-day-SEE-zoh
...prudish.	**...pudoroso.**	poo-doh-ROH-zoh
...horney.	**...allupato.**	ahl-loo-PAH-toh
We are on our honeymoon.	**Siamo in luna di miele.**	seeAH-moh een LOO-nah dee meeEH-lay
I have a boy friend / girl friend.	**Ho il ragazzo / la ragazza.**	oh eel rah-GAHT-tsoh / lah rah-GAHT-tsah
I am (not) married.	**(Non) sono sposato.**	(nohn) SOH-noh spoh-ZAH-toh
I am rich and single.	**Sono ricco e singolo.**	SOH-noh REEK-koh ay SEENG-goh-loh
I am lonely.	**Sono solo.**	SOH-noh SOH-loh
I have no diseases.	**Non ho malattie.**	nohn oh mah-laht-TEE-ay
I have many diseases.	**Ho molte malattie.**	oh MOHL-tay mah-laht-TEE-ay
Can I see you again?	**Ti posso rivedere?**	tee POS-soh ree-vay-DAY-ray
You are my most beautiful souvenir.	**Sei il mio più bel ricordo.**	SEHee eel MEE-oh peeOO behl ree-KOR-doh
Is this an aphrodisiac?	**È un afrodisiaco questo?**	eh oon ah-froh-dee-ZEE-ah-koh KWAY-stoh
This is (not) my first time.	**Questa (non) è la mia prima volta.**	KWAY-stah (nohn) eh lah MEE-ah PREE-mah VOHL-tah
Do you do this often?	**Lo fai spesso?**	loh FAHee SPAYS-soh

How's my breath?	**Com'è il mio fiato?**	koh-MEH eel MEE-oh feeAH-toh
Let's just be friends.	**Solo amici.**	SOH-loh ah-MEE-chee
I'll pay for my share.	**Pago per la mia parte.**	PAH-goh pehr lah MEE-ah PAR-tay
Would you like a massage...?	**Vorresti un massaggio...?**	vor-RAY-stee oon mahs-SAH-joh
...for your feet	**....ai piedi**	AHee peeAY-dee
Why not?	**Perchè no?**	pehr-KEH noh
Try it.	**Provalo.**	PROH-vah-loh
It tickles.	**Fa il solletico.**	fah eel sohl-LAY-tee-koh
Oh my God.	**Oh mio Dio.**	oh MEE-oh DEE-oh
I love you.	**Ti amo.**	tee AH-moh
Darling, will you marry me?	**Cara, mi vuoi sposare?**	KAH-rah mee VWOHee spoh-ZAH-ray

The Rolling Rosetta Stone Word Guide

For centuries, Egyptian hieroglyphics were considered undecipherable -- until 1799, when a black slab known as the Rosetta Stone was unearthed in the Egyptian desert. By repeating identical phrases in hieroglyphics, Greek, and a newer form of Egyptian, Rosetta helped scientists break the ancient hieroglyphic code, and thus she became the grandmother of all phrasebooks.

As you roll through Italy, our thoroughly modern, portable Rosetta will help you translate key English words into Italian. These are in English alphabetical order, from left to right.

English	Italian	English	Italian
A		**A**	
above	**sopra**	accident	**incidente**
adaptor	**adattatore**	address	**indirizzo**
adult	**adulto**	afraid	**spaventato**
after	**dopo**	afternoon	**pomeriggio**
aftershave	**dopobarba**	afterwards	**più tardi**
again	**ancora**	age	**età**
agency	**agenzia**	aggressive	**aggressivo**
agree	**d'accordo**	AIDS	**AIDS**
air	**aria**	air-conditioned	**aria condizionata**
airline	**aeroplano**	air mail	**via aerea**
airport	**aeroporto**	alarm clock	**sveglia**
alcohol	**alcool**	allergic	**allergico**
allergies	**allergie**	all together	**tutt'uno**
alone	**solo**	always	**sempre**
am (to be)	**sono (essere)**	ancestor	**antenato**

English	Italian	English	Italian
ancient	**antico**	and	**e**
angry	**arrabbiato**	animal	**animale**
another	**un altro**	answer	**risposta**
antibiotic	**antibiotico**	antiques	**antichità**
apartment	**appartamento**	apology	**scuse**
appetizers	**antipasto**	apple	**mela**
appointment	**appuntamento**	approximately	**più o meno**
area	**regione**	arrest	**arresto**
arrivals	**arrivi**	art	**arte**
artificial	**artificiale**	artist	**artista**
ask	**domandare**	aspirin	**aspirina**
at	**a**	Austria	**Austria**
autumn	**autunno**		

B

B

baby	**bambino**	babysitter	**bambinaia**
backpack	**zainetto**	bad	**cattivo**
baggage	**bagaglio**	bakery	**fornaio**
balcony	**balcone**	ball	**palla**
banana	**banana**	Band-Aid	**cerotto**
bank	**banca**	barber	**barbiere**
basement	**seminterrato**	basket	**cestino**
bath	**bagno**	bathroom	**bagno**
bathtub	**vasca da bagno**	battery	**batteria**
beach	**spiaggia**	beard	**barba**
beautiful	**bello**	because	**perchè**
bed	**letto**	bedroom	**camera da letto**
bed sheet	**lenzuolo**	beef	**manzo**
beer	**birra**	before	**prima**
begin	**cominciare**	behind	**dietro**

English	Italian	English	Italian
below	**sotto**	belt	**cintura**
best	**il migliore**	better	**meglio**
bicycle	**bicicletta**	big	**grande**
bill (payment)	**conto**	bird	**uccello**
birthday	**compleanno**	bite (n)	**morso**
black	**nero**	blanket	**coperta**
bleed	**sanguinare**	blond	**biondo**
blood	**sangue**	blue	**blu**
boat	**barca**	body	**corpo**
boil (v)	**bollire**	boiling	**bollente**
bomb	**bomba**	book	**libro**
book shop	**libreria**	boots	**stivali**
border	**frontiera**	borrow	**prendere in prestito**
boss	**capo**	bottle	**bottiglia**
bottom	**fondo**	bowl	**boccia**
box	**scatola**	boy	**ragazzo**
bra	**reggiseno**	bread	**pane**
breakfast	**colazione**	bridge	**ponte**
briefs	**mutandoni**	Britain	**Britannia**
broken	**rotto**	brother	**fratello**
brown	**marrone**	browsing	**sfogliare libri**
bucket	**secchio**	building	**edificio**
bulb	**bulbo**	burn (n)	**bruciatura**
bus	**autobus**	business	**affari**
button	**bottone**	by (via)	**in**

English	Italian	English	Italian
C		**C**	
calendar	**calendario**	calorie	**calorie**
camera	**macchina fotografica**	camping	**campeggio**
can (v)	**potere**	can opener	**apriscatola**
canal	**canale**	candle	**candela**
candy	**caramella**	canoe	**canoa**
cap	**berretto**	captain	**capitano**
car	**macchina**	carafe	**caraffa**
card	**cartina**	cards (deck)	**carte**
careful	**prudente**	carpet	**tappeto**
carrots	**carote**	carry	**portare**
cashier	**cassiere**	cassette	**cassetta**
castle	**castello**	cat	**gatto**
catch (v)	**prendere**	cathedral	**cattedrale**
cave	**grotta**	cellar	**cantina**
center	**centro**	century	**secolo**
chair	**sedia**	change (n)	**cambio**
cheap	**economico**	check	**assegno**
Cheers!	**Salute!**	cheese	**formaggio**
chicken	**pollo**	children	**bambini**
chin	**mento**	Chinese (adj)	**cinese**
chocolate	**cioccolato**	Christmas	**Natale**
church	**chiesa**	cigarette	**sigarette**
cinema	**cinema**	city	**città**
city hall	**municipio**	class	**classe**
clean (adj)	**pulito**	clear	**chiaro**
cliff	**dirupo**	closed	**chiuso**
clothesline	**marca**	clothes pins	**spilla**
cloudy	**nuvoloso**	coast	**costa**

English	Italian	English	Italian
coffee	**caffè**	coins	**monete**
cold (adj)	**freddo**	colors	**colori**
comb (n)	**pettine**	come	**venire**
comfortable	**confortevole**	complain	**protestare**
complicated	**complicato**	computer	**computer**
concert	**concerto**	condom	**preservativo**
conductor	**conducente**	congratulations	**congratulazioni**
connection (train)	**coincidenza**	constipation	**stitichezza**
cook (v)	**cuocere**	cool	**fresco**
cork	**sughero**	corkscrew	**cavatappi**
corner	**angolo**	corridor	**corridoio**
cost (v)	**costare**	cot	**lettino**
cotton	**cotone**	cough (v)	**tossire**
cough drops	**pasticche**	country	**paese**
countryside	**campagna**	cousin	**cugino**
cow	**mucca**	crafts	**arte**
cream	**panna**	credit card	**carta di credito**
crowd (n)	**folla**	cry (v)	**piangere**
cup	**tazza**		

D

D

English	Italian	English	Italian
dad	**papà**	dance (v)	**ballare**
danger	**pericolo**	dangerous	**pericoloso**
dark	**scuro**	daughter	**figlia**
day	**giorno**	dead	**morto**
dear	**caro**	delay	**ritardo**
delicious	**delizioso**	dental floss	**filo interdentale**
dentist	**dentista**	deodorant	**deodorante**
departures	**partenze**	deposit	**deposito**
dessert	**dessert**	detour	**deviazione**

English	Italian	English	Italian
diabetic	**diabetico**	diamond	**diamante**
diarrhea	**diarrea**	dictionary	**dizionario**
difficult	**difficile**	dinner	**cena**
direct	**diretto**	direction	**direzione**
dirty	**sporco**	discount	**sconto**
disease	**malattia**	disturb	**disturbare**
divorced	**divorziato**	doctor	**dottore**
document	**documento**	dog	**cane**
doll	**bambola**	donkey	**asino**
door	**porta**	dormitory	**camerata**
double	**doppio**	down	**giù**
dream (n)	**sogno**	dress (n)	**vestito**
drink (n)	**bevanda**	drive (v)	**guidare**
driver	**autista**	drunk	**ubriaco**
dry	**asciutto**		

E

E

English	Italian	English	Italian
each	**ogni**	ear	**orecchio**
early	**presto**	earplugs	**tappi per le orecchie**
earrings	**orecchini**	earth	**terra**
east	**est**	Easter	**Pasqua**
easy	**facile**	eat	**mangiare**
elbow	**gomito**	elevator	**ascensore**
embarrassing	**imbarazzante**	embassy	**ambasciata**
empty	**vuoto**	English	**inglese**
enough	**abbastanza**	entrance	**ingresso**
entry	**entrata**	envelope	**busta**
especially	**specialmente**	Europe	**Europa**
evening	**sera**	every	**ogni**

English	Italian	English	Italian
everything	**tutto**	exactly	**esattamente**
example	**esempio**	excellent	**eccellente**
except	**eccetto**	exchange (n)	**cambio**
excuse me	**mi scusi**	exhausted	**esausto**
exit	**uscita**	expensive	**caro**
explain	**spiegare**	eye	**occhio**

F

F

English	Italian	English	Italian
face	**faccia**	factory	**fabbrica**
fall (v)	**cadere**	false	**falso**
family	**famiglia**	famous	**famoso**
fantastic	**fantastico**	far	**lontano**
farm	**fattoria**	fashion	**moda**
fat (adj)	**grasso**	father	**padre**
faucet	**rubinetto**	ferry	**traghetto**
fever	**febbre**	few	**poco**
field	**campo**	fight (n)	**lotta**
fine	**bene**	finger	**dito**
finish (v)	**finire**	fireworks	**fuochi d'artificio**
first	**primo**	first aid	**primo soccorso**
first class	**prima classe**	fish	**pesce**
fix (v)	**aggiustare**	fizzy	**frizzante**
flag	**bandiera**	flashlight	**torcia**
flavor (n)	**aroma**	flea	**pulce**
flight	**volo**	flower	**fiore**
flu	**influenza**	food	**cibo**
foot	**piede**	football	**calcio**
for	**per**	forbidden	**vietato**
foreign	**straniero**	forget	**dimenticare**
fork	**forchetta**	fountain	**fontana**

English	Italian	English	Italian
France	**Francia**	free (no cost)	**gratis**
fresh	**fresco**	Friday	**venerdì**
friend	**amico**	friendship	**amicizia**
from	**da**	fruit	**frutta**
fun	**divertimento**	funeral	**funerale**
funny	**divertente**	furniture	**mobili**
future	**futuro**		

G

G

English	Italian	English	Italian
gallery	**galleria**	game	**gioco**
garage	**garage**	garden	**giardino**
gas	**benzina**	gas station	**stazione di servizio**
gay	**omosessuale**	gentleman	**signore**
genuine	**genuino**	Germany	**Germania**
get off	**scendere**	get out	**uscire**
gift	**regalo**	girl	**ragazza**
give	**dare**	glass	**bicchiere**
glasses (eye)	**occhiali**	gloves	**guanti**
go	**andare**	go away	**andare via**
God	**Dio**	gold	**oro**
golf	**golf**	good	**buono**
goodbye	**arrivederci**	good day	**buongiorno**
go through	**attraversare**	grammar	**grammatica**
grandfather	**nonno**	grandmother	**nonna**
gray	**grigio**	greasy	**grasso**
great	**ottimo**	Greece	**Grecia**
green	**verde**	grocery store	**alimentari**
guarantee	**garantito**	guest	**ospite**
guide	**guida**	guidebook	**guida**

English	Italian	English	Italian
guitar	**chitarra**	gun	**pistola**

H

H

English	Italian	English	Italian
hair	**capelli**	haircut	**taglio di capelli**
hand	**mano**	handicapped	**andicappato**
handicrafts	**artigianato**	handle (n)	**manico**
handsome	**attraente**	happy	**contento**
harbor	**porto**	hard	**duro**
hat	**cappello**	hate (v)	**odiare**
he	**lui**	head	**testa**
headache	**mal di testa**	healthy	**sano**
hear	**udire**	heart	**cuore**
heat (n)	**calore**	heaven	**paradiso**
heavy	**pesante**	hello	**ciao**
help (n)	**aiuto**	her	**lei**
here	**qui**	hi	**ciao**
high	**alto**	highway	**autostrada**
hill	**collina**	history	**storia**
hitchhike	**autostop**	hobby	**hobby**
hold (v)	**tenere**	hole	**buco**
holiday	**giorno festivo**	homemade	**fatto in casa**
homesick	**nostalgico**	honest	**onesto**
honeymoon	**luna di miele**	horrible	**orribile**
horse	**cavallo**	horse riding	**equitazione**
hospital	**ospedale**	hot	**caldo**
hotel	**hotel**	hour	**ora**
house wine	**vino della casa**	how many	**quanti**
how much ($)	**quanto costa**	how	**come**
hungry	**affamato**	hurry (v)	**avere fretta**
husband	**marito**		

English	Italian	English	Italian
I		**I**	
I	**io**	ice cream	**gelato**
ice	**ghiaccio**	ill	**malato**
immediately	**immediatamente**	important	**importante**
imported	**importato**	impossible	**impossibile**
in	**in**	included	**incluso**
incredible	**incredibile**	independent	**indipendente**
indigestion	**indigestione**	industry	**industria**
inedible	**immangiabile**	information	**informazioni**
injured	**infortunato**	innocent	**innocente**
insect	**insetto**	inside	**dentro**
instant	**istante**	instead	**invece**
insurance	**assicurazione**	intelligent	**intelligente**
interesting	**interessante**	invitation	**invito**
is	**è**	island	**isola**
Italy	**Italia**	itch (n)	**prurito**
J		**J**	
jacket	**giubbotto**	jaw	**mascella**
jeans	**jeans**	jewelry	**gioielleria**
job	**lavoro**	jogging	**footing**
joke (n)	**scherzo**	journey	**viaggio**
juice	**succo**	jump (v)	**saltare**
K		**K**	
keep	**tenere**	key	**chiave**
kill	**uccidere**	kind	**gentile**
king	**re**	kiss (v)	**baciare**

English	Italian	English	Italian
kitchen	**cucina**	knee	**ginocchio**
knife	**coltello**	know	**sapere**

L

L

English	Italian	English	Italian
ladder	**scala**	ladies	**signore**
lake	**lago**	lamb	**agnello**
language	**lingua**	large	**grande**
last	**ultimo**	late	**tardi**
later	**più tardi**	laugh (v)	**ridere**
laundromat	**lavanderia**	lawyer	**avvocato**
lazy	**pigro**	leather	**pelle**
left	**sinistra**	leg	**gamba**
letter	**lettera**	library	**biblioteca**
life	**vita**	light (n)	**luce**
light bulb	**lampadina**	lighter (n)	**accendino**
lip	**labbro**	list	**lista**
liter	**litro**	little (adj)	**piccolo**
local	**locale**	lock (v)	**chiudere**
lock (n)	**serratura**	lockers	**armadietti**
look	**guardare**	lost	**perso**
loud	**forte**	love (v)	**amare**
lover	**amante**	low	**basso**
luck	**fortuna**	lungs	**polmoni**

M

M

English	Italian	English	Italian
macho	**macho**	mad	**arrabbiato**
magazine	**rivista**	maggots	**verme**
mail (n)	**posta**	main	**principale**
make (v)	**fare**	man	**uomo**

English	Italian	English	Italian
manager	**direttore**	many	**molti**
map	**cartina**	market	**mercato**
married	**sposato**	matches	**fiammiferi**
maximum	**massimo**	maybe	**forse**
meat	**carne**	medicine	**medicina**
medium	**medio**	men	**uomini**
menu	**menu**	message	**messaggio**
metal	**metallo**	midnight	**mezzanotte**
mineral water	**acqua minerale**	minimum	**minimo**
minutes	**minuti**	mirror	**specchio**
Miss	**Signorina**	misunderstanding	**incomprensione**
mix (n)	**misto**	modern	**moderno**
moment	**momento**	Monday	**lunedì**
money	**soldi**	month	**mese**
monument	**monumento**	moon	**luna**
more	**ancora**	morning	**mattina**
mosquito	**zanzara**	mother	**madre**
mother-in-law	**suocera**	mountain	**montagna**
moustache	**baffi**	mouth	**bocca**
movie	**film**	Mr.	**Signore**
Mrs.	**Signora**	much	**molto**
muscle	**muscolo**	museum	**museo**
music	**musica**	my	**mio / mia**

N

N

English	Italian	English	Italian
nail clipper	**tagliaunghie**	naked	**nudo**
name	**nome**	napkin	**salvietta**
narrow	**stretto**	nationality	**nazionalità**
natural	**naturale**	nature	**natura**
nausea	**nausea**	near	**vicino**

English	Italian	English	Italian
necessary	**necessario**	necklace	**collana**
needle	**ago**	nervous	**nervoso**
never	**mai**	new	**nuovo**
newspaper	**giornale**	next	**prossimo**
nice	**bello**	nickname	**soprannome**
night	**notte**	no	**no**
noisy	**rumoroso**	non-smoking	**vietato fumare**
noon	**mezzogiorno**	normal	**normale**
north	**nord**	nose	**naso**
not	**non**	notebook	**blocco note**
nothing	**niente**	no vacancy	**completo**
now	**adesso**		

O

O

English	Italian	English	Italian
occupation	**lavoro**	occupied	**occupato**
ocean	**oceano**	of	**di**
office	**ufficio**	oil (n)	**olio**
OK	**d'accordo**	old	**vecchio**
on	**su**	once	**una volta**
one way (street)	**senso unico**	one way (ticket)	**andata**
only	**solo**	open (adj)	**aperto**
open (v)	**aprire**	opera	**opera**
operator	**centralinista**	or	**o**
orange (color)	**arancione**	orange (fruit)	**arancia**
original	**originale**	other	**altro**
outdoors	**all'aria aperta**	oven	**forno**
over (finished)	**finito**	owner	**padrone**

English	Italian	English	Italian

P

English	Italian	English	Italian
package	**pacco**	page	**pagina**
pail	**secchio**	pain	**dolore**
painting	**quadro**	palace	**palazzo**
panties	**mutande**	pants	**pantaloni**
paper	**carta**	parents	**genitori**
park (v)	**parcheggiare**	park (garden)	**parco**
party	**festa**	passenger	**passeggero**
passport	**passaporto**	pay	**pagare**
peace	**pace**	pedestrian	**pedone**
pen	**penna**	pencil	**matita**
people	**persone**	pepper	**pepe**
percent	**percentuale**	perfect	**perfetto**
perfume	**profumo**	period (of time)	**periodo**
period (woman's)	**mestruazioni**	person	**persona**
pharmacy	**farmacia**	photo	**foto**
pick-pocket	**saccheggiatore**	picnic	**picnic**
piece	**pezzo**	pig	**maiale**
pill	**pillola**	pillow	**cuscino**
pin	**spilla**	pink	**rosa**
pity, it's a	**che peccato**	pizza	**pizza**
plane	**aereoplano**	plain	**semplice**
plant	**pianta**	plastic	**plastica**
plastic bag	**sacchetto di plastica**	plate	**piatto**
platform (train)	**binario**	play (v)	**giocare**
play	**teatro**	please	**per favore**
pliers	**pinzette**	pocket	**tasca**
point (v)	**indicare**	police	**polizia**
poor	**povero**	pork	**porco**

English	Italian	English	Italian
possible	**possibile**	postcard	**cartolina**
poster	**poster**	pot	**pentola**
practical	**pratico**	pregnant	**incinta**
prescription	**prescrizione**	present (gift)	**regalo**
pretty	**carino**	price	**prezzo**
priest	**prete**	prince	**principe**
princess	**principessa**	private	**privato**
problem	**problema**	prohibited	**proibito**
pronounce	**pronuncia**	public	**pubblico**
pull	**tirare**	purple	**viola**
purse	**borsa**	push	**spingere**

Q

Q

quality	**qualità**	quarter (¼)	**quarto**
queen	**regina**	question (n)	**domanda**
quiet	**tranquillità**		

R

R

rabbit	**coniglio**	radio	**radio**
railway	**rotaie**	rain (n)	**pioggia**
rainbow	**arcobaleno**	raincoat	**impermeabile**
rape (n)	**violenza carnale**	raw	**crudo**
razor	**rasoio**	ready	**pronto**
receipt	**ricevuta**	receive	**ricevere**
receptionist	**centralinista**	recipe	**ricetta**
recommend	**raccomandare**	red	**rosso**
refill (v)	**riempire**	refund (n)	**rimborso**
relax (v)	**riposare**	religion	**religione**
remember	**ricordare**	rent (v)	**affittare**

English	Italian	English	Italian
repair (v)	**riparare**	repeat (v)	**ripetere**
reservation	**prenotazione**	rich	**ricco**
right	**destra**	ring (n)	**anello**
ripe	**maturo**	river	**fiume**
rock (n)	**pietra**	roller skates	**pattini a rotelle**
romantic	**romantico**	roof	**tetto**
room	**camera**	rope	**corda**
rotten	**marcio**	round trip	**ritorno**
rowboat	**barca a remi**	rucksack	**zaino**
rug	**tappeto**	ruins	**rovine**
run (v)	**correre**		

S

S

English	Italian	English	Italian
sad	**triste**	safe	**sicuro**
sale	**liquidazione**	same	**stesso**
sandals	**sandali**	sandwich	**panino**
sanitary napkins	**assorbenti**	Saturday	**sabato**
scandalous	**scandaloso**	school	**scuola**
science	**scienza**	scissors	**forbici**
scream (v)	**strillare**	screwdriver	**cacciaviti**
sculptor	**scultore**	sculpture	**scultura**
sea	**mare**	seafood	**frutti di mare**
seat	**posto**	second class	**secondo classe**
secret	**segreto**	see	**vedere**
self-service	**self-service**	sell	**vendere**
send	**spedire**	separate (adj)	**separato**
serious	**serio**	service	**servizio**
sex	**sesso**	sexy	**sexy**
shampoo	**shampoo**	shaving cream	**crema da barba**
she	**lei**	sheet	**lenzuolo**

English	Italian	English	Italian
shell	**conchiglia**	ship (n)	**nave**
shirt	**camicia**	shoes	**scarpe**
shopping	**fare spese**	shore	**spiaggia**
short	**corto**	shorts	**pantaloncini**
shoulder	**spalle**	show (v)	**mostrare**
show (n)	**spettacolo**	shower	**doccia**
shy	**timido**	sick	**malato**
sign	**segno**	silence	**silenzio**
silk	**seta**	silver	**argento**
similar	**simile**	simple	**semplice**
sing	**cantare**	singer	**cantante**
sink	**lavandino**	sir	**signore**
sister	**sorella**	size	**taglia**
ski (v)	**sciare**	skin	**pelle**
skinny	**magro**	skirt	**gonna**
sky	**cielo**	sleep (v)	**dormire**
sleepy	**assonnato**	slice	**fettina**
slide (photo)	**diapositiva**	slippery	**scivoloso**
slow	**lento**	small	**piccolo**
smell (n)	**odore**	smile (v)	**sorriso**
smoking	**fumare**	snack	**merendina**
sneeze (v)	**starnutire**	snore	**russare**
soap	**sapone**	socks	**calzini**
something	**qualcosa**	son	**figlio**
song	**canzone**	soon	**subito**
sorry	**mi dispiace**	sour	**acerbo**
south	**sud**	speak	**parlare**
specialty	**specialità**	speed	**velocità**
spend	**spendere**	spider	**ragno**
spoon	**cucchiaio**	sport	**sport**
spring	**primavera**	square	**piazza**

English	Italian	English	Italian
stairs	**scale**	stamp	**francobolli**
star (in sky)	**stella**	state	**stato**
station	**stazione**	stomach	**stomaco**
stone	**sasso**	stop (n)	**stop / alt**
stop (v)	**fermare**	storm	**temporale**
story (floor)	**storia**	straight	**dritto**
strange (odd)	**strano**	stream (n)	**corrente**
street	**strada**	string	**filo**
strong	**forte**	stuck	**incastrato**
student	**studente**	stupid	**stupido**
sturdy	**resistente**	style	**stile**
suddenly	**improvvisamente**	suitcase	**valigia**
summer	**estate**	sun	**sole**
sunbathe	**abbronzarsi**	sunburn	**bruciatura del sole**
Sunday	**domenica**	sunglasses	**occhiali da sole**
sunny	**assolato**	sunset	**tramonto**
sun screen	**crema protettiva**	sunshine	**sole**
sunstroke	**insolazione**	suntan (n)	**abbronzatura**
suntan lotion	**crema per il sole**	supermarket	**supermercato**
supplement	**supplemento**	surprise (n)	**sorpresa**
swallow (v)	**ingoiare**	sweat (v)	**sudare**
sweater	**maglione**	sweet	**dolce**
swim	**nuotare**	swimming pool	**piscina**
swim suit	**costume da bagno**	swim trunks	**costume de bagno**
Switzerland	**Svizzera**	synthetic	**sintetico**

English	Italian	English	Italian
T		T	
table	**tavolo**	tail	**coda**
take out (food)	**portare via**	take	**prendere**
talcum powder	**borotalco**	talk	**parlare**
tall	**alto**	tampons	**tamponi**
tape (cassette)	**cassetta**	taste (n)	**gusto**
taste (v)	**assaggiare**	tax	**tasse**
teacher	**insegnante**	team	**squadra**
teenager	**adolescente**	telephone	**telefono**
television	**televisione**	temperature	**temperatura**
tender	**tenero**	tennis shoes	**scarpe da tennis**
tent	**tenda**	terrible	**terribile**
thanks	**grazie**	theater	**teatro**
thermometer	**termometro**	thick	**spesso**
thief	**ladro**	thigh	**coscia**
thin	**sottile**	thing	**cosa**
think	**pensare**	thirsty	**assetato**
thread	**filo**	throat	**gola**
through	**attraverso**	throw	**tirare**
Thursday	**giovedì**	ticket	**biglietto**
tight	**stretto**	timetable	**orario**
tired	**stanco**	tissues	**fazzolettini**
to	**a**	today	**oggi**
toe	**dito del piede**	together	**insieme**
toilet paper	**carta igienica**	toilet	**gabinetto**
tomorrow	**domani**	tonight	**stasera**
too	**troppo**	tool	**arnese**
tooth	**dente**	toothbrush	**spazzolino da denti**
toothpaste	**dentifricio**	toothpick	**stuzzicadenti**

English	Italian	English	Italian
total	**totale**	touch (v)	**toccare**
tough	**duro**	tour	**giro**
tourist	**turista**	towel	**asciugamano**
tower	**torre**	town	**città**
toy	**giocattolo**	track (train)	**binario**
traditional	**tradizionale**	traffic	**traffico**
train	**treno**	translate	**tradurre**
travel	**viaggiare**	travel agency	**agenzia di viaggi**
traveler's check	**traveler's check**	tree	**albero**
trip	**viaggio**	trouble	**guaio**
T-shirt	**maglietta**	Tuesday	**martedì**
tunnel	**tunnel**	turn (v)	**girare**
tweezers	**pinzette**	twins	**gemelli**

U

U

English	Italian	English	Italian
ugly	**brutto**	umbrella	**ombrello**
under	**sotto**	underpants	**mutandine**
understand	**capire**	underwear	**mutande**
unemployed	**disoccupato**	unfortunately	**sfortunatamente**
United States	**Stati Uniti**	university	**università**
up	**su**	upstairs	**di sopra**
urgent	**urgente**	us	**noi**
use	**usare**		

V

V

English	Italian	English	Italian
vacant	**libero**	vacancy (hotel)	**camare libere**
valley	**valle**	vegetarian (n)	**vegetariano**
very	**molto**	vest	**panciotto**

English	Italian	English	Italian
video	**video**	video recorder	**video registratore**
view	**vista**	village	**villaggio**
vineyard	**vigneto**	virus	**virus**
visit (n)	**visita**	vitamins	**vitamine**
voice	**voce**	vomit (v)	**vomitare**

W

W

waist	**vita**	wait	**aspettare**
waiter	**cameriere**	waitress	**cameriera**
wake up	**svegliarsi**	walk (v)	**camminare**
wallet	**portafoglio**	want	**volere**
warm (adj)	**caldo**	wash	**lavare**
watch (v)	**guardare**	watch (n)	**orologio**
water	**acqua**	water, tap	**acqua del rubinetto**
waterfall	**cascata**	we	**noi**
weather forecast	**previsioni del tempo**	weather	**tempo**
wedding	**matrimonio**	Wednesday	**mercoledì**
week	**settimana**	weight	**peso**
welcome	**benvenuto**	west	**ovest**
wet	**bagnato**	what	**che cosa**
wheel	**ruota**	when	**quando**
where	**dove**	whipped cream	**panna**
white	**bianco**	who	**chi**
why	**perchè**	widow	**vedova**
widower	**vedovo**	wife	**moglie**
wild	**selvaggio**	wind	**vento**
window	**finestra**	wine	**vino**

English	Italian	English	Italian
wing	**ala**	winter	**inverno**
wire (money)	**spedire**	wish (v)	**desiderare**
with	**con**	without	**senza**
women	**donne**	wood	**legno**
wool	**lana**	word	**parola**
work (n)	**lavoro**	world	**mondo**
worse	**peggio**	worst	**peggiore**
wrap	**incartare**	wrist	**polso**
write	**scrivere**		

Y

Y

year	**anno**	yellow	**giallo**
yes	**sì**	yesterday	**ieri**
you (formal)	**Lei**	you (informal)	**tu**
young	**giovane**	youth hostel	**ostello della gioventù**

Z

Z

zero	**zero**	zipper	**chiusura lampo**
zoo	**zoo**		

Hurdling the Language Barrier

Don't be afraid to communicate

Even the best phrase book won't satisfy your needs in every situation. To really hurdle the language barrier, you need to leap beyond the printed page, and dive into contact with the locals. Never, never, never allow your lack of foreign language skills to isolate you from the people and cultures you traveled halfway 'round the world to experience. Remember that in every country you visit, you're surrounded by expert, native-speaking tutors. Spend bus and train rides letting them teach you. Always start a conversation by asking politely, "Do you speak English?"

When you communicate in English with someone from another country, speak slowly, clearly, and with carefully chosen words. Use what the Voice of America calls "simple English." You're talking to people who are wishing it was written down, hoping to see each letter as it tumbles out of your mouth. Pronounce each letter, avoiding all contractions and slang. For bad examples, listen to other tourists.

Keep things caveman-simple. Make single nouns work as entire sentences ("Photo?"). Use internationally understood words ("auto kaput" works in Sicily). Butcher the language if you must. The important thing is to make the effort. To get air mail stamps you can flap your wings and say "tweet, tweet." If you want milk, moo and pull two imaginary udders. If you're attracted to someone, pant. Risk looking like a fool.

Go ahead and make educated guesses. Many situations are easy-to-fake multiple choice questions. Practice. Read timetables, concert posters and newspaper headlines. Listen to each language on a multi-lingual tour. Be melodramatic. Exaggerate the local accent. Self-consciousness is the deadliest communication-killer.

Choose multi-lingual people to communicate with, like business people, urbanites, young well-dressed people, or anyone in the tourist trade. Use a small note pad to keep track of handy phrases you pick up -- and to help you communicate more clearly with the locals by scribbling down numbers, maps, and so on. Some travelers carry important messages written on a small card (I'm a vegetarian, boiled water, your finest ice cream, and so on).

Easy cultural bugaboos to avoid
- When writing numbers, give your sevens a cross (7) and give your ones an upswing (1).
- European dates are different: Christmas is 25-12-94, not 12-25-94.
- Commas are decimal points and decimals are commas, so a dollar and a half is 1,50 and there are 5.280 feet in a mile.
- The Italian "first floor" is not the ground floor, but the first floor up.
- When counting with your fingers, start with your thumb. If you hold up only your first finger, you'll probably get two of something.

Italian tongue twisters

Tongue twisters are a great way to practice a language -- and break the ice with the locals. Here are a few that are sure to challenge you, and amuse your hosts:

Trentatrè trentini arrivarono a Trento tutti e trentatrè trotterellando.

Thirty-three people from Trent arrived in Trent, all thirty-three trotting.

Chi fù quel barbaro barbiere che barberò così barbaramente a Piazza Barberini quel povero barbaro di Barbarossa?

Who was that barbarian barber in Barberini Square who shaved that poor barbarian Barbarossa?

Sopra la panca la capra canta, sotto la panca la capra crepa.

On the bench the goat sings, under the bench the goat dies.

Tigre contro tigre.

Tiger against tiger.

English tongue twisters:

After your Italian friends have laughed at you, let them try these tongue twisters in English:

The sixth sick sheik's sixth sheep's sick.

One smart fellow he felt smart, two smart fellows they felt smart, three smart fellows they all felt smart.

I'm a pleasant mother pheasant plucker. I pluck mother pheasants. I'm the most pleasant mother peasant plucker that ever plucked a mother pheasant.

International words

As our world shrinks, more and more words hop across their linguistic boundaries and become international. Savvy travelers develop a knack for choosing words most likely to be universally understood ("auto" instead of "car," "kaput" rather than "broken," "photo," not "picture"). They also internationalize their pronunciation. "University," if you play around with its sound (Oo-nee-vehr-see-tay) will be understood anywhere. Practice speaking English with a heavy Italian accent. Wave your arms a lot. Be creative.

Here are a few internationally understood words. Remember, cut out the Yankee accent and give each word a pan-European sound.

Stop	Kaput	Vino	Restaurant
Ciao	Bank	Hotel	Bye-bye
Rock 'n roll	Post	Camping	OK
Auto	Picnic	Amigo	Autobus (boos)
Nuclear	Macho	Tourist	English (Engleesh)
Yankee	Americano	Mama mia	Michelangelo
Beer	Oo la la	Coffee	Casanova (romantic)
Chocolate	Moment	Sexy	Disneyland
Tea	Coca-Cola	No problem	Mañana
Telephone	Photo	Photocopy	Passport
Europa	Self-service	Toilet	Police
Super	Taxi	Central	Information
Pardon	University	Fascist	Rambo
American profanity			

Italian Gestures

Gestures say a lot

In your travels, gestures can either raise or lower the language barrier. For instance, pointing to your head can mean smart in one country and crazy in another. And if you shake your head "no" in Bulgaria, you've just said "yes." Gesture boundaries often follow linguistic ones, but not always. Occasionally a gesture which is very popular in one town or region is meaningless or has a completely different meaning a few miles away.

Here are a few common Italian gestures, their meaning and where you're likely to see them:

The Hand Purse: Straighten the fingers and thumb of one hand, bringing them all together to make an upward point. Your hands can be held still or moved a little up and down at the wrist. This is a common and very Italian gesture for query. It is used to say "what do you want?" or "what are you doing?" or "what is it?" or "what's new?" It can also be used as an insult to say "You fool!"

The Cheek Screw: Make a fist, stick out your forefinger and screw it into your cheek. The cheek screw is used widely and almost exclusively in Italy to mean good, lovely, beautiful. Many Italians also use it to mean clever.

The Eyelid Pull: Place your extended forefinger below the center of your eye, and pull the skin downward. In Italy and Spain this is a friendly warning, meaning "Be alert, that guy is clever."

The Chin Flick: Tilt your head back slightly, and flick the back of your fingers forward in an arc from under your chin. In Italy and France this means "I'm not interested, you bore me," or "you bother me." In southern Italy it can mean "no".

The Forearm Jerk: Clench your right fist, and jerk your forearm up as you slap your bicep with your left palm. This is a rude phallic gesture that men throughout southern Europe often use the way Americans give someone "the finger." This extra-large version says "I'm superior" (it's an action some monkeys actually do with their penis to insult their peers).

Counting on fingers: In most of Europe, counting begins with the thumb, so if you hold up two fingers, someone will sell you three of something.

To beckon someone: Remember that in northern Europe you bring your palm up, and in the south you wave it down. While most people greet each other by waving with their palm out, you'll find many Italians wave "at themselves," with their palm towards their face. Bye-bye.

Let's Talk Telephones

Using Italephones

Smart travelers use the telephone every day. Making a hotel reservation by phone the morning of the day you plan to arrive is a snap. If there's a language problem, ask someone at your hotel to talk to your next hotel for you.

The key to long distance is understanding area codes and having an Italian phone card. Hotel room phones are reasonable for local calls, but a terrible rip-off for long-distance calls. Never call home from your hotel room (unless you are putting the call on your credit card).

For calls to other European countries, dial the international access code (00 in Italy), followed by the country code, followed by the area code without its zero, and finally the local number (four to seven digits). When dialing long distance within Italy, start with the area code (including its zero), then the local number. Post offices have fair, metered long distance booths.

Italian telephone cards are much easier to use than coins for local and long distance calls. Buy one on your first day to force you to find smart reasons to use the local phones. The L. 5000 or L. 10,000 phone cards are worth from $4 to $8. You can buy them at post offices, *tabacci* shops, and machines near phone booths (many phone booths indicate where the nearest phone card sales outlet is located). The old vandal-plagued coin- and token-operated phones, which are getting more and more difficult to find, work if you have the necessary pile of coins or *gettoni* (slotted tokens which also function as L200 coins). One *gettone* gets you about 5 minutes of local talk.

Dial patiently in Italy, as if the phone doesn't understand numbers very well. Sometimes you'll need to try again and again. When you finally get through, don't hesitate to nearly scream to be heard.

Calling the USA from a pay phone is easy if you have an Italian phone card, or an ATT, MCI or SPRINT credit card. Or you can call using coins ($1 for 15 seconds) to have the other person call you back at your hotel at a specified time. From the States, they would dial 011-39-your Italian area code without the zero-and the local number. Italy-to-USA calls are twice as expensive as direct calls from the States. Midnight in California is breakfast in Rome.

If you plan to call home much, get an ATT, MCI or SPRINT card. Each card company has a toll-free number in each European country which puts you in touch with an American operator who takes your card number and the number you want to call, puts you through and bills your home phone number for the call (at the cheaper USA rate of about a dollar a minute plus a $2.50 service charge). If you talk for at least 3 minutes, you'll save enough to make up for the service charge. ATT, MCI and SPRINT numbers in Italy are listed on the next page.

Important Italian phone numbers:

Italy's international access code: (calling from Italy)	00
Italy's country code: (calling to Italy)	39
ATT operator:	172-1022
MCI operator:	172-1011
SPRINT operator:	172-1877
Emergency: (English-speaking help)	113
Emergency (police):	112
Road service:	116
Directory assistance:	12
Telephone help in English:	170

Country codes:

France:	33	Germany:	49	USA/Canada:	1
Austria:	43	Britain:	44	Switzerland:	41
Belgium:	32	Spain:	34		

To call Italy from the USA, dial 011-39-Italian area code (without the zero)-local number.

To call the USA from Italy, dial 00-1-area code-local number.

Weather

First line is average daily low (°F.); 2nd line average daily high (°F.); 3rd line, days of no rain.

	J	F	M	A	M	J	J	A	S	O	N	D
Rome	39	39	42	46	55	60	64	64	61	53	46	41
	54	56	62	68	74	82	88	88	83	73	63	56
	23	17	26	24	25	28	29	28	24	22	22	22

Metric conversions (approximate)

1 inch = 25 millimeters   1 foot = .3 meter
1 yard = .9 meter   1 mile = 1.6 kilometers
1 sq. yard = .8 sq. meter   1 acre = 0.4 hectare
1 quart = .95 liter   1 ounce = 28 grams
1 pound = .45 kilo   1 kilo = 2.2 pounds
1 centimeter = 0.4 inch   1 meter = 39.4 inches
                                 36-24-36 = 90-60-90

1 kilometer = .62 mile
Miles = kilometers divided by 2 plus 10%
(120 km/2 = 60, 60 +12 = 72 miles)

Fahrenheit degrees = double Celsius + 30
32° F = 0° C, 82° F = about 28° C

Your tear-out cheat sheet

Keep this sheet of the most essential Italian words and phrases in your pocket. That way you can memorize them during idle moments, or quickly refer to them if you're caught without your phrase book.

The essentials:

Hello. / Goodbye.	**Ciao.**	chow
Do you speak English?	**Parla inglese?**	PAR-lah een-GLAY-zay
Yes.	**Sì.**	see
No.	**No.**	noh
I don't understand.	**Non capisco.**	nohn kah-PEE-skoh
I'm sorry.	**Mi dispiace.**	mee dee-speeAH-chay
Please.	**Per favore.**	pehr fah-VOH-ray
Thanks.	**Grazie.**	GRAH-tseeay

Where?

Where is...?	**Dov'è...?**	doh-VEH
...a hotel	**...un hotel**	oon oh-TEHL
...a youth hostel	**...un ostello**	oon oh-STEHL-loh
	della gioventù	DAY-lah joh-vehn-TOO
...a restaurant	**...un ristorante**	oon ree-stoh-RAHN-tay
...a grocery store	**...un negozio**	oon nay-GOH-tsoh
	di alimentari	dee ah-lee-mayn-TAH-ree
...the train station	**...la stazione**	lah stah-tseeOH-nay
...tourist	**...informazioni**	een-for-mah-tseeOH-nee
information	**per turisti**	pehr too-REE-stee
...the toilet	**...il gabinetto**	eel gah-bee-NAYT-toh
men	**uomini, signori**	WAW-mee-nee,
		seen-YOH-ree

women	**donne, signore**	DON-nay, seen-YOH-ray

How much?

How much?	**Quanto costa?**	KWAHN-toh KOS-tah
Wil you write it down?	**Lo può scrivere?**	loh pwoh SKREE-vay-ray
Cheap.	**Economico.**	ay-koh-NOH-mee-koh
Cheaper.	**Più economico.**	peeOO ay-koh-NOH-mee-koh
Included?	**È incluso?**	eh een-KLOO-zoh
I would like...	**Vorrei....**	vor-REHee
We would like...	**Vorremo...**	vor-RAY-moh
Just a little. /	**Un pochino. /**	oon poh-KEE-noh /
More.	**Di più.**	dee peeOO (say "P.U.")
A ticket.	**Un biglietto.**	oon beel-YAYT-toh
A room.	**Una camera.**	OO-nah KAH-may-rah
The bill.	**Il conto.**	eel KOHN-toh

Number crunching:

one	**uno**	OO-noh
two	**due**	DOO-ay
three	**tre**	tray
four	**quattro**	KWAHT-troh
five	**cinque**	CHEENG-kway
six	**sei**	SEHee
seven	**sette**	SEHT-tay
eight	**otto**	OT-toh
nine	**nove**	NOV-ay
ten	**dieci**	deeEH-chee
hundred	**cento**	CHEHN-toh
thousand	**mille**	MEEL-lay

The Europe Through the Back Door Catalog

All of these items have been specially designed for independent budget travelers. They have been thoroughly field tested by Rick Steves and his globe-trotting ETBD staff, and are completely guaranteed. Prices include shipping, tax, and a free subscription to our quarterly newsletter/catalog.

Back Door Bag convertible suitcase/backpack $70

At 9"x21"x13" this specially-designed, sturdy, functional bag is maximum carry-on-the-plane size (fits under the seat), and your key to foot-loose and fancy-free travel. Made from rugged, water-resistant Cordura nylon, it converts from a smart-looking suitcase to a handy backpack. It has hide-away padded shoulder straps, top and side handles, and a detachable shoulder strap (for toting as a suitcase). Lockable perimeter zippers allow easy access to the roomy (2500 cubic inches) central compartment. Two large outside pockets are perfect for frequently used items. Also included is one nylon stuff bag. Over 40,000 Back Door travelers have used these bags around the world. Rick Steves helped design this bag, and lives out of it for 3 months at a time. Comparable bags cost much more. Available in black, grey, navy blue and teal green.

Eurailpasses

...cost the same everywhere, but only ETBD gives you a free 90-minute "How to get the most out of your railpass" video, free advice on your itinerary, and your choice of one of Rick Steves' "22 Day" books. No wonder why ETBD has become the second largest Eurailpass retailer in the USA. It's easy to order your pass by mail -- call 206/771-8303, and we'll send you a full description of the types of Eurailpasses available, pass prices, our unique map for comparing Eurail and pay-as-you-go rail prices, and our user-friendly Eurailpass order form.

Moneybelt $8

Absolutely required no matter where you're traveling! An ultra-light, sturdy, under-the-pants, one-size-fits-all nylon pouch, our svelte moneybelt is just the right size to carry your passport, airline tickets and traveler's checks comfortably. Made to ETBD's specifications, this moneybelt is your best defense against theft -- when you wear it, feeling a Gypsy's hand in your pocket will become just another interesting cultural experience.

Prices are good through 1993. Orders will be processed within 2 weeks. For rush orders (which we process within 48 hours), please add $10. Send your check to:

Europe Through the Back Door
109 Fourth Ave. N, PO Box 2009
Edmonds, WA 98020

More books by Rick Steves...

Now more than ever, travelers are determined to get the most out of every mile, minute and dollar. That's what Rick's books are all about. He'll help you have a better trip **because** *you're on a budget, not in spite of it. Each of these books is published by John Muir Publications, and is available through your local bookstore, or the Europe Through the Back Door newsletter/catalog.*

Europe Through The Back Door

Now in its 11th edition, *ETBD* has given thousands of people the skills and confidence they needed to travel through the less-touristed "back doors" of Europe. You'll find chapters on packing, itinerary-planning, transportation, finding rooms, travel photography, keeping safe and healthy, plus individual chapters on Rick's 40 favorite back door discoveries. 1993 edition.

Mona Winks: Self-Guided Tours of Europe's Top Museums

Let's face it, museums can ruin a good vacation. But *Mona Winks* takes you by the hand, giving you fun and easy-to-follow self-guided tours through Europe's 20 most frightening and exhausting museums and cultural obligations. Packed with more than 200 maps and illustrations. 1993 edition.

Europe 101: History and Art for the Traveler

A lively, entertaining crash course in European history and art, *101* is the perfect way to prepare yourself for the rich cultural smorgasbord that awaits you.

2 to 22 Days in Europe
2 to 22 Days in Great Britain
2 to 22 Days in France
2 to 22 Days in Italy
2 to 22 Days in Germany, Austria & Switzerland
2 to 22 Days in Norway, Sweden & Denmark
2 to 22 Days in Spain & Portugal
Planning an itinerary can be the most difficult and important part of a trip -- and you haven't even left yet. To get you started, Rick gives you a day-by-day plan linking his favorite places in Europe, complete with maps, descriptions of sights, and recommended places to stay. Some people follow a 22-day route to the letter, and others use it as a general outline. Either way, your *2 to 22 days in...* guidebook will help you structure your trip so you'll get the most out of every moment. These guides are updated every year.

Europe Through the Back Door Phrase Books:
French, Italian and German
Finally, a series of phrase books written specially for the budget traveler! Each book gives you the words, phrases and easy-to-use phonetics you need to communicate with the locals about room-finding, transportation, food, health -- you'll even learn how to start conversations about politics, philosophy and romance -- all spiced with Rick Steves' travel tips, and his unique blend of down-to-earth practicality and humor. All are 1993 editions.

What we do at Europe Through the Back Door

At ETBD we value travel as a powerful way to better understand and contribute to the world in which we live. Our mission at ETBD is to equip travelers with the confidence and skills necessary to travel through Europe independently, economically, and in a way that is culturally broadening. To accomplish this, we:

Teach do-it-yourself travel seminars (often for free);

Research and write guidebooks to Europe and a public television series;

Sell Eurailpasses, our favorite guidebooks, maps, travel bags, and other travelers' supplies;

Provide travel consulting services;

Organize and lead unique Back Door tours of Europe;

Sponsor our Travel Resource Center in Edmonds, WA;

...and we travel a lot.

Back Door 'Best of Europe' tours

If you like our independent travel philosophy but would like to benefit from the camaraderie and efficiency of group travel, our Back Door tours may be right up your alley. Every year we lead friendly, intimate 'Best of Europe in 22 Days' tours, free-spirited 'Un-Tours' and special regional tours of Turkey, Britain, France and other places that we especially love. For details, dates and prices, call 206/771-8303 and ask for our free newsletter/catalog.

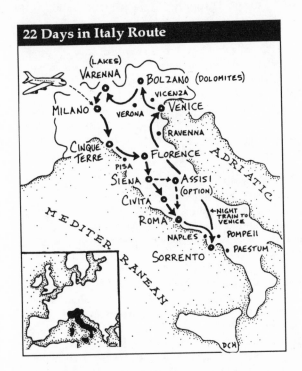

22 Days in Italy Route

(LAKES) VARENNA
BOLZANO (DOLOMITES)
VICENZA
MILANO
VERONA
VENICE
CINQUE TERRE
RAVENNA
PISA
FLORENCE
ADRIATIC
SIENA
ASSISI (OPTION)
CIVITA
ROMA
← NIGHT TRAIN TO VENICE
NAPLES
POMPEII
SORRENTO
PAESTUM
MEDITERRANEAN
DCH

You've got your phrase book, but have you planned your itinerary yet?
If this route looks good to you, pick up a copy of Rick Steves' *2 to 22 Days in Italy*. You'll get the most productive day-by-day itinerary through Italy, with up-to-date listings of Rick's favorite budget accomodations along the way.

Reader feedback pages

Your feedback will do a lot to improve future editions of this phrase book. To help tomorrow's travelers travel smarter, please use the blank pages at the end of this book to jot down ideas, phrases, and suggestions as they hit you during your travels, and then send them to me. Grazie!

Rick Steves
Europe Through the Back Door
109 Fourth Ave. N, PO Box 2009
Edmonds, WA 98020

Other Great Travel Books by Rick Steves

Asia Through the Back Door, 3rd ed., 326 pp. $15.95 (4th ed. avail. 6/93 $16.95)

Europe 101: History & Art for the Traveler, 4th ed., 372 pp. $15.95

Europe Through the Back Door, 11th ed., 432 pp. $17.95

Europe Through the Back Door Phrase Book: French, 168 pp. $4.95

Europe Through the Back Door Phrase Book: German, 168 pp. $4.95

Mona Winks: Self-Guided Tours of Europe's Top Museums, 2nd ed., 456 pp. $16.95

2 to 22 Days in Europe, 1993 ed., 288 pp. $13.95

2 to 22 Days in France, 1993 ed., 192 pp. $10.95

2 to 22 Days in Germany, Austria, & Switzerland, 1993 ed., 224 pp. $10.95

2 to 22 Days in Great Britain, 1993 ed., 192 pp. $10.95

2 to 22 Days in Italy, 1993 ed., 208 pp. $10.95

2 to 22 Days in Norway, Sweden, & Denmark, 1993 ed., 192 pp. $10.95

2 to 22 Days in Spain & Portugal, 1993 ed., 192 pp. $10.95

Kidding Around Seattle: A Young Person's Guide to the City, 64 pp. $9.95 (Ages 8 and up)

More European Travel Books Available from John Muir Publications

Great Cities of Eastern Europe, 256 pp. $16.95

Opera! The Guide to Western Europe's Great Houses, 296 pp. $18.95

22 Days Around the World, 1993 ed., 264 pp. $13.95

Understanding Europeans, 272 pp. $14.95

Undiscovered Islands of the Mediterranean, 2nd ed., 256 pp. $10.95

A Viewer's Guide to Art: A Glossary of Gods, People, and Creatures, 144 pp. $10.95

For Young Readers Traveling Abroad, Consider Our "Kidding Around" Travel Guides (Ages 8 and up)

Kidding Around London, 64 pp. $9.95

Kidding Around Paris,
64 pp. $9.95
Kidding Around Spain,
108 pp. $12.95

These are just a sampling of the many titles we have to offer. Whether you are traveling within the U.S. or around the world, turn to John Muir Publications for unique travel titles to practically any location.

Call or write for our *free* catalog listing our complete selection of travel and young readers titles. All the necessary information is listed below.

Ordering Information

If you cannot find our books in your local bookstore, you can order directly from us. If you send us money for a book not yet available, we will hold your money until we can ship you the book. Your books will be sent to you via UPS (for U.S. destinations). UPS will not deliver to a P.O. Box; please give us a street address. Include $3.75 for the first item ordered and $.50 for each additional item to cover shipping and handling costs.

For airmail within the U.S., enclose $4.00. All foreign orders will be shipped surface rate; please enclose $3.00 for the first item and $1.00 for each additional item. Please inquire about foreign airmail rates.

Method of Payment

Your order may be paid by check, money order, or credit card. We cannot be responsible for cash sent through the mail. All payments must be made in U.S. dollars drawn on a U.S. bank. Canadian postal money orders in U.S. dollars are acceptable. For VISA, MasterCard, or American Express orders, include your card number, expiration date, and your signature, or call **(800) 888-7504**. Books ordered on American Express cards can be shipped only to the billing address of the cardholder. Sorry, no C.O.D.'s. Residents of sunny New Mexico, add 6.125% tax to the total.

Address all orders and inquiries to:
John Muir Publications
P.O. Box 613
Santa Fe, NM 87504
(505) 982-4078
(800) 888-7504